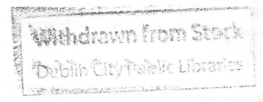
The 100

The 100

Insights and lessons from 100 of the
greatest speeches ever delivered

Simon Maier and Jeremy Kourdi

 Marshall Cavendish
Business

Reprinted twice in 2010

First published in 2010 by Marshall Cavendish Business
An imprint of Marshall Cavendish International
PO Box 65829
London EC1P 1NY
United Kingdom
sales@marshallcavendish.co.uk
and

1 New Industrial Road
Singapore 536196
genrefsales@sg.marshallcavendish.com
www.marshallcavendish.com/genref

Marshall Cavendish is a trademark of Times Publishing Limited

Other Marshall Cavendish offices:
Marshall Cavendish International (Asia) Private Limited, 1 New Industrial
Road, Singapore 536196 • Marshall Cavendish Corporation. 99 White Plains
Road, Tarrytown NY 10591–9001, USA • Marshall Cavendish International
(Thailand) Co Ltd. 253 Asoke, 12th Floor, Sukhumvit 21 Road, Klongtoey
Nua, Wattana, Bangkok 10110, Thailand • Marshall Cavendish (Malaysia)
Sdn Bhd, Times Subang, Lot 46, Subang Hi-Tech Industrial Park, Batu Tiga,
40000 Shah Alam, Selangor Darul Ehsan, Malaysia

A CIP record for this book is available from the British Library

ISBN 978-0-462-09969-9

Printed and bound in Great Britain by
CPI William Clowes, Beccles NR34 7TL

Dedicated to Edward B. Fairman,
who knew a great speech when he heard one

Contents

Introduction

In 1896 Henry Hardwicke wrote: "Oratory is the parent of liberty. By the constitution of things it was ordained that eloquence should be the last stay and support of liberty, and that with her she is ever destined to live, to flourish and to die. It is to the interest of tyrants to cripple and debilitate every species of eloquence. They have no other safety. It is, then, the duty of free states to foster oratory."

In recent years, we both realized that oratory (composing and delivering a speech in public) and rhetoric (the art of using language as a means to persuade) were making something of a return. We had talked often about their demise and the reasons for it. But politicians, particularly in the United States, were beginning to again regard speechwriting and excellent oratory as "must haves". Conversely, business speakers around the world seemed to be getting worse at making speeches. We found that the average executive prepares for a presentation poorly and speaks badly – a generalization certainly, but evidence suggests that there is very little care or due diligence about political, business or general public speaking.

With our experience of the corporate world and of witnessing speakers on the international stage, it was clear to us that many people find making a speech or delivering a presentation difficult or boring. Difficult certainly, absolutely, without any question, but boring? We noted that many people simply couldn't be bothered. They had little interest in the topic and even less in the audience. They felt that speechmaking was an odious duty that got in the way of "proper work". This view was shared, in the corporate world, by executive advisors and consultants, advertising agency representatives, PR specialists and indeed a whole gamut of people who we always thought would support the value of rhetoric and oratory.

We also concluded, not for the first time, that speeches often fall short of audience aspirations or expectations. There are, of course, notable exceptions to this, with some individuals delivering well-crafted speeches incorporating personal style and great power, but it is as if most people – even (very) senior, influential figures – view speechmaking if not as boring then as simple or routine, and so their preparation and attention to the task are often perfunctory. While many speeches are weak, some are certainly good, but only a few are truly great. This prompts the question then, of course: what is it that makes a speech great? And does it matter?

Speeches do matter and so does speechmaking. Watching a great speaker and hearing a great speech is a heart-warming, inspirational and spine-tingling experience. It can make us believe and understand something infinitely better (or just make us believe and understand it). It can help us take heart when all around us are in despair. It can embolden us. It can be superb theatre. It can make a difference. When we leave and re-enter the real world, we feel that what we've witnessed was "real world" too, so we feel doubly uplifted and refreshed. To appreciate this, you have only to look at Barack Obama's audiences in the speaking engagements he undertook in the run-up to the presidency. It is worth watching how people are before his speeches and how they seem after them.

Conversely, it is disappointing and utterly dispiriting to witness a speech, any speech, that has been ill-conceived, poorly prepared or lazily delivered, with little understanding of the audience or, sometimes, even of the event's purpose. How can that happen? It is arrogant or complacent to believe that one can simply get up and deliver a speech with little or no preparation. Very, very few people can ever do that and even fewer should take the risk. Certainly, there are those such as Bill Gates whose easy, engaging style makes it look as if he is speaking without preparation, but that is not the case: he practised hard to achieve that "look".

Great oratory should inspire and enlighten. World history shows time and time again that speeches can soothe a nation or encourage a faction. Speeches can inspire a people to fight battles or injustice. Speeches can get people to make huge sacrifices or overcome the shackles of prejudice or poverty. Speeches can help people fight against oppression, racism, bigotry. Alternatively, speeches can perpetrate terrible acts of inhumanity, hate, torture, prejudice, violence and extraordinary destruction. Great speeches have a powerful effect on the listener – from revolution to revulsion – and the cleverly written and well-delivered phrase can for ever be imprinted upon our individual memories and on the collective memory of society. Add to that an emotional charge that simply moves us, brings tears to our eyes and makes us feel humble, angry or vindicated, and the speech or speaker will be consequential, long-lasting and for ever remembered.

Of course, not all great speeches have to make us cry and not all great speeches have to make us want to fight someone or something. But they do have to make us feel comfortable about the message and good about the messenger. In fact, they have to make us want to care very much indeed about both.

Several elements combine to make a great speech: the power to define the times, to inspire, to make an impact and to motivate. A great speech needs a great speaker. That doesn't mean picture perfect; many great orators didn't or don't look particularly great. Not by a long shot. They don't always sound consistently great offstage either, but they do something on that platform which has audiences entranced and motivated.

When we began writing this book, colleagues and friends often commented that people rarely use oratory or rhetoric these days, apart from Barack Obama. And he, they declared, was a "one-off". Those from our (admittedly limited) sample poll would mostly cite historical figures such as Socrates, Churchill or Lincoln as examples of great public speakers, only very rarely including a modern politician or business leader. Our straw poll participants would often declare, in an effort to give an example of public speaking excellence, the name of a popular business headliner. We knew, having witnessed many business speeches, that such famous names were invariably not great, or even good, public speakers. The assumption of our unofficial table-top ballots was that all successful business people must be great speakers. This is compounded by the rise of the soundbite, the quickly prepared 24-hour rolling news and the growth of the internet. Colleagues remarked that people around the world, in whatever walk of life, didn't require or respond to speeches. Executives, politicians, all of us, were quite happy dipping into radio or TV and clutching a BlackBerry. They believed that all we needed was a short email, a text, a blog or a Twitter. We had all become an international set of headline readers.

Certainly, the expectations of modern audiences have changed and speechmakers have had to adapt. It was ever thus. Public meetings cease to be the draw they once were and attention spans have declined, in some cases dismally so. The same applies to the modern nature of conferences, business seminars and events of all shapes and sizes. Face-to-face communication is regarded as important – as against the predominant view in business a decade ago when managers thought that email and intranets would do the job instead. But oratory of any type has changed. No modern political leader would write a speech running to tens of thousands of words, as Emmeline Pankhurst and Nikita Khrushchev did, when audiences were prepared (or required) to listen for hours at a time. And nobody's suggesting that they should. Speed and brevity are much more important than they were fifty years ago or indeed ten years ago. Yet this led us to pose an interesting question: is there oratory in the humble soundbite? The answer is yes, because the best soundbites rely on classical techniques and old tricks. And most good (as opposed to trite) soundbites aren't remotely humble. An example is phrase reversal, as in John F. Kennedy's phrase: "Ask not what your country can do for you, but what you can do for your country." Another is the adaptation of an established cliché. Margaret Thatcher, Britain's "Iron Lady", took the well-worn phrase of Labour's "winter of discontent" and added a promise of "an autumn of understanding". "Read my lips: no new taxes" from presidential candidate George H. W. Bush is another example, as is Ronald Reagan's Berlin wall speech of 1987 which included this gem: "Mr Gorbachev, tear down this wall." Newspapers and blogs, websites and rolling news programmes around the world are full of soundbites. Some are good, but most are just cheap shots with little inner meaning and, truth be told, not a great deal of face-value meaning either.

If it's obvious to say that a great speech needs a speaker (and preferably one with more to offer than a simple soundbite) then two other qualities are equally apparent: a clear, compelling message and passion. It's surprising how many people stand vainly (in both senses of the word) in front of an audience with an unclear, unfocused message, a complete lack of empathy or understanding of who sits before them (or, heaven forfend, why) and an array of distracting or incomprehensible PowerPoint visuals. The very best speakers, as well as those from the mists of history, use the stage to present an argument. They prepare and practise their craft. They want to say something useful and say it well, even if they find the process hard. They make their message clear and spend a great deal of time in preparation to ensure complete clarity – and they have a real, immovable passion for their subject.

Great oratory and rhetoric seek to convince the listener of something, perhaps to accept a certain definition of freedom, to assert a "right", to offer hope, inspiration, practical support or simple guidance. These things are still required. Despite its value, oratory is sometimes conspicuous by its absence in contemporary speeches. Why? With the problems and opportunities of the modern world, surely more and better oratory is overdue? Oratory has been called the highest or finest form of art. It benefits from knowledge of literature, the ability to construct clear prose, empathy and an ear for rhythm and harmony. Maybe that's the problem. Do we know enough about these elements? Do we understand these ingredients? Do we care?

Other attributes of great oratory include emotion and timeliness. Oratory is not merely speaking; it is speech that has noble sentiments, clear ideals, values, stirring emotions, highlighting passions and inspiring action. Oratory is often at its finest when used during times of tragedy, pain, crisis and turmoil. In these situations it serves as a light, a guide to those who cannot make proper sense of the chaos or confusion and are looking for a leader to point the way. (All things are relative and the "leader" can of course be a middle manager presenting to thirty people.)

A great speech reflects the times in which it is delivered, but it can also work in other times – as a whole or in parts. That is what many of the speeches that we talk about in this book have in common: the speakers offered an idea or course of action that resonated with their times and with their audience, but which also had definitive value long after the words were first spoken.

Several of the speeches upon which we comment show how simple words can establish the importance of a speaker in the public mind. In any language and in any place. For example, Charles de Gaulle's wartime broadcasts were the first step to his being regarded as France's saviour. Likewise, Margaret Thatcher's determination and personality were firmly established when she insisted, despite high unemployment, that "the lady's not for turning". Nationalism is a powerful and recurring theme in many of the speeches we like. Other speeches rally opponents of the powerful by welding arguments together into a devastating weapon. This was achieved, for example, in very different ways, both by Nelson Mandela's speech from the dock in his 1964 treason trial and Aneurin Bevan's masterly parliamentary demolition of Anthony Eden's case for waging war on Egypt in 1956. In a different age, Earl Spencer's eulogy to his sister, Princess Diana, gently but coldly condemned the encroaching media and the seeming disinterest of the establishment, in particular the royal family.

Other speeches of note paint a picture, sometimes a detailed and true picture, of what a better world might be like. It is the communication of this vision around the world that can give a speech momentous political consequence. For example, the famous and superb "I Have a Dream" speech from Martin Luther King Jr was daring, beautifully constructed and delivered with absolute belief and passion. Some might say that this was preaching at its very best and, indeed, many of the world's greatest speakers emanated from pulpits or versions of pulpits or learned their craft from the preacher's pen and voice. King's speech painted a picture of a different world, an achievable world. The worldwide transmission of this speech has since given it even greater impact, inspiring generations.

Even where great speeches have very different form and purpose, there are some rhetorical tools that are used regularly. These are the tricks of the speaker's trade, many known to orators for centuries.

One of the most basic is the "rule of three". Speakers have always found that by putting things together in threes they can hit home their message. Charles de Gaulle put the rule to particularly good use. Instead of calling on people who served in "any of France's armed forces", he issued his summons in sequence to people of the army, navy and air force ("de terre, de mer et de l'air" – with the added advantage of course that it rhymed in French). The rhythm reinforces the call for everyone to take up arms and support the cause. Another example of that device is in President Obama's victory address in Grant Park, Chicago, in November 2008. He refers to his wife, Michelle, as: "The rock of our family, the love of my life, the nation's next first lady." The technique allows for a steady build of power and then an opportunity for accolade.

Anastrophe is a frequent device. This is when a speaker departs from normal word order for sake of emphasis (for example "Never in the field of human conflict was so much owed by so many to so few"). Parallelisms are also useful – using successive words or phrases with the same or similar grammatical structure. For example, on 10 November 1942, in response to the Allied victory at the Second Battle of El Alamein, Churchill said: "This is not the end. It is not even the beginning of the end. But it is, perhaps, the end of the beginning." John F. Kennedy, with his writer-in-chief Ted Sorensen's help, was also fond of parallelisms, for example: "Let every nation know, whether it wishes us well or ill, that we shall pay any price, bear any burden, meet any hardship, support any friend, oppose any foe to assure the survival and the success of liberty."

We all crave and respond to interesting and varied stimulants. Telling a story with dramatic effects – suddenly loud or suddenly soft, faster or slower, deliberate pausing – are simple, dramatic, theatrical effects. We like stories, stories that have a good fabric, an amusing conclusion, perhaps, or one that reinforces an already powerful point. Memorability is important. We want people to remember what we say long after we've said it. And an audience responds with enthusiasm to a speaker who understands the art of, well, talking. That means fits and starts for dramatic effect, short sentences in the active voice along with a few colloquial turns of phrase such as "you see", "so" or "well" – much as are used by some comedians when they stand and tell stories.

And then there is the symploce, where the first and last word or words appear in one phrase or sentence and are then repeated in one or more successive ones. John F. Kennedy again: "There are many people in the world who really don't understand, or say they don't, what is the great issue between the free world and the communist world. Let them come to Berlin. There are some who say that communism is the wave of the future. Let them come to Berlin. And there are some who say, in Europe and else-where, that we can work with the communists. Let them come to Berlin. And there are even a few who say that it is true that communism is an evil system, but it permits us to make economic progress. Lass' sie nach Berlin kommen. Let them come to Berlin." The repetition drives the narrative and the expectation is heightened. Another example is from Bill Clinton's "Oklahoma Bombing Memorial Prayer Service Address": "Let us let our own children know that we will stand against the forces of fear. When there is talk of hatred, let us stand up and talk against it. When there is talk of violence, let us stand up and talk against it." Here's one more, this time from Malcolm X: "Much of what I say might sound bitter, but it's the truth. Much of what I say might sound like it's stirring up trouble, but it's the truth. Much of what I say might sound like it is hate, but it's the truth." You get the idea and no doubt can see the power of structure. These things take time to prepare and borrow much from the style of the preacher.

But rhetoric on its own doesn't necessarily make a speech great. Speeches can be made, often fervently, with flowing and melodic language. But the net result of this is mere positioning. Content, and shaped content, is obviously important. The audience has to understand the subject or why it's important. Listeners want authenticity. When sincerity is conveyed to an audience – *and* when it isn't – it makes an impression. This is the case not just for the immediate listener, but also for those who hear it or read the speech long after it was given. For example, the greatness of Abraham Lincoln's speeches was not widely recognized when they were first delivered. Yet his eventual trademark, of course, and what made him unique as a politician, was his humility and the beauty of the written language he employed. It is in hindsight that we imagine his delivery to also have been outstanding (apparently it wasn't).

Great orators often reach back into their past, perhaps in a highly individual way, to provide their audiences with some appreciation of the significance of the present moment. They share their personal beliefs with their audiences. A classic example is Martin Luther King Jr, when he said that: "I have a dream that my four little children will one day live in a nation where they will not be judged by the colour of their skin, but by the content of their character." Modern politicians follow this line although it is less common in corporate presentations where the thinking tends to be that it's somewhat vainglorious to personalize speeches too much. That's a mistake. Personal stories count for much that a speech can inspire.

Inspiration comes in different styles and different guises. There are many speakers and speeches that extol the virtues of the distant future, not least because the speaker can paint almost any picture he or she wants and convey whatever the audience will believe. It's more difficult to inspire people to consider the significance of the "here and now". In September 1962 John F. Kennedy asserted: "We choose to go to the moon in this decade and do the other things – not because they are easy, but because they are hard. Because that goal will serve to organize and measure the best of our abilities and skills, because that challenge is one that we are willing to accept, one we are unwilling to postpone, and one which we intend to win." Many great speakers appeal to us to follow their example. They get us to buy in to their views (good or bad, agreeable or disagreeable) and we allow them to lead or simply to confirm our own thinking in a way that we find difficult to express, but which they annotate simply and superbly well.

The ability to provide a persuasive, influential vision or foretaste of the future is certainly a hallmark of a great speech. Persuasive speeches by an incoming state leader in any nation are designed to inspire hope for the future. And of course they must, but the words can't simply be disposable. For example, many American presidential inaugural speeches symbolize the philosophy of freedom in all its senses; freedom of speech, of living, of style, freedom from crime, war and strife, hunger, racism, schism and desperation. That is one of the reasons why so many of our one hundred greatest speakers and speeches are American: because for the last two centuries Americans have been thinking about their present and future. A largely immigrant society, Americans have often united around a single, compelling vision. Great speeches are invariably positive, forward-looking and successful – and the same can be said of many Americans. Circumstances have also played their part in America's contribution to oratory, often providing a dramatic platform and memorable context. For example, Franklin D. Roosevelt, speaking in the deepest, worst times of the Depression and in his first address as president, said: "The only thing we have to fear is fear itself ... These dark days will be worth all they cost us if they teach us that our true destiny is not to be ministered unto but to minister to ourselves and to our fellow men." There are many other examples of times of strife, struggles for liberty, civil war, violence against fellow men, assassination, financial meltdown and so on, when oratory counts and people want what it offers. These occasions need leadership, and people need to listen to those leaders. Sometimes, of course, the leadership is evil and people will still listen and follow. Such is the power of oratory.

Great speakers or speeches often have a moral seriousness which allows the audience to feel moved or to agree with the speaker's wit, insight or exhortation to think or do something. It is also noticeable when this doesn't work. We have all sat through a speech which should have been brilliant, but just never really worked. We willed the speaker to fly but he or she just didn't take off. Once again, it could have been a mixture of many things: poor understanding of the audience; too much reliance upon heavy-duty PowerPoint; poor audience awareness or engagement; no preparation (same speech as last week); and so on. Speakers often imagine themselves to be great orators, but there's neither depth nor form (and sometimes little ability) to what they deliver. No connection. In each case of great oratory, speakers present their personal convictions and do this in such a way that connects immediately with their audience. Bang. Immediately. This connection is absolutely key. In the preface to *Howard's End*

E. M. Forster writes "Only connect", and that phrase was, for a while, the working title of this book.

A successful speech is cleverly constructed and the writer (not always the speaker, of course) understands the real purpose of the speech and what the audience wants and needs. It can be said that the best orators are masters of both the written and spoken word; they use words to create texts that are beautiful to both hear and read. They create substance. Great rhetoric successfully persuades the audience of a fact or idea. And it is here that we declare a truism: the very best speeches really can change hearts and minds. At challenging moments in history, great speakers and speeches *have* changed minds. In a few short years the twenty-first century has already proven to be a time of conflict as well as insecurity and economic uncertainty. Recent years can also be viewed positively, with more people than ever before emerging from poverty (notably in Asia) and technological developments proving our overall capacity for ingenuity and progress. The point is that whether you believe in challenge or opportunity, both benefit from the leadership, guidance, insight, clarity, energy, consolation or support that come from great speakers and speeches.

While we have deliberately avoided any speeches from the theatre, plays, movies or television in our collection, fiction certainly did inspire us, as it includes some memorable speeches, many of which are admired and used by orators. For example, Shakespeare was undoubtedly a great speechwriter. Recall his rendition of Henry V's address at Agincourt: "We few, we happy few, we band of brothers; for he today that sheds his blood with me shall be my brother." Using this inspirational style and appeal to camaraderie is a simple and unrivalled way to rouse, enthuse and energize. The danger, of course, is over-use, which risks the quotation becoming a parody.

Military oratory, too, has given us memorable speeches. The address given in Iraq to the troops of the Royal Irish Regiment on the eve of battle by their commander, Lieutenant-Colonel Tim Collins, forms part of a long tradition of military oratory designed to galvanize the fighting spirit. In a speech full of soldierly virtues such as courage, modesty and respect for the enemy, he asked his soldiers to be "ferocious in battle and magnanimous in victory".

If a speech is to appeal to people it should be *designed* to appeal to people. This means, for example, that the speaker must allude to events and historical figures that are already known to the audience – an obvious observation, but one that is all too often forgotten or ignored. Great speakers display their passion in different ways but, however that passion is conveyed, audiences are left in no doubt as to the orator's view. The best orators use their audiences' imaginations and their knowledge of the good things and the good people of the past. Things and people that the audience will like. Talented speechmakers are also aware of the arguments that critics will raise and are able to deftly address and defuse each issue – before the issue arises or hitting it hard when it does. Preparation is required.

We have already touched on the importance of preparation in delivering a memorable speech. Cisco Systems CEO John Chambers is an example of a leader whose preparation is meticulous. He learns about his audience: who they are, what they need to know and what they like or dislike. The week before the presentation he will invariably discuss content with colleagues or specialists. The night before the presentation, he is known to review the slides and text. On the day of the presentation, he might walk onto the stage before the doors open and review the set-up of the room. Then he leaves the stage to see the lighting from the audience's perspective, taking note of where the lights are in every section of the hall to ensure that he never walks outside the lit areas. Very good.

The truth is that any speech, for any occasion, can be brilliant if you want it to be. The key is not to think of it as a chore or something that gets in the way of the day job. For a leader, even one under immense pressures, communicating with people is a core part of the overall task. Good communication should be the norm, great communication the ambition.

The qualities that make a speech or speaker better than good are also illuminated by the mediocre, weak and downright awful. "To keep silent is the most useful service that a mediocre talker can render to the public," said nineteenth-century French political thinker and historian Alexis de Tocqueville in his book *Democracy in America*. He went on to say: "Unfortunately, democratic assemblies encourage the mediocre to make dull, myopic, badly prepared, ill-performed speeches often and at length." In assessing democratic man, de Tocqueville observed: "He has only very particular and very clear ideas, or very general and very vague notions; the intermediate space is empty."

Of course, what works with one listener might not with another, but the greatest speeches seem to appeal to a majority at any one time. Something clicks; the light bulb blazes; the tear ducts swell; either the speaker says what the audience wants to hear (all too easy perhaps) or the speaker argues to change opinion (much harder). Clearly, many speeches are designed to appeal to the majority in an audience, either because someone has researched the situation accurately (a good thing), or because the time is absolutely right (also a good thing).

Hopefully, there will always be disagreements about what constitutes a great speech or speaker. This at least means that the issue occupies people's thoughts and, from our recent dinner table research, it does. The choice of one hundred greatest speeches was necessarily a subjective exercise and intended to stimulate debate. In our selection we have tried to be fair, balanced and politically neutral – so don't be surprised to find Margaret Thatcher with Aneurin Bevan, Jawaharlal Nehru with Muhammad Ali Jinnah, Bill Clinton with George H.W. Bush or his son, Barack Obama with John McCain. Most of the names that one would expect to be included are here, along with some lesser-known suggestions. Those garnering the most votes between the two of us and our friends are Abraham Lincoln, Franklin D. Roosevelt, Martin Luther King Jr, John and Robert Kennedy, Winston Churchill, Mahatma Gandhi, Frederick Douglass, Clarence Darrow, Virginia Woolf, Bill Cosby, Pericles, Nelson Mandela, Ronald Reagan and Barack Obama. But that doesn't mean a priority order – there just isn't one. All of our chosen hundred have great, but different, merits and each stands tall. Feel free to disagree.

If there is a unifying theme to our selection, it is that each speech made an impact, a huge impact, often because it was given at a crossroads in history – in hope, in business, in emergency or in chaos – and the audience heard something that helped to shake their complacency, provide guidance, inspire their actions, settle doubt or change minds. Some speeches are very specific about what change they seek to bring about. With others, it is only with hindsight that we see their full value or the strength that they brought to their audience when they were first given. One of the big issues that emerged in our selection was that of the slavery or subjugation of peoples. This issue dominates many of the speeches of our chosen few. We move from the crisis over slavery to the controversy over civil rights. This highlights another important ingredient of exceptional speeches: the need for moral courage and the need for exceptional change.

Other speakers and speeches we chose simply because we liked the speaker and knew that he or she delivered a speech in a way that always delighted an audience, while making pertinent and memorable messages abundantly clear. In such cases, it is the performance that adds huge value. In others, it's the moment and the surroundings, the theatre of the occasion, the drama. We wanted to be sure that we were being fair each time we made a choice. Choosing one speaker usually meant removing another from the list.

Not all of our inclusions are "good" people or "nice" folks. That's deliberate and for obvious reasons. Great speeches are not limited to the power of good or what we consider right. We have therefore included a speech by Adolf Hitler because, as we explain later, his first and arguably his most powerful weapon was his oratory and this enabled him to move a nation from peace to war. We believe that our common understanding of the threat posed by dictators is enhanced if we recognize the menace that comes from their simple, powerful words and communication techniques.

Surprisingly, some of the speeches we have chosen actually berate their audiences. With this sort of oratory, the attack is on society as a whole and the rhetoric gets the audience onside. The trick is to set out your logic and argument clearly so that your audience can properly understand your argument – and then lead them to the point where they can only agree with you. For example, Frederick Douglass, a great orator with a fantastic turn of phrase, must have made the abolitionists go grey with anxiety and then bright red with awkwardness when he delivered his "Fifth of July" speech. He issues a shopping list of accusations: "This fourth of July is yours, not mine. You may rejoice, I must mourn." Douglass says that to invite him as a guest Independence Day speaker is mere "mockery and sacrilegious irony". How the audience must have wondered why he had been invited to speak! He declared that he and his audience should not dare to sing a song of praise on the nation's birthday because, as he pointed out: "Above your national, tumultuous joy, I hear the mournful wail of millions!" Douglass slammed his audience hard and even now, as one reads the speech, one can only wonder how close he might have been to an ejection. After the haranguing, Douglass lets up. At his close, he gives his abolitionist audience succour and calms down the fevered ears by ending on a note of hope.

People may say: "But surely we can't say that sort of thing now?" Our answer, borrowed from Barack Obama, is "Yes, we can" and of course people do. Because of the multimedia machine surrounding us, we may not always seek out oratory to say it and we may not always assume its relevance. But, as others have widely remarked, the Obama campaign and his election showed, without doubt, what rhetoric and oratory can do. There may be different subjects, different languages, different cultural and political references, different challenges and times, but great speeches continue to have similar structure, similar power, similar emotions, similar tone – and similar results.

It takes no great scrutiny to see that modern speeches have become shorter, and that's not a bad thing. After all, we would always advise executives to keep their speeches to 20 or 30 minutes tops. Unfortunately, there are many who dictate that they should speak for an hour (or much more) for no other reason than they feel that it's about the right amount of time and, anyway, they argue, why shouldn't they? Well, it may be their toy and they can do what they want. But consider any other form where people sit in seats watching a performance when that performance is less than acceptable. Would they be obliged to stay? Would they stay? Would they come back for more? So many corporate, educational, institutional, conventional or political speeches are dull, forgettable and inconsequential. Harsh? Really, not. And more and more, the cost comes into it. Just getting an audience in, parked and ready to listen is not a cheap option. Why waste the opportunity? Who would want to? Modern speeches are often composed of dry, detailed corporate or political lists of tired delivery or non-delivery, promises, revised promises, promised programmes or historical financial details – all sandwiched between tired phrases and the management-speak of the day, along with poorly delivered hectoring. Why?

Modern phraseology doesn't always lend itself to great speechmaking. Maybe it was always so. Organizational leaders, politicians and mid-range executives of all persuasions utilize lists of phrases which are wretched as much as they are meaningless: "going forward", "low-hanging fruit", "watch this space", "from the get-go", "close of play", "110%", "paradigm shifts", "living the values", "drill down". That's just a few. The creation of long, convoluted paragraphs is also rife. This is not only an English language issue; it's a worldwide issue. It is the combination of laziness, the generation of non-verb sentences and smart phrases along with the vapid generalizations that de Tocqueville predicted. But we find the current collection anathema.

There is perhaps a new awareness of what language can do; how it can sound; what it can achieve. There is the beginning of a revised awareness of rhetoric, great writing and great delivery. People, it seems, want to listen to words. They want, it appears, to be persuaded by face-to-face communication. And, in all of our research, we have found that it is certainly true that the greatest speeches are those that were gripping precisely because they made demands on the listener.

Barack Obama sets the standard for speechmaking in our immediate times. His strengths are his sincerity and blatant ability to connect with people. He conveys a vision that appears uniquely his own but one in which his listeners can join. He is sincere and not egotistical; he does not dwell on the maudlin. It's no surprise to find that he is a student of the great orators and wordsmiths, particularly Lincoln, his favourite. The reception given to his speeches, even in office, suggest that there is a hunger for oratory (and, for the moment certainly, for him) – and not just in the United States. Everywhere he is valued and respected because of his inspirational words that touch audience ideals.

There are certainly in the corridors of all kinds of power around the world some great speakers. In India, Pakistan, China, Mexico, Korea, France, Canada, Singapore, Brazil – everywhere – there are gifted orators. Some are modest and work in schools, in colleges, in universities, in local government, in businesses. But while there are still a few great orators

Salvador Allende

Other men will overcome this dark and bitter moment when treason seeks to prevail. Go forward knowing that, sooner rather than later, the great avenues will open again and free men will walk through them to construct a better society."

Last speech: radio broadcast, La Moneda, Santiago de Chile, Tuesday 11 September 1973

Salvador Isabelino Allende Gossens was born on 26 June 1908 and allegedly committed suicide on 11 September 1973. He was president of Chile from November 1970 until his death during a coup d'état.

Allende was deeply entrenched in Chilean politics for the best part of 40 years. He unsuccessfully ran for the presidency on three occasions, 1952, 1958 and 1964. He was finally elected in 1970.

He was a fervent Marxist and believed that his country needed structural and social change on a grand scale. His policies included free milk for school children and a substantial increase in workers' wages. Part of his planned change programme also included the nationalization of the vital Chilean copper industry and broad land reform. Allende felt that this would be essential for the country to move quickly to socialism from what he believed to be a corrupt capitalist system.

Effecting change and movement on a big scale, from one edge of the political spectrum to another, was a tough task and it divided Allende's supporters. Chile's right-wing opposition forces began to regroup, receiving substantial support from America. The opposition also controlled much of the country's media. Allende was between a rock and a hard place. On the one hand his attempt at large-scale social and economic reform (including the nationalization of private industries) made him enemies in Chile and the United States. On the other, he faced factional opposition from extremists in his own party who felt that his reforms were far too mild and limited.

Lessons from Salvador Allende

Drive home key words. Repetition of certain words or phrases within a speech, particularly at the start of short sentences, frames an idea and pummels (or persuades) the audience into remembering an argument's main points. The device is called anaphora and its prime benefit is that it helps the speaker and the listener to gather together thought and the logic of an idea. It's a technique frequently used in political speeches, but we've known it to work, used wisely, in corporate life as well. Here Salvador Allende uses a simple repetition to great emotional effect: "I address you, above all, the modest woman of our land …," "I address professionals of Chile …," "I address the youth …," "I address the man of Chile, the worker, the farmer …"

Be ready to capture memorable moments with your speech. Many speeches are made before, at or shortly after historical moments. These can be big, national occasions or important only to a small audience. Whatever the case, the moment cannot be revisited, so work at the speech, its content and delivery. Not all situations are as stark as this one, of course.

Just before the capture of the presidential palace, Palacio de La Moneda, with gunfire and explosions heard clearly in the background, Salvador Allende gave his farewell live radio broadcast to the citizens of Chile.

Whether he knew that this was the end of his rule and his life, we don't know, but we can guess that he did. The speech is, as a consequence, moving and enormously poetic. The sense is political but the language is that of poetry, epitomizing his love for Chile and of his faith that the future would be better.

The speech is intense but there's no panic: "My words do not have bitterness, but disappointment. May they be a moral punishment for those who have betrayed their oath … the only thing left for me is to say to workers: I am not going to resign! Placed in a historic transition, I will pay for loyalty to the people with my life …" Allende explained that his commitment to Chile did not allow him to take an easy way out. He said that he refused to be used as a propaganda tool by those who had betrayed him and, accordingly, the country, including those on his side who had accepted safety for surrender. The implication was clear; he intended to fight to the end.

Shortly after the broadcast, Salvador Allende died. An official announcement declared that he had committed suicide.

A Legacy

Salvador Allende is seen as a hero by many around the world on the political left. For many of his supporters he is remembered for his conviction that socialism could be reached democratically and peacefully. Some view him as a martyr who died for socialism, others see him as a Marxist symbol.

The pathos of his last broadcast is obviously heightened, given the context in which his words were spoken, but his speech has lived long in hearts of many Chileans: "Surely Radio Magallanes will be silenced and the calm metal instrument of my voice will no longer reach you. It does not matter. You will continue hearing it. I will always be next to you. At least my memory will be that of a man of dignity who was loyal to his country. The people must defend themselves, but they must not sacrifice themselves. The people must not let themselves be destroyed or riddled with bullets, but they cannot be humiliated either."

Allende's name and his memory have grown in stature with time. Streets, museums and schools carry his name both in Chile and elsewhere. He is regarded as having brought prestige to Chilean politics and also a series of reforms which, to a large degree, helped shape the country's fabric. His influence was such that neighbouring countries, such as Venezuela and Bolivia, also subsequently elected socialist governments with more or less the same ambition as set out by Allende.

Susan B. Anthony

It was we, the people; not we, the white male citizens; nor yet we, the male citizens; but we, the whole people, who formed the Union. And we formed it, not to give the blessings of liberty, but to secure them; not to the half of ourselves and the half of our posterity, but to the whole people – women as well as men."

"Women's Right to the Suffrage" stump speech, after being convicted of voting, Monroe County, New York, USA, 1873

Susan Brownell Anthony was born on 15 February 1820 and died on 13 March 1906. She was a prominent American civil rights leader who played an absolutely pivotal role in the nineteenth-century movement to bring attention to American women's suffrage.

In the 1800s, women in America had very few legal rights; certainly they didn't have the right to vote. This speech was given by Susan Anthony after her arrest for casting an illegal vote in the 1872 presidential election. She was tried and subsequently fined $100; she adamantly refused to pay the penalty.

Her involvement in suffrage began when she met abolitionists Lloyd Garrison, Amelia Bloomer and Elizabeth Cady Stanton. Through their influence and companionship, she began her temperance work. On one occasion, at a temperance rally, she tried to speak, but was refused the opportunity. As a result, she and Stanton founded the first women's temperance society.

Lessons from Susan B. Anthony

Use your passion. Make it count, make it work. Controlled anger can be highly effective, but passion is not the same as anger. Passionate at the injustice of the lack of women's rights, Susan Anthony embarked on a speaking tour in support of female voting rights, during which she gave this particular speech. She had to work very hard at her speechmaking since it did not come easily and she was initially terrified of tough audiences. During the early stages of the temperance society, most of the public speaking was left to her colleague Elizabeth Stanton, who excelled at oratory. Although she may not have been the orator that Stanton was, certainly to begin with, Anthony excelled in her speechwriting.

Initially, her speaking style was slow and sometimes hesitant, but that in itself produced a power that was attractive and which she used to full effect. People (mostly) wanted to hear her talk about fairness and the right to vote. Her hesitancy added value, a modesty, a strong element of truth. They would wait for her words, which were presented with an intensity, verve and vigour that became unforgettable. Over the years, audiences quietened and people listened. The pauses became as important as the spoken words.

Set out your case, your cause. An obvious point to make but many make speeches where the peroration takes an absolute age to reach and at its end one cannot in truth recall the real message or the subtlety of any argument. Susan Anthony said: "I stand before you tonight under indictment for the alleged crime of having voted at the last presidential election, without having a lawful right to vote. It shall be my work this evening to prove to you that in thus voting, I not only committed no crime, but, instead, simply exercised my citizen's rights, guaranteed to me and all United States citizens by the National Constitution, beyond the power of any State to deny." She went on, brilliantly, to offer the basis of her argument: "It was we, the people; not we, the white male citizens; nor yet we, the male citizens; but we, the whole people, who formed the Union. And we formed it, not to give the blessings of liberty, but to secure them; not to the half of ourselves and the half of our posterity, but to the whole people – women as well as men."

A Legacy

In 1919 the United States passed the 19th Amendment to the Constitution – the "Susan B. Anthony Amendment" – extending the vote to women.

Susan Anthony did not marry and spent most of her life on her activism. She was both aggressive and compassionate by nature, with a sharp mind and an ability to inspire others, as she did in speeches like the "Women's Right to the Suffrage": "The only question left to be settled now is: are women persons? And I hardly believe any of our opponents will have the hardihood to say they are not." Her organizational genius was legendary. The canvassing plan she created is still used by grassroots organizations. There are few people who can be said to have changed social mores, to have made possible what many thought impossible, to have made a major difference for people then and for those who followed. Susan Anthony was one of these very few and her legacy is reflected in a changed society that she, and people like her, effected.

Corazón Aquino

Before we scrutinize personalities and agenda, let us look inward first. Before we try to discern whom to believe, let us be certain about what we believe. Before demanding anything of our leaders, let us first demand it of ourselves. Let us be true to ourselves and to everything that we profess to hold dear."

Speech to Jesuit priests, Ateneo de Manila University, Manila, Philippines, Tuesday 13 September 2005

María Corazón Cojuangco-Aquino (born 25 January 1933 and died 1 August 2009) was president of the Philippines from 1986 to 1992. Cory Aquino's husband was Senator Benigno Aquino, Jr, who opposed

Philippine president Ferdinand Marcos, a dangerous thing to do openly. In 1983 Senator Aquino was assassinated on his return from exile in the United States and it was left largely to Cory Aquino to oppose President Marcos for no other reason really than she was her husband's widow. Such was the expectation of her that, despite having absolutely no background in, or experience of, politics, Cory Aquino became the focal point of the opposition against Marcos. As a result of the peaceful People Power Revolution in 1986 (largely orchestrated by her), she became president. These days, Aquino spends much of her time establishing women's rights round the world and also devotes herself to a number of peace movements.

Lessons from Corazón Aquino

Use your speech to establish legitimacy and evoke sympathy or support. Cory Aquino was brand-new to politics after her husband's assassination. Her challenge was even more significant simply because her husband had been killed, probably at the behest of Marcos, and because Philippine politics was driven by violence and its threat. Aquino made a big point of presenting herself as a decent, honest and simple citizen. She reinforced this by developing or adopting a speaking style that was similarly simple and direct, using language spoken by the people. Her references were the people's references and the popular quotations and allusions she used were readily understood by her audiences. Her directness and openness were a refreshing change and obviously people liked that. Her popularity grew fast to the point that, in 1986, she was declared Woman of the Year in *Time* magazine – after less than twelve months as president of the Philippines. Also in late 1986, she was invited to speak before a joint session of the United States Congress. The occasion was a huge success – Aquino was stopped on several occasions by wild and prolonged applause. United States House Speaker Tip O'Neill apparently said that Aquino's was "the finest speech I've ever heard in my 34 years in Congress".

Accentuate a moving story or myth, particularly if one has built up around you. In the Congress speech Aquino explained her position and how it had developed. She said: "Twenty years ago, I found myself thrust into a role I did not seek. Against all odds, I consented to run for the presidency primarily because the political opposition at the time needed a candidate to unite around in order to end the Marcos dictatorship and restore our democracy. However, the elections were mired in lying, cheating, stealing and killing. When the rubber-stamp parliament proclaimed Ferdinand Marcos as the winner of the 1986 elections, around one million

Filipinos joined me in a rally proclaiming the people's victory and there I launched a non-violent protest movement ..."

Her style was always humble but firm and direct and her speeches always reinforced the position of humility and citizenship, of right versus wrong and of freedom and democracy. On one occasion she declared: "I am a plain housewife, the widow of a great man and I am simply seeking justice and to complete his work." This positioning worked on a number of levels. It presented her as representative of the downtrodden and it showed her to be weak with a defence only of moral courage. This became her strength. Her stance suggested that her motives were honourable rather than solicitous or even political. Her attitude also evoked support and empathy. It identified her personally with the benefits of democracy while showing her enemies, and therefore enemies of the Philippines, as being dangerous, oppressive and evil.

The stance rallied the people to the movement towards freedom, hope, democracy, non-violence. It could be said of course that the romance of Aquino's story had an opposite and somewhat negative side. Some saw her as protesting far too much and not advocating sufficiently detailed change; they saw this as a weakness, a weakness that a leader shouldn't have.

A Legacy

Cory Aquino's legacy was a return to democracy for the Philippines after years of dictatorship. She gave the country legitimacy and authority once more – in its own affairs and also as a respected nation. Her fight was one for fairness and democracy, something which had been sadly lacking during the dark days before her rise in influence and power. For instance, during her 2005 speech to the Jesuit priests at the Ateneo de Manila University, she said: "Those who march beside, behind or in front of me on the streets may hold views and convictions quite different from mine. I have no control over that. Such is the nature of democracy." She was also delighted and rightly proud that she had shown that a woman could succeed in the traditional, male-dominated world of politics, particularly Filipino politics. In this she became something of an important beacon to women and to a "can-do" spirit worldwide, much as did Bhutto and Gandhi, Thatcher and Meir, Chile's Bachelet and Finland's Halonen, Helen Clark of New Zealand and, of course, the Philippines' Gloria Macapagal-Arroyo. Aquino's achievement in helping to deliver a country from darkness to light was managed with a mixture of strength, grace and decency.

Mustafa Kemal Atatürk

We have accomplished great things in a short period of time. The greatest of these is the Turkish Republic ... We never think that what we have done is enough. We are determined and obliged to accomplish more and greater things."

Speech on the tenth anniversary of the foundation of the Republic of Turkey, Ankara, Turkey, Sunday 29 October 1933

Mustafa Kemal Atatürk was born in the Ottoman city of Salonika (modern-day Thessaloniki in Greece) on 19 May 1881 and he died on 10 November 1938. He was the founder of the Republic of Turkey and its first president.

In 1915 Atatürk became known as an excellent military commander, while fighting at the Battle of Gallipoli. His successful and well-documented military campaigns in the Turkish War of Independence led to the liberation of the country and to the foundation of the Turkish Republic. Almost immediately, Atatürk initiated an ambitious programme of social, political, economic and cultural reforms.

Lessons from Mustafa Kemal Atatürk

Project authority and belief. The Ottoman Empire had lasted from 1299 to 1923 but now it was at an end. Atatürk knew that there was a need for strong leadership and confidence. He believed unequivocally that Turkey could rise again and that its people could ensure that it did. In this October 1933 speech, he is indeed confident because he knows that he has delivered what he promised. This is very important. Never claim what you haven't helped to deliver. People do and it always backfires. Atatürk said: "During the last fifteen years, I have made many promises to you to be successful in our undertakings. I am pleased that I have not failed my nation in any of them and given you cause to doubt me. Today, I speak with the same faith and assurance that, within a short period of time, the whole civilized world will once again recognize that the Turkish nation, moving unified toward the national ideal, is a great nation."

Show magnanimity and exemplify your words. Atatürk's reputation was as a military leader. Some therefore expected him to manage Turkey with a strong focus on its army and something akin to a military dictatorship. He did not. He knew that all levels of Turkish society looked for guidance. He showed his people that he wanted to build a state that was modern, forward-looking and secular. Not a sad and tired ex-empire that looked with envy over its shoulder at its history. Turkey, Atatürk averred, would be a successful nation belonging firmly to the twentieth century.

Use the language and style with which you feel comfortable, provided that you know the audience will share your comfort. Atatürk's style and choice of words were sometimes old-fashioned and stilted, but his views and his example were striking and consistent. For instance, speaking in March 1923, he said: "History is made as much with emotions as with knowledge, reason and logic. It would be wrong to assume that we can erase the centuries-old emotions of our enemies with only today's developments. We will erase these feelings not with victories, but by adopting the contemporary progress, by undertaking all that is necessary for contemporary science and civilization, and by actually reaching the level of knowledge of all civilized nations."

A Legacy

From the shattering aftermath of World War I and the destruction of the Ottoman Empire, Atatürk worked determinedly to create the modern Turkish Republic. It was a great achievement considering the Empire's confusion, factions, religious differences and poor economy. For instance, he successfully led the Turkish nationalist revolt against France, Britain, Italy, Armenia and Greece in the Turkish War of Independence, lasting from 1919 to 1923. But his leadership was not about war. The principles of Atatürk's reforms formed the strong political foundations on which the modern Turkish state is built.

Atatürk's words in October 1933 gave back to the people of Turkey their self-respect. The words also emphasized the importance of peace and of growth. And of being Turkish: "In every decade which passes into eternity, I wholeheartedly wish that you celebrate this great national holiday with ever greater honour, happiness, peace and tranquillity. Happy is he who says: 'I am a Turk'." This extract from Atatürk's speech is something of which Turks are most proud.

Aung San Suu Kyi

I would like [the West] to see us not as a country rather far away whose sufferings do not matter, but as fellow human beings in need of human rights and who could do so much for the world, if we were allowed."

Mass Rally, Shwedagon pagoda, Friday 26 August 1988

Aung San Suu Kyi is Burma's pro-democracy leader and she has been under house arrest in Burma for the past nineteen years and, as we write, she is still a focus of the Burmese government. For her work and efforts in trying to bring democracy to her country, she was awarded the Nobel Peace Prize. She persistently calls on people around the world to join the struggle for freedom in Burma, famously saying to the international community: "Please use your liberty to promote ours". She was born on 19 June 1945, the daughter of Burma's independence hero, General Aung San, who was assassinated by political opponents when Suu Kyi was very young.

Lessons from Aung San Suu Kyi

Championing a cause in which you believe, but which has risk, requires enormous self-belief, preparation and courage. On 26 August 1988, Aung San Suu Kyi addressed a large rally in Rangoon, calling for Burmese democracy: "Reverend monks and people! This public rally is aimed at informing the whole world of the will of the people. Therefore at this mass rally the people should be disciplined and united to demonstrate the very fact that they are a people who can be disciplined and united. Our purpose is to show that the entire people entertain the keenest desire for a multi-party democratic system of government ..." Half a million people participated in the protest, despite the danger from the military government, which did in fact respond by killing or incarcerating hundreds of dissident leaders.

On the day of the rally, the grounds of the golden Shwedagon pagoda of Rangoon were packed. A huge picture of Aung San Suu Kyi's father looked down from the stage, along with a vast flag of the resistance movement he had led. It was this movement that in 1948 had brought Burma its independence, a few months after he had been assassinated. In 1988, though, Burma was again in the midst of unrest and political upheaval.

An audience's curiosity is a valuable lever. The vast crowds at the pagoda heard that Suu Kyi had responded to the government's violent stance by calling for an immediate stop to any force against unarmed demonstrators. She had proposed a People's Consultative Committee to help resolve the crisis. People knew almost nothing about her apart from the fact that she was her father's daughter. And her father was regarded as a hero. The crowd also knew that she had been educated abroad and wondered if she had any idea about their plight or would even understand Burmese. However, when she began to speak in perfect Burmese, they listened with rapt attention and, at the end of the speech, they gave her huge applause. She had dared to say what they had long thought.

The oratory is brilliant. The context, the absolute conviction, the carefully built argument, the passion and the delivery are all superb. Obviously, it does help if a speaker says what the audience wants to hear but, when times are tough, that's not at all easy. Some, many, certainly wanted to hear what Suu Kyi had to say in 1988. Others were far less sure of her credibility and they had less than encouraging views of her ability as a leader. However, a great speaker can also convert audience opinion from a minus view to a positive. It falls to many who take the stage – in business, in politics – to do just that.

Inspire your audience with an emotive challenge. Suu Kyi described the crisis as being Burma's "second struggle for national independence", the first being her father's. "I could not, as my father's daughter, remain indifferent," she said. What the people wanted was the freedom and democracy for which he had so desperately fought. The country had been divided, group against group, faction fighting faction; division had ruled. She asked the Burmese people to work together with the many ethnic minorities in the country and called upon them not only for unity and discipline, but also to "demonstrate clearly and distinctly their capacity to forgive".

Always be straightforward. Aung San Suu Kyi spoke frankly about personal criticisms: "It is true that I have lived abroad. It is also true that I am married to a foreigner. These facts have never interfered and will never interfere with or lessen my love and devotion for my country by any measure or degree." With this speech, her first major political address, Aung San Suu Kyi became the leader of what had previously been a spontaneous popular movement. The people saw her as a reincarnation of her father. Even her name, which means "a bright collection of strange victories", made (and makes) them feel hopeful.

A Legacy

Since 1988 Suu Kyi has directly, but mostly indirectly, agitated for the restoration of democratic rights in Burma and fought for the human rights of victims of Burmese army rule. When she won the Nobel Peace Prize in 1991, her son gave a very powerful and moving acceptance speech on her behalf. That fact alone guaranteed a huge amount of press coverage and the world's media continues to thwart Burma's military government's attempts to try to cover up any aspect of revolt in that country.

The 1988 Rangoon speech by Aung San Suu Kyi marked the beginning of her campaign against the Burmese military regime. While her house arrest has limited her ability to drive the campaign, it has focused the world's media upon her and Burma's position. Even now, her liberty is at further risk and her country more isolationist than ever.

Her 1988 speech reflects a great plea for a country denied the opportunity to be free in many ways. On that day in August 1988 she said plaintively, but powerfully: "If my words meet with your approval, please support me ..."

Henry Ward Beecher

Let us look for a true humanity, let us look for the true fruit of religion, not in the associated body of this or that denomination, but in the majesty and power of love in the individual hearts ..."

Sermon, Plymouth Church, New York, USA, Thursday 18 November 1869

Henry Ward Beecher was born on 24 June 1813. An outstanding preacher and abolitionist, he was possibly the best-known and certainly the most influential American Protestant minister between 1850 and his death on 8 March 1887. Like his novelist sister, Harriet Beecher Stowe (author of the hugely successful novel *Uncle Tom's Cabin*), Henry Beecher had a brilliant flair for getting audiences to listen. He was able to enthral people and to ensure that all his messages, political or spiritual, were remembered, not least because he used language and references readily understood and liked by all, an obvious device that is, quite astonishingly, still only rarely used by speechmakers today.

Lessons from Henry Ward Beecher

View speaking as an opportunity – not a curse. In 1847 Beecher moved to Brooklyn, New York, to become the pastor of the new Plymouth Church. He stayed there for the rest of his life and made it one of the most admired and influential American pulpits, attracting huge crowds of around 2,500 each Sunday. His dynamic, powerful delivery and his ability to speak on topics of popular, relevant interest gained him a wide audience. His sermons were regularly copied down, then published on a national basis and read by all levels of society.

Reflect your audience's mood and concerns. If the mood is low, lift it. Beecher had a natural empathy with both his immediate parish and the wider audience. He was sensitive to local and national issues and he understood what people wanted to hear. He was a natural showman and enjoyed preparing and giving his speeches. He knew that he could lift an apathetic audience or calm an excited one. He also knew that his ministry exerted huge power and he was as well known for his Republican Party affiliation and advocacy of political matters as for his theological opinions. Politicians would seek his support, parishioners his opinion.

Always show that you are there for your audience. Make the audience feel that you are talking to them personally and not just exercising a duty. Many speakers care not a jot that they are repeating the same presentation time after time. It shows. Beecher carefully planned his sermons shortly before delivering them, leaving his audience with the impression that he was preaching extemporaneously. His deliveries were always regarded as fresh – week upon week. About which and how many speakers can we say the same? His sermons were always regarded as inspirational, emotional and theatrical performances. It has been said that as many people would have turned up had Beecher offered sermons every day of the week. Even if that's hearsay, it's some hearsay.

Use dramatic language when appropriate. Building to a point is a powerful technique: "Let us look for a true humanity, let us look for the true fruit of religion, not in the associated body of this or that denomination, but in the majesty and power of love in the individual hearts of those who are gathered into sects. Let us look no more into books, merely ..." The repeated use of "let us look" allows the speech to gain power, crest like a wave and wash over the audience.

Humour is good – with care. Beecher's humour was anticipated with glee by his admirers and even grudgingly acknowledged by his critics. He brought good cheer and he was able to poke fun at targets that most found hard to criticize. His notoriety was such that politicians were wary and sometimes fearful of Beecher's broadsides. He was also notorious for the anecdotes and amusing quips that he inserted into his sermons and he was more than willing to induce laughter by mimicry or ridicule. Beecher's vitality and love of life were infectious and it would be fair to say that many of the nation's speakers, preachers, actors, politicians, teachers and writers were more than a little jealous (and certainly admiring) of his ability.

Detail, the right detail, matters. Beecher's anecdotes, his stories, his illustrations, his descriptions were superb. He kept notes on all sorts of detail and these reveal an extraordinary mind. His imagination was obviously vivid and he shared it to the full. He assimilated material from nature, domestic life, society, literature and politics: "The States are so many points of vitality. The nation, like a banyan tree, lets down a new root when each new State is established and when centuries have spread this gigantic commercial tree over a vast space, it will be found that the branches most remote from the centre do not draw their vitality through the long intricate passages from the parent trunk, but each outlying growth has roots of its own and draws from the ground by organisms of its own, all the food it wants, without dissociating its top from the parent branches ..." The result was that audiences listened, entranced.

A Legacy

According to Abraham Lincoln's biographer, Carl Sandburg, Beecher was "the most accomplished artist of them all if stump oratory was required from the pulpit". Without question, Beecher set a standard for preaching and public speaking, one that has been rarely matched.

Beecher firmly believed that it was the role of Christianity to adapt itself to the changing culture of the times. He brought to the attention of a large number of people across America and later in Britain the plight of slaves, the struggle of women's suffrage and Darwin's theory of evolution. In particular, he was adamant that slavery was abhorrent and that it shamed the new nation of America. Quite openly, and encouraged by many politicians, he raised considerable amounts of money to buy weapons so that slavery could be opposed in a number of States. The guns bought with this money became known as "Beecher's Bibles".

Ralph Waldo Emerson, Henry David Thoreau and Mark Twain were all avid Beecher fans. Mark Twain described a particular event: "Beecher went marching up and down the stage, sawing his arms in the air, howling sarcasms this way and that, discharging rockets of poetry and exploding mines of eloquence ..."

Beecher was said to have been integral to the Union victory in the Civil War. Lincoln himself wanted the preacher to give an important Fort Sumter address: "We had better send Beecher down to deliver the address on the raising of the flag because if it had not been for Beecher, there would be no flag to raise," he said. Lincoln also later observed that if it hadn't been for Beecher's sister, Harriet Beecher Stowe, and her novel *Uncle Tom's Cabin*, there might not have been a Civil War.

Aneurin Bevan

We cannot run the processes of modern society by attempting to impose our will upon nations by armed force. If we have not learned that, we have learned nothing."

The "Severed Weapons for Squalid and Trivial Ends" speech on Suez, House of Commons, London, UK, Wednesday 5 December 1956

Aneurin (often called Nye) **Bevan** was born on 15 November 1897 and died on 6 July 1960. He was a British politician with a reputation as an awesome orator and also known predominantly as the founder of the UK's National Health Service – a huge achievement after World War II and a great example of a political vision becoming a reality, despite its modern difficulties. He championed the poor and the political left, most of his speaking engagements being made in support of both causes. His fiery language and firm views often got Bevan into political hot water and much of what he said was, at the very least, controversial.

Lessons from Aneurin Bevan

Make your language inspiring. Bevan's words have inspired many – a phrase from one of his speeches, "This is my truth, tell me yours", provided the Welsh rock band, the Manic Street Preachers, with the title of their fifth album. It's a powerful, pithy, memorable and engaging phrase, the likes of which Bevan used to pepper most of his public oratory. His audiences thirsted for these phrases and a serving of what Bevan offered – a developed language that sang, soared and inspired.

Use your background to help tell stories. Many public speakers assume that their audiences will know all about them and their histories. If relevant, positioning your personal history, within the context of your message, can help the force of your speech. Bevan's childhood had been very tough and his family were poor; one of ten children, he left school four days before his fourteenth birthday to work in a coalmine. While he did not milk this background during his political career, he did make a point of showing his understanding and knowledge of the plight of poor people – of Wales in particular but also of the whole of Britain. The poor in turn knew unequivocally that he was one of them.

Voice and style and a sense of the theatre are vital. Bevan was a natural actor and studied body language carefully. He enjoyed the theatre of public speaking. Along with his lilting Welsh accent, he used a range of physical techniques to his advantage. His language was imaginative and his imagery colourful and relevant. People understood and delighted in his references. He talked *to* his audiences not at them. He understood what they wanted to hear and know and he grasped what would encourage and motivate them.

His timing within his speeches was excellent and, like many orators before him, he used his stammer (that he'd had since childhood) to advantage rather than pretending it wasn't there. His stammer became part of his speechmaking methodology. Many people who suffer a stammer often hate the process of others completing their words or sentences. Conversely, Bevan liked the fact that audiences would complete his thought process. It became a method of binding him with them.

Create a style. To reinforce a point Bevan would invariably use his arms to embrace or push away an argument. Sometimes, he would feign exhaustion, wearily pausing, looking about him or stopping to brush his hair back with a sweep of a hand and perhaps giving a long-suffering sigh – instantly gathering sympathy and empathy all in one. Interestingly, his manners were superb and gentlemanly. His behaviour was always impeccable, even when he was doing his opponents the most harm with his wrath, sarcasm, wit or withering pity.

Speeches benefit from being straightforward, robust and with a single, powerful message or argument. When quizzed about the art of his own speechmaking, Bevan said that by and large he would take the strongest part of an opponent's case or an opposing view, not the weakest. Damage that, he thought, and you sink the argument. For example, Bevan's 1956 Suez speech made in the House of Commons was directed at outdated, but still current and popular, imperialist assumptions. The speech deconstructed each point of these assumptions and very carefully damaged and then destroyed each one.

Educate your audience. Bevan felt it incumbent upon leaders and politicians to educate and develop people's thinking. Bevan never meant this in a condescending way but rather he believed that people, working people, often had little opportunity to express real views. He felt that he had a duty to release any shackles that held people's thinking tight. He thought that if his speeches contained some strong, sometimes surprising, hooks, then listeners would be able to follow an argument to its conclusion and, in the process, learn something.

Conclude your speech with a sharp point – it helps people to remember your main proposition. What you say at the end of a speech should echo in people's minds, make them think, get them to consider the argument long after you've gone. In the Suez speech, the ending makes Bevan's main argument crystal-clear: "The social furniture of modern society is so complicated and fragile that it cannot support the jackboot. We cannot run the processes of modern society by attempting to impose our will upon nations by armed force. If we have not learned that, we have learned nothing … It may be that the dead in Port Said are 100, 200 or 300. If it is only one, we had no business to take it … It will take us very many years to live down what we have done. It will take us many years to pay the price. I know that tomorrow evening honourable and right honourable members will probably, as they have done before, give the government a vote of confidence, but they know in their heart of hearts that it is a vote which the government do not deserve."

A Legacy

Aneurin Bevan is still considered one of the best political orators of modern times. His style of delivery often changed from paragraph to paragraph. One moment he could be affable and wit incarnate and the next much darker. One minute he would sound angry, the next persuasive and the next doom-laden and threatening. His speeches were never lazy and were always well thought through and well prepared. His turn of phrase was clever and fresh. Audiences wanted more.

Bevan's speaking skills were held in awe by many British politicians long after he had left day-to-day politics and indeed for many years after his death.

Benazir Bhutto

The Mujahideen would later morph into the Taliban. The Taliban would morph into Al-Qaeda. And the rest is ugly, painful history. But it was not necessarily unpredicted. The danger of the short-term strategy undermining long-term goals was apparent even then. When I met with President George H. Bush in the White House in June of 1989, I told him, 'Mr. President, we have created a Frankenstein.'"

International Institute for Strategic Studies (IISS) address "The Future of Democracy in Pakistan", London, Friday 20 July 2007

Benazir Bhutto was born on 21 June 1953 and assassinated on 27 December 2007. She was the first woman elected to lead a Muslim country, twice as prime minister of Pakistan (1988–1990 and 1993–1996). She was mentored and tutored for a life in politics by her politician father, Zulfikar Ali Bhutto, who was the country's president from 1971 to 1973.

After a turbulent political life as prime minister and also as exiled leader of the opposition, Benazir Bhutto was granted a long-sought amnesty and returned to Pakistan to fight the general election in October 2007. Many of her supporters believed this to be a huge error of judgement given the risks to her life. She was killed in Rawalpindi while campaigning, two weeks before the scheduled Pakistani general election of 2008 where she was the leading opposition candidate. There are a variety of views about who carried out the assassination.

In 1977 Benazir Bhutto returned to Pakistan from her education abroad, intending to begin a career in the Foreign Service. Shortly after her return, martial law was declared and her father was arrested on a murder charge. Benazir was placed under house arrest. She became the focus for her father's followers and, from prison, he continued to advise her. In particular, he taught her what to say in speeches and how to say it. They both knew what was to happen. He was executed in 1979 and Benazir was convinced by her father's followers that she must follow him as leader of the Pakistan People's Party (PPP). We said in our introduction that powerful speeches often emanate from extraordinary situations and circumstances. Speeches can of course be highlighted by the circumstances in which they are made and many of Bhutto's were made at the height (and in the midst) of embattled election campaigns.

Lessons from Benazir Bhutto

Share the difficulties you face, but only so that your audiences can identify with them – and understand you better. If your audience can identify with you in some way, communication becomes much easier. As the first Muslim woman prime minister, Bhutto considered (rightly) that she would experience discrimination. Many of the Muslim religious leaders believed she had taken a man's place and they made their views very clear. Such criticism was always something she found hard to understand and it made her extremely angry. However, she used the discriminatory views to a powerful and positive effect in many of her speeches. All through her adult life, and particularly towards its end, she was under threat. These were not idle musings or empty political threats. After one severe attack, she said: "We are prepared to risk our lives. We're prepared to risk our liberty. But we're *not* prepared to surrender this great nation to militants. The attack was on what I represent. The attack was on democracy and the very unity and integrity of Pakistan."

Understand your audience and meet (or exceed) their expectations. Bhutto went to great pains to understand and know detail about her different audiences – their political leanings obviously, but also their background, education, and world awareness, along with their needs and aspirations. Her speeches included accurate references and allusions to facts and views with which she knew her audiences would readily identify. Journalists and western politicians liked her for her sense of humour, her ability to synthesize complex political processes and her preparedness. They liked the fact that she was bold (sometimes verging on arrogant) and was always strong in her views. She also had film-star looks and spoke very good English.

If necessary, begin a speech with a stark fact or admission. Shock people into listening. Benazir Bhutto begins her 2007 "Future of Democracy in Pakistan" speech at the IISS in London with: "As we meet, Pakistan is in crisis … As we gather together, much to the dismay of the people of Pakistan, Islamabad is the primary training and staging area for Al Qaeda … Ladies and Gentlemen … The voices of moderation have been silenced …" Bhutto was very much aware of the world's general opinion of Pakistan's alleged role in world terrorism. Rather than deny it or refute it, she was open. Such openness is a good stance when you know your audience is aware of a particular wider view. Acknowledge such views as did Bhutto: "It pains me, and I know it pains every Pakistani, when the terrorist trail always seems to lead back to Pakistan …" Danger is much more prevalent when senior politicians deny an obvious fact or likelihood.

Aim to make your speeches memorable. Many of Bhutto's speeches are regularly quoted. In her IISS speech, made with passion, energy, charisma, character and conviction, she uses very simple devices – setting out her cause, picking on a few strong, memorable and, what she clearly knows will be, emotive factors. She repeats them in different ways and uses connecting devices, such as the repetition of "Ladies and gentlemen", which both slows down the pace and allows the voice to lower in register, ensuring that the audience is listening carefully and hard.

A Legacy

This "daughter of destiny" (the title of her autobiography) had a clear and (we must believe) genuine belief – the need to bring full democracy to Pakistan. She was also keen to get Pakistan to take its place in the world as a regional (nuclear) power that could influence international affairs. To do that she knew that internal strife and relationships with warring and hard-nosed factions would need to be properly managed. This did not happen in her lifetime and it still has not.

It is hard to doubt the bravery of a woman whose family members were destroyed, who saw death more than a few times and saw bombs explode before her. Bhutto sought out a safe haven but she did not put aside her duty. There were very few people inside Pakistan or indeed outside the country who had the determination or courage to stand up and be counted as she did. It was clear to her and to others that Pakistan was in a parlous position. The country had no money, politically the divisions had become huge rifts and democracy had all but disappeared. On the dissolution of freedoms and democracy, she said on one occasion: "You can imprison a man, but not an idea. You can exile a man, but not an idea. You can kill a man, but not an idea."

Lee Bollinger

I am only a professor ... and today I feel all the weight of the modern civilized world yearning to express the revulsion at what you stand for. I only wish I could do better."

Introductory remarks at the World Leaders' Forum with Iranian President Mahmoud Ahmadinejad, The School of International and Public Affairs, Columbia University, New York City, USA, Monday 24 September 2007

Lee Bollinger, born 7 August 1946, is president of Columbia University. He is also a lawyer and is a highly respected legal scholar of the United States First Amendment and international freedom of speech.

Bollinger has attempted to expand the international scope of Columbia, inviting world leaders to address students, politicians and academics. However, he received harsh criticism from many when the university invited Iranian president Mahmoud Ahmadinejad to speak at its campus in New York. Some politicians, including John McCain, Barack Obama and Hillary Clinton, denounced Columbia for hosting Ahmadinejad, possibly for different reasons. Bollinger described the event as part of "Columbia's long-standing tradition of serving as a major forum for robust debate, especially on global issues" and he delivered this (some think brave) memorable introduction to the controversial Iranian president.

Lessons from Lee Bollinger

Deliver a powerful introduction. Start firmly and grab attention. Lose the beginning of a speech and it's almost impossible to catch up. Audiences lose interest fast. In his introduction, Bollinger explained to the student body that the "free speech" afforded to President Ahmadinejad was for the sake of the students and the faculty, rather than for the benefit of Ahmadinejad himself. Bollinger does not much hide his disgust and distaste of that for which the Iranian leader stood. The address is direct and bold – honest to the point of pain. But it echoed the views of a very large number of people around the world, not just in the USA. If you make a speech saying what some or all in the audience are thinking, then you create a groundswell of support in thought and maybe action. That action, of course, can go either way, depending on a speaker's purpose. You simply cannot get this wrong. If you say what the audience isn't thinking and won't be persuaded to consider, you have a tough and nigh on impossible task.

Be brave. Shock by all means if you know it'll work and if it supports your cause. Lee Bollinger was courting controversy by inviting the Iranian president, a highly controversial and unpopular figure, but it was also evident from Bollinger's speech that he passionately believed in his argument. He had arguments ready to support his main peroration and he was able to deliver a strong and brave speech that had many squirming with embarrassment or inwardly cheering. Some of what Bollinger said was truthful and clearly designed to shock: "According to Amnesty International, 210 people have been executed in Iran so far this year … Iran hanged up to thirty people this past July and August during a widely reported suppression of efforts to establish a more open, democratic society … Let's, then, be clear at the beginning, Mr President, you exhibit all the signs of a petty and cruel dictator."

A Legacy

Lee Bollinger's introduction received both praise and condemnation in equal measure. He described Ahmadinejad as a "cruel dictator" who denied the Holocaust. In response, President Ahmadinejad called the remarks "an insult", indicating that more research was needed on the Holocaust. Mr Ahmadinejad was denied a visit to the site of the 9/11 attacks in New York, with US secretary of state Condoleezza Rice saying that "it would have been a travesty".

Bollinger increased international focus on the current reality of Iran and its domestic behaviour. He created a focus and pinpointed the danger of a country led, in his view, by a dangerous man.

Napoleon Bonaparte

Adieu, my friends. Would I could press you all to my heart."

"Farewell to the Old Guard" speech, The Courtyard, Fontainebleau, France, Wednesday 20 April 1814

Napoleon Bonaparte was born on 15 August 1769 and died on 5 May 1821. As Emperor Napoleon I, he was the French military and political leader whom many consider one of the (perhaps the) most influential in French history. Born in Corsica, he trained at military school in France and rose through the ranks with astonishing speed, becoming politically powerful and with a reputation as a brilliant campaign planner and soldier.

He became Emperor during the chaos following the French Revolution, in which the established order of nobility and royalty had been all but totally eliminated. At his peak, Napoleon had established a 500,000-strong Grand Army that, under his leadership, conquered much of Europe.

But due to mistakes, politics and strain on the military front, cracks appeared in the Emperor's armour. On 30 March 1814 Paris was captured by the Allies. Napoleon lost the support of most of his generals and was obliged to abdicate on 6 April 1814. In the courtyard at the Palace of Fontainebleau, he bade farewell to his remaining faithful officers, the veterans of the French Army's Imperial Guard. These officers, The Old Guard, were utterly loyal to their Emperor, despite the fact that the invasion of Russia had failed and that the Allies had inflicted a humiliating military defeat.

Lessons from Napoleon

Stand tall and "own the room". Napoleon himself was not particularly tall and not particularly striking in his bearing or appearance (although his uniform was impressive). However, his reputation was remarkable and it was said that he "owned the room" when he entered any social occasion, conference or military briefing. He was also a fervent speaker who used personal charisma, great charm, a dry humour on occasion and emotion, mostly about France, extraordinarily well. When he spoke, people listened.

Short speeches work better than rambling ones. For whom is your speech – you or the listener? The old adage that a speaker has to fill a slot, often a long, long slot, is nonsense. Speakers should speak for as long as it takes to get a message across in a well-argued, entertaining, engaging, powerful way. The amount of time this requires varies of course, and the more engaging and exciting the speaker and the message, the more that an audience will want to hear. But simplicity, great writing, great structure and great phraseology are key.

This speech of Napoleon's is simple, but still highly emotional. Speeches don't have to be long, but they do need to make a point, sell an idea and provoke a reaction.

Choose words with care. In this speech Napoleon is careful to address the emotions that his soldiers would have felt about the imminent loss of their adored leader. He praises his soldiers for their courage, their heart and their ability to lead – and follow: "Soldiers of my Old Guard: I bid you farewell ... I have sacrificed all of my interests to those of the country. I go, but you, my friends, will continue to serve France. Her happiness was my only thought. It will still be the object of my wishes. Do not regret my fate; if I have consented to survive, it is to serve your glory. I intend to write the history of the great achievements we have performed together. Adieu, my friends. Would I could press you all to my heart." The last phrase says it all. And he meant it.

A Legacy

In 1814 Napoleon was exiled to the island of Elba off the coast of Italy. But ten months later, in March of 1815, he managed to escape and made his way back to France. Accompanied by a thousand men from his Old Guard, he then marched toward Paris and gathered an army of supporters along the way. Once again, Napoleon assumed the position of Emperor, but a few months later, on 18 June 1815, at the battle of Waterloo, he was finally defeated by the English and Prussian armies. The Allies restored Louis XVIII to the French throne. A month later Napoleon was again exiled, this time to the island of St Helena off the African coast. On 5 May 1821, Napoleon died.

One of Napoleon's greatest legacies is a code establishing the rule of law in France. It's essentially a text indicating to all what could and could not be done in society and in commerce. The Code Napoléon is unique in that it is a straightforward detail of clearly written, fair and accessible law, something that was essential in giving back order to the country after the Revolution. Before the Code, France did not have a single set of laws but a vast range of often conflicting regional principles based on local customs with more exemptions than inclusions and relying upon privileges that had been agreed by the nobility or royalty.

The Napoleonic Code was adopted throughout much of Europe and remained in force long after Napoleon's defeat and final exile. He said: "My true glory is not to have won forty battles ... Waterloo will erase the memory of so many victories ... But what will live for ever is my Civil Code." The Code is still valid today and versions of it are used in provinces, states and countries of Europe, Africa and the Americas.

Neville Bonner

I worry for my children and my grandchildren. I worry that what has proven to be a stable society, which now recognizes my people as equals, is about to be replaced. How dare you? I repeat: how dare you?"

Address to the Constitutional Convention, Canberra, Australia, Thursday 4 February 1998

Neville Thomas Bonner was born on 28 March 1922 and died on 5 February 1999 and was the first indigenous Australian to become a member of Australia's Parliament. He was an elder of the Jagera people and had a tough upbringing. His education had been minimal, yet Bonner became an excellent speaker as well as a powerful advocate for the rights of Aborigines and others who lacked a governmental mouthpiece.

Bonner was a fervent boomerang thrower and tried hard to get more recognition for the skill involved. Soon after making his maiden speech, and much to most of his colleagues' delight or surprise, he gave a boomerang throwing demonstration in order to prove that Aboriginal boomerangs were much better than those made for tourists.

In July 1998 Bonner was invited to address the opening of the 49th State Parliament just before the State Governor's speech. Bonner's tribe was the traditional owner of the land on which Parliament House was built and he said with much emotion that delivering the address was a moment of great honour and enormous pride.

In many ways, the speech was Bonner's opportunity to thank (and bid adieu to) the country. It is thought that he was already quite ill and becoming frail. It was also a call to the country to preserve and protect the Constitution of the Commonwealth of Australia.

Bonner was vehemently opposed to the idea of Australia becoming a republic. He gave vent to his anger in a way that also made clear his sense of betrayal, his sadness and his disappointment: "But my heart is heavy. I worry for my children and my grandchildren. I worry that what has proven to be a stable society, which now recognizes my people as equals, is about to be replaced. How dare you? I repeat: how dare you? You told my people that your system was best. We have come to accept that. We have come to believe that ... Now you say that you were wrong and that we were wrong to believe you." He repeats the refrain later in the speech; it's like a staccato shot that pierces all defences and it would have made listeners, other politicians, squirm: "Fellow Australians, what is most hurtful is that after all we have learned together, after subjugating us and then freeing us, once again you are telling us that you know better. How dare you? How dare you?"

Lessons from Neville Bonner

Believe in what you say and explain your passion. This does not mean that you should shout. Project yes, shout no. It means showing why and how you care and, moreover, why your audience should care. Bonner was passionate about making a difference and firmly believed that to do that one had to work hard. In his case, that included learning how to make powerful speeches. His love of the monarchy is something on which this speech focuses. His language is blunt and it is clear, even from reading the speech, that he felt passionately and firmly about what he considered was right and just.

A Legacy

After his speech, Sir Neville Bonner, as he'd become, received a standing ovation. Many who listened were visibly moved by a man who had spent his life fighting for one cause. He said later: "I made people aware, the lawmakers in this country; I made them aware of indigenous people. I think that was an achievement." Bonner probably did more than any other politician to ensure that indigenous peoples had more of a fair hearing and received fairer treatment.

Adrien Brody

My experiences of making this film made me very aware of the sadness and the dehumanization of people at times of war and the repercussions of war. And whomever you believe in, if it's God or Allah, may He watch over you ..."

Best Lead Actor Acceptance Speech, Academy (Oscar) Awards, Kodak Theater, Hollywood, California, USA, Sunday 23 March 2003

Adrien Brody was born on 14 April 1973 and is the youngest person to receive the Academy Award for Best Actor. He is also the only American to have won a César Award (the French equivalent of the "Oscars"). Other films in which Brody has acted include *King Kong, Fade to Red, Hollywood-land, The Darjeeling Limited* and *The Brothers Bloom.*

It was after starring in Roman Polanski's 2002 film *The Pianist* that Brody gained worldwide recognition. To prepare for the role of a success-ful Jewish musician, Wladyslaw Szpilman, whose family is caught up in the Warsaw occupation by the Nazis in 1939, the ensuing pogroms and the horrors that follow, Brody learned how to play Chopin on the piano and lost a great amount of weight. During his preparation for the part, and for many months, he lived alone and very simply – without a car or distractions.

The humiliation, the complete sense of loss and the horror portrayed in the film are terrifying and shocking. Brody's physical transformation as the character and the story progressed was extraordinary. Equally, he managed to convey sorrow superbly well, not just through the words in the script but also by what he didn't say.

Brody is probably equally well known for giving Academy Awards pre-senter Halle Berry a lavish kiss before accepting his Best Actor Oscar.

Lessons from Adrien Brody

Rise to the occasion (whatever it is) and make your speech memorable. Each year there are many awards ceremonies and many more awards accep-tance speeches, most of them abysmal or embarrassing in the extreme. It is strange, perhaps, that in an arena where words and theatre are sup-posedly second nature, speechmaking skills are few and far between. Of course, you could argue that off-the-cuff speeches are hard to make, but if you are nominated for something it is highly likely that you will at least have prepared something.

On this occasion, Brody was skilful in keeping his short speech to the point and, while he acknowledges the emotive angle of the movie, he's at great pains to also acknowledge the fact that the opportunity was a privilege. There is a humility that shines through and his self-effacement ensures that the speech is moving and powerful. He makes the subject of the film personal and the poignancy makes us consider very carefully the plight of a soldier, many soldiers and a war. At the close of his speech, Brody paid particular tribute to his boyhood friend who at the time of the speech was serving in the Gulf. "I have a friend from Queens who's a soldier in Kuwait right now, Tommy Zarobinski."

Be poignant when the occasion demands it. But make any speech count. If you're standing there and people are sitting ready to listen to what you have to say, there is an unquestionable duty to care about what you say. Why wouldn't you? Brody's speech is concise but he focuses on a special moment that relates to the pathos of the film. The organizers are clearly trying to stop him speaking: "And you know, this – wait one second, one second – please one second. Cut it out – Cut it out. I got one – one shot at this. This is – This is – I'm sorry … But I am also filled with a lot of sadness tonight, because I'm accepting an award at – at such a strange time. And you know my experiences of making this film made me very aware of the sadness and the dehumanization of people at times of war and the repercussions of war. And whomever you believe in, if it's God or Allah, may He watch over you, and let's pray for a peaceful and swift resolution. Thank you."

A Legacy

There are few actors who can portray sensitive roles with conviction; not just to show a moving moment or two but to convey real in-depth character development. It can of course be argued that managing careful character portrayal is much more difficult on stage than it is in movies. Whether that is so or not, there are rare occasions when an actor succeeds so very well in portraying a huge welter of emotions as does Brody in *The Pianist*.

Brody set a standard in *The Pianist* matched by Liam Neeson's performance in Steven Spielberg's *Schindler's List* and Roberto Benigni in *Life is Beautiful*. These actors have set a benchmark, and the acting profession survives only because people like Brody raise the bar. That's a true legacy.

William Jennings Bryan

The humblest citizen in all the land, when clad in the armor of a righteous cause, is stronger than all the hosts of error."

Address, Democratic National Convention in Chicago, Chicago, USA, Wednesday 8 July 1896

William Jennings Bryan was born on 19 March 1860 and died on 26 July 1925. He was the Democratic Party presidential nominee in 1896, 1900 and 1908. He was also a successful lawyer and secretary of state in President Woodrow Wilson's administration.

One of the most popular and successful orators in American history, Bryan was noted for a rich, deep, powerful voice and a speech delivery of eloquence and style that demanded attention.

Bryan was religious (a Presbyterian), a passionate supporter of democracy for all people, a prohibitionist and also a populist. Indeed, because he fought for and had faith in basic, good values, he was often called by the press "The Great Commoner". During his lifetime he took issue with large institutions – including banks and railway companies – for their treatment of the smallholder or the faceless worker.

For every speech, there is a moment when that speech counts, when its point is so valid and clear and when you know, just know, that the message has hit home. Some people call Bryan's Democratic Convention speech the most famous ever in American political history. That's some accolade. In it he said: "The individual is but an atom; he is born, he acts, he dies; but principles are eternal, and this has been a contest over a principle." At the time of the Convention, the Democratic Party wanted to standardize the value of the dollar to that of silver and not to a gold standard alone. The Democrat argument was that the inflation resulting from the silver standard would make it far easier for farmers in particular, but also those running small businesses, to settle their debts by increasing their earnings.

Lessons from William Jennings Bryan

Build your case, attack what needs attacking, but have solutions. Too many reasonable speeches fall flat because they offer no new thinking, no solutions. Bryan attacked the widely held view that gold was the only reliable currency. He admitted to speaking out for small businesses and farmers. His speech extolled their virtues. He railed against a government that, he claimed, ignored the smallholder and favoured large corporations in a way that was ruining the country and destroying the hopes and aspirations of the working population. The result was that Bryan was nominated by the Democratic delegates as their candidate for president. And he was only 36.

Be generous. In his speech, Bryan removed personality from the contest. This can be a healthy technique. If a speech becomes personal, the danger is that audiences will not warm to it. They might, depending on their view of the individual or individuals, but too much spite or invective can cause a discomfort which reflects poorly on the speaker. Bryan said: " ... I would be presumptuous, indeed, to present myself against the distinguished gentlemen to whom you have listened if this were mere measuring of abilities;

but this is not a contest between persons. The humblest citizen in all the land, when clad in the armor of a righteous cause, is stronger than all the hosts of error. I come to speak to you in defense of a cause as holy as the cause of liberty – the cause of humanity ..."

A Legacy

Many consider Bryan to be a celebrity, better known for his vibrant and vivid personality and oratorical skill than for his political outlook, beliefs and action. It is notable, however, that Bryan did not appear to attack the South's racism. Such tacit support sat ill with his other liberal thinking. Nevertheless, had he attacked the South and slavery he could never have hoped for high office.

Bryan is given credit for making the Democratic Party strong in opposition and powerful in government. His oratorical prowess created a speaking style from which politicians have since learned. Those who want to discover excellent speech structure, great language, and wonderful resonance that truly leaps from the page have only to read Bryan's speeches. Start with this one.

George H. W. Bush

Some see leadership as high drama, and the sound of trumpets calling, and sometimes it is that. But I see history as a book with many pages, and each day we fill a page with acts of hopefulness and meaning."

Inaugural address, Washington DC, USA, Tuesday 20 January 1989

George Herbert Walker Bush, the 41st president of the United States, was born on 12 June 1924 and occupied the White House during a time of dramatic change – from the collapse of the Soviet Union to the Iraqi invasion of Kuwait. Bush's style was thoughtful, warm and optimistic, as well as bold when so required.

Bush recognized the opportunity provided by a period of change and his well-written, beautifully constructed speeches sought to capitalize on this. For example, in his inaugural address he said: "I come before you and assume the presidency at a moment rich with promise. We live in a peaceful, prosperous time, but we can make it better. For a new breeze is blowing and a world refreshed by freedom seems reborn ... The totalitarian era is passing, its old ideas blown away like leaves from an ancient, lifeless tree ... There is new ground to be broken and new action to be taken."

Lessons from George H. W. Bush

Show your warmth and interest in people. President Bush understood that the priority for a leader is to connect with people. Although not a naturally gifted orator, Bush had a warm, generous and disarming style that was consistent and authentic, whether speaking to one person or 300 million. He begins his inaugural speech with an analogy that exudes warmth: "We meet on democracy's front porch, a good place to talk as neighbors and as friends. For this is a day when our nation is made whole, when our differences, for a moment, are suspended ..." Bush was good at extemporizing without going off the point and he told easily recalled and often amusing stories to make a point. A number of his speeches contained lists, and "groups of three" that built and reinforced an emotive argument. He said to his inaugural audience: "My friends, we have work to do. There are the homeless, lost and roaming. There are the children who have nothing, no love, no normalcy. There are those who cannot free themselves of enslavement to whatever addiction – drugs, welfare, the demoralization that rules the slums."

Let people clearly see what matters to you – your principles and values – and use that to get them to think about the future. George H. W. Bush was the last United States president to have served in World War II; his love of country and belief in national safety were consistent themes in his speeches. His openness and empathy with his audience helped him to challenge audience thinking. In his inaugural address, he said: "America today is a proud, free nation, decent and civil, a place we cannot help but love. We know in our hearts, not loudly and proudly, but as a simple fact, that this country has meaning beyond what we see, and that our strength is a force for good." Rather than stopping there, he continues: "But have we changed as a nation even in our time? Are we enthralled with material things, less appreciative of the nobility of work and sacrifice?" He first connects with people and then takes them with him as he asks them to think, to consider a new thought or revisit an old one. This is a clever, but not always well-delivered, technique and one that sets great speakers apart from good ones. Bush ensures that people leave feeling comfortable: "I see history as a book with many pages and each day we fill a page with acts of hopefulness and meaning. The new breeze blows, a page turns, the story unfolds. And so today a chapter begins, a small and stately story of unity, diversity, and generosity – shared, and written, together."

A Legacy

Bush's presidency was dominated by international affairs. The Berlin Wall fell in 1989 and the Soviet Union was dissolved two years later. The Bush administration negotiated the North American Free Trade Agreement (NAFTA), but in domestic policy he was seen as reneging on a 1988 campaign promise to keep taxes low by signing an increase that Congress had passed. The country became disenchanted and Bush lost the 1992 presidential election to Democrat Bill Clinton.

Leaders like George H. W. Bush show that there is no "great man" theory of management, but a preference instead for empathy, sincerity, warmth, erudition and personal style. This contrasts with more directive or autocratic approaches, such as those displayed by British prime minister Margaret Thatcher who famously warned George H. W. Bush during the first Gulf War not to "go wobbly". Following the relative popularity and success of the Reagan years, Bush highlighted and reinforced the need for CEOs to show empathy and to connect with people, a technique that became firmly and widely established in politics and business in the 1990s.

John Chambers

What we are now seeing is a world that is connected."

"The Economy and the Internet" presentation to the Commonwealth Club, California, USA, Monday 23 April 2001

John Chambers was born on 23 August 1949 in Charleston, USA. He is Chairman of the Board and CEO of Cisco Systems, Inc. No other hardware company has been so closely involved with building and designing the internet's infrastructure and much of the company's huge growth and success is down to Chambers.

Chambers has been celebrated for making Cisco one of the fastest-growing companies in the computing industry and in 1999 ABC's *20/20* featured him as "The Best Boss in America". However, he was pilloried in 2001 when Cisco shares fell fast and very badly. In response, Chambers made some big changes, including cutting staff levels by 8,500 and his own salary to one dollar, and managed to resurrect and strengthen Cisco.

Chambers finds any opportunity to extol the virtues of education and how it can be improved and reinforced by the internet, which is his absolute passion: "Education and the internet must go hand in hand ... It will serve as one of the great equalizers," he says.

Lessons from John Chambers

If your style works, then hone it. Chambers is known for delivering Cisco's sales pitch (which he does at every opportunity) in the style of a revivalist preacher. Indeed, he is referred to by some as "the Reverend". He has a Southern Baptist style – complete with walking away from the podium and touching audience members on the shoulder, often to the delighted surprise of the recipients. Chambers is a gifted orator. Some believe that he speaks perhaps a bit too swiftly and with an accent that reveals his West Virginian roots, but this has not held him back. Sometimes his ideas run away with him, but his passion is always evident, particularly when he is talking about how the internet will unequivocally support and drive education for all purposes and at all levels. He may talk to crowds of 5,000, but each person present feels as if Chambers is speaking to him or her directly and personally. Chambers works hard to make people feel emotionally connected to him, for instance through careful repetition, looking directly at individuals (something many executives and politicians fail to do) and using language that his audiences understand.

Speaking in public doesn't always come easily: it needs patience and practice. Growing up, Chambers struggled with dyslexia but, like many who suffer from this condition, he has an extraordinary memory; he recalls virtually everything he hears in meetings and always presents without notes. But he does prepare. When it comes to preparation, Chambers rehearses properly, no matter how full his diary. If he uses a Power-Point presentation, he will memorize the bullet points of which, please note, there will be very few. He knows where the moments of inflection are, when he's going to leave the stage and walk into the audience, when he's going to praise people by name and when he's going to pause.

A Legacy

Chambers has been described as an "e-business emissary". Some say that he sells dreams and peddles hope. In the words of Philip J. Lawlor of internet service provider AGIS: "What Bill Gates is to PCs, John Chambers has become for the Net." Chambers continues to have a huge impact on the digital economy and he also uses his influence to improve access to education. He has served on advisory councils for presidents George W. Bush and Bill Clinton.

As can be imagined, he is a much sought-after speaker and, wherever he presents, the venue is packed. Greeting his own managers, Chambers apparently often asks: "Are you having fun?" And he really wants to know whether they are or not. Turning the tables on his questioners during a conference is a Chambers trademark, as he suddenly asks them "What do *you* think?"

César Estrada Chávez

We don't ask for words. We ask for deeds."

Speech at the Second Annual Mexican Conference, Sacramento, California, USA, Sunday 10 March 1968

César Estrada Chávez was born on 31 March 1927 in Yuma, Arizona, USA. He died on 23 April 1993. He was a Mexican-American civil rights activist who co-founded the National Farm Workers Association, which later became the United Farm Workers. Chávez enabled huge and long-lasting improvements for union members; as a result he is honoured in the United States, with many civil and public buildings and amenities named after him.

Lessons from César Chávez

A great speaker has to be passionate. This sounds obvious, of course, but many speakers are not passionate; perhaps that's why they're not great. Think about it – you really can't make any speech without having a passion for your subject, your argument or your message. That doesn't mean behaving exuberantly, extravagantly and certainly not arrogantly; it just means showing that you have belief. After all, why are you standing there making a speech? Chávez was, in Robert F. Kennedy's words, "one of the heroic figures of our time". In his speeches, he told straightforward, simple stories about what was fair and unfair. There were few other farm workers like him who were sufficiently prepared or able to stand up for colleagues. Many were frightened, most wanted to be helped. Chávez led a historic, non-violent movement for farm workers' rights and dedicated himself to building that movement.

Very quickly the movement spread beyond the farms and into cities and towns across America. Chávez inspired farm workers (and many others) to understand and then commit to social action and change. It was this inspiration, quietly expressed in his speeches, that helped spread the word that, politically, things needed to change.

A speech does not have to prove that you can change everything yourself. Change is rarely achieved by one person. Your speeches about change should show that you're working together with others, not planning on doing (or taking credit for) everything on your own. You should not talk about change without explaining how it will happen and how its success will be measured. Your audience can then see that there is a shared belief. Chávez focused on showing that his movement needed religious and spiritual support. His speech was inclusive and inclusion was key. As he says in this Second Annual Mexican Conference speech: "Though we were not allowed to have our own priest, the power of the ecumenical body of the Church was tremendous ... When poor people get involved in a long conflict, such as a strike or a civil rights drive, and the pressure increases each day, there is a deep need for spiritual advice. Without it we see families crumble, leadership weaken, and hard workers grow tired."

If you are there to lead, keep showing your audience what leadership means and, equally, what it means not to be part of "the team". This speech was originally an article prepared by Chávez during a 25-day spiritual fast. Chávez was then invited to present the piece to a meeting on Mexican-Americans and the Church at the Second Annual Mexican Conference in Sacramento, California. In it Chávez explains that the movement for change had to support everyone and be supported by government and by employers: "The leadership of the Mexican-American Community must admit that we have fallen far short in our task of helping provide spiritual guidance for our people. We may say, I don't feel any such need. I can get along. But that is a poor excuse for not helping provide such help for others. For we can also say, I don't need any welfare help. I can take care of my own problems. But we are all willing to fight like hell for welfare aid for those who truly need it, who would starve without it ..."

A Legacy

Chávez's influence, much like that of Martin Luther King Jr, continues to inspire, educate and empower people from all of society's strata. On another occasion Chávez said: "We believe that unions have always been about much more than the industries in which they operate. The fight is never about grapes or lettuce ... it is always about people."

Chávez is justifiably famous because he rallied thousands to improve terrible working conditions in the fields. He did so at some risk. Employers did not take kindly to "trouble-makers", people who could lead workers to demonstrate against poor working conditions and equally poor pay. His efforts were tireless but always non-violent and eventually the boycotts of farm products, hunger strikes, increased political awareness, and newspaper coverage ensured that farmers treated workers better.

Chávez is remembered affectionately and there is a single, common phrase that acts as a constant reminder of his influence: "Sí, se puede" ("Yes, you can"). US President Barack Obama used a similar refrain in his 2008 election campaign to great effect.

The most compelling and often most overlooked aspect of Chávez's leadership was that he chose to live in voluntary poverty. He did this so that he could readily identify (and be seen to be identified) with the very real poverty of agricultural workers. Apart from the admiration that he gained from this, the stance gave him moral authority that in turn led to respect and increased support.

Winston Churchill

We shall fight on the beaches, we shall fight on the landing grounds, we shall fight in the fields and in the streets, we shall fight in the hills; we shall never surrender."

House of Commons speech, Westminster, London, UK, Tuesday 4 June 1940

Winston Leonard Spencer Churchill (born 30 November 1874; died 24 January 1965) is possibly Britain's most popular prime minister, famed for his strength of character and exemplary leadership during World War II and for his oratory which inspired Britain during periods when all seemed lost. He was twice prime minister, from 1940 to 1945 and 1951 to 1955. On his own admission later in life, he claimed to have much enjoyed being a soldier, a journalist, a historian, a Nobel Prize-winning writer, a water colourist and, to provide himself with therapy during World War II, a bricklayer.

On oratory, the effects of which he observed in Italy and Germany during the 1930s, he said: "Understand that rhetorical power is neither wholly bestowed nor wholly acquired, but cultivated." He was convinced that the power to inspire audiences could be learned; Churchill had a stutter and found public speaking both nerve-racking and difficult.

Churchill's first speech in the House of Commons as prime minister was given after the withdrawal of British forces from Dunkirk, France. In the speech, Churchill had to balance the fact that the nation was relieved at the safe withdrawal (and rescue) of its troops with relatively little loss of life with the need for determination in the hard struggle ahead: "Even though large parts of Europe and many old and famous States have fallen or may fall into the grip of the Gestapo and all the odious apparatus of Nazi rule, we shall not flag or fail. We shall go on to the end, we shall fight in France, we shall fight on the seas and oceans, we shall fight with growing confidence and growing strength in the air, we shall defend our Island, whatever the cost may be, we shall fight on the beaches, we shall fight on the landing grounds, we shall fight in the fields and in the streets, we shall fight in the hills; we shall never surrender, and if, which I do not for a moment believe, this Island or a large part of it were subjugated and starving, then our Empire beyond the seas, armed and guarded by the British Fleet, would carry on the struggle, until, in God's good time, the New World, with all its power and might, steps forth to the rescue and the liberation of the Old."

Lessons from Winston Churchill

View oratory as both an art and a science. Churchill understood the effect that could be achieved by combining structure with rhythm, hard reason with flowing language, facts with humour. He used various rhetorical devices, such as anaphora, the repetition of a phrase at the beginning of a series of short sentences ("We shall fight ..."), or asyndeton, the joining together of related phrases without conjunctions, allowing the speaker to pick up pace, tell a narrative, add facts – to build an argument or a point. For example, in this speech: "In a long series of very fierce battles, now on this front, now on that, fighting on three fronts at once, battles fought by two or three divisions against an equal or sometimes larger number of the enemy, and fought very fiercely on old ground so many of us knew so well, our losses in men exceed 30,000 in killed, wounded and missing ..."

Use structure to full effect. Sir Winston Churchill won the Nobel prize for literature in 1953 and his speeches display many literary techniques: a strong introduction, quotations, rhetorical questions, literary paraphrasing, and powerful conclusions that both summarize the speech and provide a memorable final point. For example, on 18 June 1940 Churchill concluded a powerful speech to parliament with the words: "Let us therefore brace ourselves to our duties, and so bear ourselves, that if the British Empire and its Commonwealth last for a thousand years, men will still say, 'This was their finest hour'."

Find memorable metaphors and images. This requires confidence and bold imagination. When Churchill spoke in Fulton, Missouri, on 5 March 1946 he used several phrases that are still in popular use, referring to "the sinews of peace" and "the special relationship", for example. He also said: "From Stettin in the Baltic to Trieste in the Adriatic, an iron curtain has descended across the Continent."

Refer to others' great oratory. It's highly likely that Churchill will have known Pericles's funeral speech well and certainly he must have had it in mind for some of his wartime speeches. According to some translations, Pericles uses the phrase "blood and toil", which seems very like a hint of Churchill's famous phrase.

A Legacy

In a long political career Churchill made many mistakes – for example, launching the ill-fated Gallipoli landings. He also held views that have since proved to be outdated. For example, during the first half of the 1930s, he was outspoken in his opposition to granting Dominion status to India.

What he left, however, is enormous and undiminished; it can be divided into two areas. First, his practical accomplishments, notably leading the free world and rallying people to defeat fascism, and, second, his intangible successes. Prominent among these is his legacy, permanently embraced by the British people, of a "bulldog spirit" or "spirit of the blitz" – an attitude that would not allow defeat to enter the lexicon. He has come to symbolize a tough, intelligent, principled and ultimately successful defiance – and his words were vital in achieving this success. Without him, it is frequently argued, Britain (and indeed other nations) might well have succumbed during World War II.

Marcus Tullius Cicero

The great numbers in which you are here met this day, O Romans, and this assembly, greater, it seems to me, than I ever remember, inspires me with both an exceeding eagerness to defend the republic, and with a great hope of re-establishing it."

The Fourth Oration against Marcus Antonius, also called the Fourth Philippic, Rome, Italy, 44 BC

Marcus Tullius Cicero was born on 3 January 106 BC and murdered on 7 December 43 BC. He was a lawyer, consul, philosopher (he studied in Greece), an academic, sceptic and a stoic. He devoted much of his life to the application of philosophical theory to politics with the ambition of improving the Republic. In 64 BC Cicero became a consul, one of the highest offices in Rome. It was then that his reputation for oratory spread far and wide.

It is said that Cicero's main contribution to Rome was to help transform the Republic into a larger and more powerful Empire. However, he bitterly came to terms with the fact that after civil war, the Roman Republic was badly damaged and could not be sustained.

Cicero is regarded as one of the greatest orators of all time, perhaps *the* greatest.

Lessons from Marcus Tullius Cicero

Borrow from previous, successful speech forms – if it helps your case. But do so with care, otherwise your audience may become lost. Many great orators have borrowed techniques from others and made them their own, often with huge success. A Philippic is a damning speech form specifically delivered to condemn a political personality or enemy of the state. This can be a therapeutic technique, but is dangerous in the extreme if the object of the Philippic has power and is still close at hand!

Cicero must have been aware of the risks, even though he throws caution to the wind in *The Fourth Oration*: "Although my courage indeed has never failed; what has been unfavourable is the time; and the moment that that has appeared to show any dawn of light, I at once have been the leader in the defence of your liberty … For the senate has no longer been content with styling Antonius an enemy in words, but it has shown by actions that it thinks him one. And now I am much more elated still, because you too with such great unanimity and with such a clamour have sanctioned our declaration that he is an enemy ..." He goes on: "For he does not now desire your [Romans'] slavery, as he did before, but he is angry now and thirsts for your blood ..." It's not surprising that, when there was nobody left to protect Cicero politically, he was murdered on Mark Antony's instructions.

A Legacy

Cicero's speeches are outstanding for their quality, vigour, variety of tone and the clarity with which a complicated series of facts are often presented. As was common at the time, Cicero considered that skilled orators should also show the best of human qualities. The building of a decent society was the basis, the bedrock, of how an orator should live.

Cicero's writings still provide us with a close view of Roman society and history. Of his letters, an extraordinary 800 or so survive. It's clear that Cicero had no idea that they would have a wide readership (and, of course, so very many years later) because most of the letters record moods, feelings, thoughts and activity with an abandon that is both fascinating and open. All his writings are lucid, logical, coherent and, even in translation, it's easy to see why his rhetoric is regarded as superb. His oratorical structures are still copied today and his poetry, prose and speeches studied by those training for the law or studying politics.

Cicero is sometimes called "Rome's Greatest Politician". Even now his writing is fresh. For example: "It is the responsibility of the judge always to seek the truth in trials; while it is the advocates' to make out a case for what is probable, even if it doesn't precisely correspond to the truth."

Bill Clinton

There is nothing wrong with America that cannot be cured by what is right with America."

First inaugural address, Washington DC, USA, Wednesday 21 January 1993

William (Bill) Jefferson Clinton was born William Jefferson Blythe III in Hope, Arkansas, on 19 August 1946. He was the 42nd president of the United States, occupying the White House from 1993 to 2001.

On the whole, Clinton's time in office is seen as a period of domestic growth and prosperity. In foreign policy the result was less positive, with adventures in Somalia (1993), for example, and Kosovo (1999) meeting with mixed views at home and abroad. However, Clinton was lauded for having negotiated the Oslo Accords of the early 1990s which attempted to draw Israel and Palestine together, even though nothing material was achieved. There were also a number of financial scandals and, of course, the infamous Lewinsky affair for which Clinton was all but impeached. What is undeniable is that Clinton was, and indeed is, a superb communicator, brilliant at managing public relations for himself, the presidency and the United States. He left office with one of the highest approval ratings in US history (66%).

Lessons from Bill Clinton

If relevant, promote a brighter vision of the future. This does not need to be a blue-sky nirvana, but one that has realism and, more than anything, connects with your audience. Clinton did this and more. He used poetic language to do it. In his inaugural speech, he said: "This ceremony is held in the depth of winter. But, by the words we speak and the faces we show the world, we force the spring. A spring reborn in the world's oldest democracy, that brings forth the vision and courage to reinvent America ... When our founders boldly declared America's independence to the world and our purposes to the Almighty, they knew that America, to endure, would have to change. Not change for change's sake, but change to preserve America's ideals – life, liberty, the pursuit of happiness. Though we march to the music of our time, our mission is timeless ..."

Clinton was greatly influenced by President Kennedy and it was the humanity and hopeful visions of earlier presidents that Clinton liked to evoke, saying, for example: "Let us resolve to make our government a place for what Franklin Roosevelt called 'bold, persistent experimentation', a government for our tomorrows, not our yesterdays."

Inspire confidence. Clinton used all his charm, experience, intellect and exuberance to achieve his dream of succeeding in politics. What made him successful as a speaker also made him highly successful as a politician: he genuinely liked people, was well-grounded and had a large capacity for empathy. His comfortable and confident speaking style contrasted with the more formal manner of his predecessor, George H. W. Bush. He smiled easily and made people feel comfortable, with language that was straightforward. His style of presentation meant that you wanted to trust him. His delivery has always been powerful but not in a loud way, more in a "we can do this" sort of way – a commitment to delivery.

Use simple, honest and open charm. During his second term, Clinton was accused of misleading the American people about an extra-marital affair he conducted while in office. Although managing to avoid the very real threat of impeachment, he did acquire, at least temporarily, a reputation for being less than honest. It may seem strange, therefore, to claim that one of Clinton's great attributes was his open, homespun and, yes, honest style. Yet that was exactly what he offered. What was unusual was that he managed to combine warmth, humour and humanity with gravitas, intelligence and, when required, seriousness. He also knew how to work a room and the camera.

A Legacy

Compared with many other contemporary political leaders of his time (such as Al Gore and Bob Dole in the USA and Jacques Chirac, Boris Yeltsin and John Major in Europe) Clinton's style was compelling, authoritative and natural. The others were often regarded as stiff and a little uncomfortable when facing various audiences. Emotion was lacking.

Clinton also pioneered the use of technology and the internet to raise funds and to communicate with people in his election campaigns, a technique that has been taken much further by other politicians in the 21st century, notably Barack Obama. In fact, other leaders, including the UK's Tony Blair and the USA's Barack Obama, owe much to Clinton's natural style. Without doubt, one of Clinton's greatest legacies was the standard he set for connecting with the electorate and communicating clearly, in a way that supports strong, reassuring leadership. He ended his inaugural speech with poetic language and people drew huge strength from his allusions to the scriptures: "And so, my fellow Americans, at the edge of the 21st century, let us begin with energy and hope, with faith and discipline, and let us work until our work is done. The scripture says, 'And let us not be weary in well-doing, for in due season, we shall reap, if we faint not.' From this joyful mountaintop of celebration, we hear a call to service in the valley. We have heard the trumpets. We have changed the guard. And now, each in our way, and with God's help, we must answer the call."

George Clooney

So, after September 30th, you won't need the UN. You will simply need men with shovels and bleached white linen and headstones."

United Nations Security Council address on Darfur, United Nations, New York, USA, Thursday 14 September 2006

George Clooney, born on 6 May 1961, is an Academy Award-winning American actor, director, producer and, more recently, a political activist. On 31 January 2008, the United Nations honoured him as a "Messenger of Peace".

The background to Clooney's address at the UN is important. On 30 September 2006, the poorly financed African Union (AU) peacekeeping force in Darfur was about to leave the country. They had been allowed there for only a set period of time and that time was up. The AU troops – only 7,000 of them and spread thinly over a vast area – were the only barriers to the genocidal violence in Darfur, in which civilians had been attacked, displaced or killed in large numbers since the conflict began in 2003. It is estimated that over 300,000 people have died and more than 2,000,000 have been driven from, or have fled, their homes since then. Just before the AU force left, the Sudanese government intensified its air strikes and tried hard to remove or eliminate witnesses, including aid workers and foreign journalists. It was the plight of those left on the ground, at the mercy of the Sudanese forces, that dismayed and infuriated many in the West, particularly since few nations were prepared to do much to alter the situation.

Lessons from George Clooney

Dramatic situations or messages need a dramatic impact and approach.
Speechmaking, to be great, needs to have impact – that much is obvious. Sometimes drama helps and sometimes shocking imagery is necessary to make a point that would not otherwise be heard. Unfortunately, there are situations where important speeches can have no or little impact to the listener. Unhappily, given the lack of courage on the part of the United Nations, little changed as a result of Clooney's speech and the response was lukewarm.

Clooney's speech was made at a special informal session hosted by the United Nation's American ambassador, John Bolton. Clooney makes it very plain in this address that he and others hold the United Nations account-able for the continuing deterioration of safety to the population of Sudan and the easy distribution of death. The speech is blunt and designed to be a direct call to at least some action. He told council members that geno-cide was taking place "on your watch" and how they responded would be their legacy. His words demanded a response.

Sometimes creating guilt is effective. Making an audience feel guilty can be a powerful motivator if the topic is urgent. People won't always accept guilt, however, and any warmth towards the speaker and the subject can cool … and then freeze. Clooney said that if the United Nations force didn't go into Darfur on 1 October, when the mandate of the under-resourced African Union force ended, then: "aid workers will have to leave and, if they leave, that leaves a couple of million people with absolutely nothing … How you deal with it is your legacy … It's your Rwanda – your Cambodia, your Auschwitz. We are one 'yes' away from ending it."

A Legacy

Diplomats baulked at the suggestion the United Nations should "shoot its way in" to Darfur without the consent of Sudan.

In March 2009 Sudanese president Omar al-Bashir was the first head of state to be indicted for war crimes by the International Criminal Court. At the time of writing it is not certain whether there will be a trial. Darfur is still a place of violence, cruelty, political unease and huge poverty. The United Nations has recently disclosed that the Darfur death toll may have been underestimated by 50 per cent.

For Clooney, acknowledgement of the atrocities by the United Nations wasn't sufficient. He closed his speech by saying, simply: "If not the UN, then who?"

Sebastian Coe

Today's children live in a world of conflicting messages and competing distractions. Their landscape is cluttered. Their path to Olympic sport is often obscured. But it's a world we must understand ..."

IOC presentation, International Olympic Committee (IOC) General Assembly, Singapore, Wednesday 6 July 2005

Sebastian Newbold Coe, better known as Seb Coe, was born on 29 September 1956 and is one of Britain's greatest athletes. Coe won the 1500m gold medal at the 1980 and 1984 Olympic Games and established eight outdoor and three indoor world records. He was the first man to run 1 minute 43 seconds and 1 minute 42 seconds in the 800m event. Some commentators would say that he is the greatest middle distance runner of all time.

Following his retirement from athletics, Coe became a Conservative Party MP from 1992 until 1997. In 2000 he became a life peer. He has been successful in business, with a series of health clubs, and in 2005 he led the London bid to host the 2012 Summer Olympics. Subsequent to the announcement by the International Olympic Committee that London would be the 2012 host city, Coe was appointed chairman of the London Organizing Committee for the Games.

Seb Coe's presentation at the critical IOC meeting is held as being one of the prime factors in winning IOC support for London's bid – in a close and highly competitive contest, with Paris the major challenger.

Lessons from Sebastian Coe

Practise like an athlete. The speech was rehearsed in the same way that an athlete would train for an event: long and hard. Coe regarded preparation for the presentation as important as for any athletics competition he had ever entered. The presentation platform was shared with then Prime Minister Tony Blair and other prominent British politicians and sports representatives, but it is Coe's speech in particular that stands out for its simplicity, expression of belief, passion and aspiration.

Personal storytelling works. Interestingly, this speech was almost entirely a personal story. It was a risky approach, particularly to an international audience. Yet using personal stories is invariably a good device because it allows you to be more passionate, emotive and compelling. Coe knew this and drew his audience in: "... I stand here today because of the inspiration of the Olympic Movement. When I was 12 ... I was marched into a large school hall with my classmates. We sat in front of an ancient, black and white television and watched grainy pictures from the Mexico Olympic Games. Two athletes from our home town were competing. John Sherwood won a bronze medal in the 400m hurdles. His wife Sheila narrowly missed gold in the long jump ... That day a window to a new world opened for me ... My journey here to Singapore started in that school hall and continues today in wonder and in gratitude ... And that gratitude drives me and my team to do whatever we can to inspire young people to choose sport. Whoever they are, wherever they live and whatever they believe."

Based on the applause (the longest for any of the teams) and the single technical question following the London presentation, the speech was clearly received very well. And, most importantly, it worked.

A Legacy

Seb Coe was appointed a Member of the Order of the British Empire in 1982 and an Officer of the Order of the British Empire in 1990. In December 2005 he was given a special award at the BBC Sports Personality of the Year awards ceremony. In 2006 he was also promoted to be a Knight Commander of the Order of the British Empire for services to sport. In August 2007 Lord Coe was elected a vice-president of the International Association of Athletics Federations and it is widely felt that he could be a future president of the IOC.

He has made sport accessible and shows a confidence and a statesman-like quality when addressing issues relating to sport, sports funding and the way in which sports are taught and managed. Of course, the Olympic Games legacy for London is currently his greatest legacy.

Colonel Tim Collins

Iraq is steeped in history. It is the site of the Garden of Eden, of the Great Flood and the birthplace of Abraham. Tread lightly here."

Eve of Battle speech to British troops, Fort Blair Mayne camp, Kuwaiti Desert, Wednesday 19 March 2003

Colonel **Tim Collins** OBE, born in April 1960, was a colonel in the British Army. He is best known for his role in the Iraq War and his inspirational eve-of-battle speech in 2003. Colonel Collins's address was given to men of the Royal Irish Regiment at their Fort Blair Mayne camp in the Kuwaiti desert, around twenty miles from the Iraqi border.

Lessons from Colonel Tim Collins

If you know your subject, you may not need notes. However, this does not mean zero preparation. It's insulting to listen to a speech that is unprepared. This particular speech was a moving occasion, delivered without notes, but it would have required some research and certainly preparation. What began as a pep talk turned into a credible, mature and thoughtful positioning of the job of the British soldier. One observer said later that had Shakespeare's Henry V been real ("Once more unto the breach, dear friends…") then he would have sounded like Colonel Collins during his address: "We go to liberate, not to conquer. We will not fly our flags in their country. We are entering Iraq to free a people and the only flag which will be flown in that ancient land is their own. Show respect for them … There are some who are alive at this moment who will not be alive shortly. Those who do not wish to go on that journey, we will not send. As for the others, I expect you to rock their world. Wipe them out if that is what they choose. But if you are ferocious in battle remember to be magnanimous in victory."

Let your setting help you to deliver your speech. Delivered using short phrases and immediately understood, dynamic language, the speech combined Biblical imagery and poetical phraseology with the language of the street: "tread lightly" but "rock their world". Many of the soldiers were very young and Colonel Collins's aim was to explain something of the history and culture of Iraq to them. He knew, and so did they, that the British public had doubts about the war. Collins therefore wanted to reassure these soldiers and tell them why they were there and something about the battle's aim. He spoke of history, respect, dignity, family, warfare and the individual moral choice between fighting for a cause and murder. Perhaps the speech made the soldiers under his command think twice about what they were about to do. Some reported that it put the task in context, others that it made them feel better, stronger.

A Legacy

Colonel Collins's words undoubtedly influenced the way in which the public viewed their soldiers and the "eve of battle" speech became famous, as did the Colonel. That, of course, was not his aim. The speech drew widespread praise, with the Prince of Wales describing it as "extraordinarily stirring, civilized and humane".

Did the speech make a difference? Well, it helped shape how the world saw the conflict and led us to think of it in much more human and responsible terms. And, possibly, it caused the British government to consider (even for a short while) whether the troops' presence in Kuwait and Iraq was beneficial.

Emperor Constantine

"We believe in one God, the Father Almighty, Maker of all things visible and invisible."

Original Nicene Creed, First Council of Nicaea, Turkey, Saturday 19 June AD 325

Could you arrange for a group of colleagues, friends or advisors to agree a short speech for you, say 118 words, that would reflect your views and sustain your influence for hundreds of years (actually, over 1600 years)? A tough call. This extraordinary achievement was delivered at the First Council of Nicaea by the first Christian Roman Emperor, **Constantine I (Flavius Valerius Aurelius Constantinus),** who lived from AD 272 until 337. He was Roman Emperor from 306 (despite violent claims against the post from others) and from 324 until his death, unequivocal sole ruler.

Constantine (the Great as he became known – after his death) was born in Nis, Serbia. His father was a senior officer in the Roman army and his mother, Helena, was Greek. It was at the court of Emperor Diocletian that Constantine received his education which enabled him to mix comfortably with pagan and Christian intellectuals. He is thought to have had a good intellect and an excellent grasp of prose and the power of oratory. He knew that speeches, if delivered superbly, could win or lose important political battles. As a soldier, he fought for the Empire in Syria, Mesopotamia, on the Danube and in Britannia. In 303 he returned to Rome in time to witness the start of Diocletian's "Great Persecution", the bloodiest illtreatment of Christians in Roman history. The extent of this persecution and its eventual failure, combined with other influences, led Constantine to announce tolerance of Christianity in the Edict of Milan in 313. These other influences included his undoubted personal faith (probably inspired by his mother's belief in Christianity) and his own desire to unify pagans and Christians within the Empire.

Lessons from Emperor Constantine

People like unity. Great speechmakers have always been able to emphasize the factors that bring people together, and to identify who will spread the speaker's message and argument once they are gone. Great speakers recognize that people respond to the comradeship of like-minded thinking, placing value on community and conformity, and often find these easier and more comfortable to accept than change and the unfamiliar. The Creed was expressly designed to remove doubt and create an enduring sense of unity and shared belief. To achieve great unity, messages have to be simple and straightforward.

The original Nicene Creed, a commitment to the unification of faith, was first agreed and used at the Council of Nicaea in June 325. There are a large number of variations of the text and some bear substantial revisions, the earliest of which was made by the second Ecumenical Council in 381. Here, the sections we show in square parentheses are the portions of the 325 text that were omitted or moved in 381. "We believe in one God, the Father Almighty, Maker of all things visible and invisible. And in one Lord Jesus Christ, the Son of God, begotten of the Father [the only-begotten; that is, of the essence of the Father, God of God], Light of Light, very God of very God, begotten, not made, being of one substance with the Father; by whom all things were made [both in heaven and on earth]; who for us men, and for our salvation, came down and was incarnate and was made man; he suffered, and the third day he rose again, ascended into heaven; from thence he shall come to judge the quick and the dead. And in the Holy Ghost."

Capture and sell an enduring idea. Many speakers change their messages or cram too much into one presentation. The Greek and Roman civilizations understood the enduring power of ideas, giving us as they did such concepts as democracy and the republic. Christianity provided Constantine with a powerful idea that he knew could endure – after all, he had seen it survive the mightiest Roman persecution by Emperor Diocletian. In short, Constantine recognized a powerful idea when he saw one and he skilfully turned it to his advantage. The Creed has a practical purpose: it makes absolutely clear the fundamental tenets of Christianity. This may seem obvious now, but in 325 there were major schisms and different beliefs as to what constituted Christianity. Constantine and the Church realized that uncertainty and confusion could not be allowed to persist or it would undermine support for their religion, their unifying idea and, fundamentally, the source of their influence. Politically, clarity was needed. The Creed provided it and, in various shapes and forms, it has continued so to do ever since.

A Legacy

The words that Constantine spoke in June 325 (or words similar to the original) are still repeated passionately today by millions of people in a variety of different languages. Constantine gave unity, clarity and influence to a religion that has, for good or otherwise, shaped western civilization. Since 325, Church and State have worked together, in a more or less supportive manner (though with some clear exceptions), to influence and govern western societies. Whichever way we look at the power of the Creed, its legacy has been one of unifying strength. The simplicity of the language similarly increases its force.

Constantine was one of the most significant of all Roman emperors – and they were a pretty influential bunch. Not everything he did, however, is regarded so highly now. He founded the city of Constantinople (Istanbul) and made it into a powerful centre of the Empire; he led the first intra-Christian war; passed laws that began to formalize anti-semitism; resolved doctrinal Christian disputes that might have split the religion; made Christianity both acceptable and then influential within a generation; decided which gospels should be in the Bible; and began dismantling, sidelining and co-opting other pagan religions. Constantine's Council of Nicaea agreed, for example, that Christianity's greatest festival should fall on the first Sunday after the first full moon after the Spring equinox – not an obvious date for Easter, but certainly one that has proved as enduring as his words.

Bill Cosby

I'm telling you Christians – what's wrong with you? Why can't you hit the streets? Why can't you clean it out yourselves?"

Address at the NAACP (National Association for the Advancement of Colored People), sometimes called "The Pound Cake" speech, given on the 50th anniversary of the Brown versus Board of Education, Constitution Hall, Washington DC, USA, Monday 17 May 2004

William (Bill) Henry Cosby Jr (born 17 July 1937) is an American comedian, author, activist and actor. He is most famous for starring in *The Cosby Show*, a television sitcom which ran from 1984 to 1992 with nearly two hundred episodes. It is said that this show single-handedly revived the sitcom genre in the USA. Cosby has a doctorate in education and has always had a passion for supporting inner city African-American youth. His image is kind and fatherly; he is without question seen as caring and understanding. His popularity was such that at one point over 70 million viewers watched a single episode of *A Different World*, a spin off of *The Cosby Show*.

Lessons from Bill Cosby

If you have a passion to share, be passionate. In May 2004, Cosby received an award at the celebration of the 50th anniversary commemoration of the Brown versus Board of Education ruling (which was the decision by the US Supreme Court that made school segregation illegal). In his speech of thanks, Cosby criticized African-Americans who put higher priorities on violence, posturing, intimidation, sport, fashion and greed than on education, manners, care, civic awareness and self-respect. Cosby has a great voice, gentle when necessary and commanding and hectoring as required. In this speech he uses his voice, his personality, evident dismay and huge anger to extraordinary power and effect: "I'm talking about these people who cry when their son is standing there in an orange suit. Where were you when he was two? Where were you when he was twelve? Where were you when he was eighteen and how come you don't know he had a pistol? And where is his father and why don't you know where *he* is? … The church is only open on Sunday … You can't keep asking that God will find a way. God is *tired* of you …"

Use language that is firm, colourful and direct. Above all, don't prevaricate, don't be indirect. Mean what you say. And include your audience; make the listener feel that you are being inclusive. Cosby had a hard message with which many in America (and elsewhere) readily agreed, but were perhaps too afraid to voice: "Looking at the incarcerated, these are not political criminals. These are people going around stealing Coca Cola. People getting shot in the back of the head over a piece of pound cake! Then we all run out and are outraged: 'The cops shouldn't have shot him.' What the hell was he doing with the pound cake in his hand? ... We are *not* parenting."

If you are to persuade your audiences, sometimes you may need to shock and surprise. Certainly it's essential to use language with which the audience can readily identify. An obvious point? Perhaps, but not one that's regularly followed. In 'The Pound Cake' speech, as it became widely known, Cosby asked (actually demanded that) inner-city African-American parents start teaching their children considerably better morals at a younger age. He was critical of those who had forgotten the sacrifices made by their forebears. He berated the emphasis on one-parent families, loose morals and anti-social behaviour. Cosby uses humour and "street" language to reinforce his points: "Ladies and gentlemen ... Are you not paying attention? People with their hat on backwards, pants down around the crack ... Is it a sign of something when she's got ... all kinds of needles and things going through her body. What part of Africa did this come from? We are not Africans. Those people are not Africans; they don't know a damned thing about Africa. With names like Shaniqua, Shaligua, Mohammed and all that crap and all of them are in jail ..."

You don't have to repeat the same thing over and over again but you should reinforce and illustrate your main points. Cosby's language is strong. He tells a story for each point he makes and each little story is scorchingly stark, for example: "We've got to take the neighborhood back. We've got to go in there ..." Cosby pushes the points hard and drives the pain: "I'm telling you Christians, what's wrong with you? Why can't you hit the streets? Why can't you clean it out yourselves? It's our time now, ladies and gentlemen. It is our time. And I've got good news for you. It's not about money. It's about you doing something ..."

A Legacy

Cosby was awarded the Bob Hope Humanitarian Award in 2003. He has also won numerous Grammy Awards and an Emmy. In 1994, Cliff Huxtable, his character in *The Cosby Show*, was ranked number one by Television Guide in its list of the top fifty Greatest Television Dads of All

Time. In the same year he was inducted into the American Academy of Television Arts and Sciences Hall of Fame.

Cosby has continued to lecture to African-American and other communities (including politicians) about serious problems in underprivileged urban communities. He remains angry that many African-Americans fail to live up to the ideals of Frederick Douglass, Martin Luther King Jr and others who worked hard and sacrificed so much for civil rights and a better, safer, fairer society. This particular speech is incredibly strong and you can imagine the smiles and perhaps a laugh or two as Cosby joked, but only to draw the audience in – not to safety, but to be mauled. Then shock on people's faces as what he had to say sank in. And it wasn't just what he said but the way he said it. An angry, passionate and distressed individual expounding on realities and hard-edged truths with powerful language that must have made that audience squirm in discomfort.

The ending is strong indeed and would bring up short an audience that was in all likelihood church-going and decent: "When you go to the church, look at the stained glass things of Jesus. Look at them. Is Jesus smiling? Not in one picture. So, tell your friends. Let's try to do something. Let's try to make Jesus smile. Let's start parenting ..." This is a truly remarkable speech, truly remarkable and it is but one of several that Cosby has made on the same subject.

In 1997 one of Cosby's sons was murdered, aged 28, in Los Angeles as he was changing a tyre by the roadside. After Bill Cosby spoke out following the incident, the death penalty for the murderer was dropped in favour of a life sentence.

Walter Cronkite

Let us hear the peal of a new international liberty bell that calls us all to the creation of a system of enforceable world law in which the universal desire for peace can place its hope and prayers ..."

Speech on accepting the Norman Cousins Global Governance Award, United Nations, New York, USA, Tuesday 19 October 1999

Walter Leland Cronkite Jr (born 4 November 1916 and died 17 July 2009) was a retired American broadcast journalist, probably best known throughout the United States and beyond as the CBS Evening News anchorman, a job he did for 19 years between 1962 and 1981. During the height of its popularity, CBS News, led by Cronkite, set the bar for American news coverage. He was known as trustworthy, honourable, safe, professional, unbiased and well mannered. His pet phrase was at the end of each broadcast: "Well, that's the way it is on ...."

In 1999 Cronkite was presented with the Norman Cousins Global Governance Award at a United Nations ceremony. In his acceptance speech, he argued for a global federal government, a view which some observers found astoundingly naïve, coming from a well-seasoned newsman. However, Cronkite had apparently long held the view that the world would be better managed by a world government. He referred to the political courage displayed by the American founders in 1787, when the notion of establishing a United States seemed impossible and unlikely.

Cronkite's major argument was that the world was a dangerous place, many parts of which faced warfare, persecution, starvation and strife of some sort or another. It was time to call a halt to extremism: "For how many thousands of years now have we humans been what we insist on calling 'civilized'? And yet, in total contradiction, we also persist in the savage belief that we must occasionally, at least, settle our arguments by killing one another." Whatever our own views on its content, this is a speech that sought vast change. It's not an angry speech necessarily, but one which set out an impassioned reasoning that warranted a hearing.

Lessons from Walter Cronkite

Recognize that controversy is sometimes hard to avoid. If controversy is inevitable, then make sure that you back up your position with facts and give your audience enough information to be convinced.

Cronkite had long been associated with the World Federalist Movement and this speech was a golden opportunity to test his thinking. Here he calls for a world government: "It seems to many of us that if we are to avoid the eventual catastrophic world conflict, we must strengthen the United Nations as a first step toward a world government ... To do that, of course, we Americans will have to yield up some of our sovereignty. That would be a bitter pill. It would take a lot of courage, a lot of faith in the new order. But the American colonies did it once and brought forth one of the most nearly perfect unions the world has ever seen ..." In political terms, Cronkite must have known that abandoning American sovereignty, even a little of it, was never going to happen, but he wanted to air views on settling the world's differences in a way that had yet to be tried – getting the United Nations to behave in a way for which (he felt) it had been established.

Use your experience. Cronkite shows us the value of referring to our own experience in order to reinforce opinion. He uses personal anecdotes as well as wit – and he excelled at both. He told those assembled, including Hillary Clinton, that he was speaking out because he was now free so to do. He could, he said, use his experience of nations, of huge conflicts, of the United States, to conclude that the world was able to manage the world. Not now, not soon, but one day.

A Legacy

Walter Cronkite's ideas did not meet with action and few were surprised by this. However, what he said underlined what many thought (and still think) about a federal world. It set a context. And, because of what people like Cronkite said, pressure increased on the United Nations to behave in a collegiate, federal way in order to properly manage, and possibly stop, some of the world's most troublesome conflicts. With forums like the G7, G8, G20 and world leadership organizations like the World Bank, IMF, WHO, International Court of Justice, and International Criminal Court, the federalist global movement is gathering momentum. True global federalism and a world government have yet to take root, however.

Severn Cullis-Suzuki

If you don't know how to fix it, please stop breaking it!"

Address to the Plenary Session, Earth Summit, Rio Centro, Brazil, 9 June 1992

Severn Cullis-Suzuki was born on 30 November 1979 in Vancouver, Canada. She is an environmental activist, speaker, academic, television host and author. She speaks frequently on environmental issues, urging governments, agencies, businesses and individuals with influence to take responsibility for environmental awareness and, where necessary, change.

At nine years of age, she founded the Environmental Children's Organization (ECO). The organization comprised of a group of children dedicated to helping other children learn more about the environment.

In 1992, aged twelve, Cullis-Suzuki attended the Earth Summit in Rio de Janeiro and was offered only six minutes to present environmental issues from a youth perspective. She spoke with confidence and aplomb, after which she received a standing ovation: "We raised all the money ourselves to come six thousand miles to tell you adults you must change your ways. Coming here today, I have no hidden agenda. I am fighting for my future." It wasn't just because she was a child that the delegates liked her; it was because of what she said. Most of it was common sense; it was also a very clear statement that the future was hers but that the present was being ruined.

Lessons from Severn Cullis-Suzuki

If you have a belief, then you can make a speech. Cullis-Suzuki's is a remarkable speech, not only because it was made by one so young, but also because it is direct and uses youth as a lever to get commitment from the audience or, at least, a hearing. She makes and reinforces cogent arguments which are emotive rather than emotional and, more than anything, personal. Her attitude is appealing and refreshing. Here was an example of a young person speaking on behalf of something in which she and other children passionately believed: "In my life, I have dreamt of seeing the great herds of wild animals, jungles and rainforests full of birds and butterflies, but now I wonder if they will even exist for my children to see. Did you have to worry about these little things when you were my age? All this is happening before our eyes and yet we act as if we have all the time we want and all the solutions. I'm only a child and I don't have all the solutions, but I want you to realize, neither do you! You don't know how to fix the holes in our ozone layer ... If you don't know how to fix it, please stop breaking it!"

Make your arguments simple. Cullis-Suzuki's language was simple, her argument straightforward. You don't have to be twelve to make a simple, straightforward speech. Clarity is all. If you're clear, the likelihood is that your audience will also be clear. For example, read this from her speech: "I am here to speak on behalf of the starving children around the world whose cries go unheard. I am here to speak for the countless animals dying across this planet because they have nowhere left to go. We cannot afford to be not heard. I am afraid to go out in the sun now because of the holes in the ozone. I am afraid to breathe the air because I don't know what chemicals are in it."

A Legacy

In 1993 Cullis-Suzuki was honoured in the United Nations Environmental Programme's Global 500 Roll of Honour. In the same year, still only thirteen, she published *Tell the World*, a book on the environmental steps for families to follow.

Severn Cullis-Suzuki, and her views on the environment, became noticed. The platform was used well. She caused enormous discomfort amongst the Brazilian Earth Summit but also amongst a wider audience. She helped focus more attention on worldwide environmental issues. It cannot be said that her speech moved nations to behave differently. It cannot even be said that she was remembered by everyone attending the event in Brazil. But it *can* be said that she made a powerful difference to some people's awareness of the issues facing the planet.

Cullis-Suzuki graduated from Yale in 2002 in ecology and evolutionary biology. In that year she also co-hosted *Suzuki's Nature Quest*, a children's television series on the Discovery Channel. As a member of Kofi Annan's Special Advisory Panel, she and members of The Skyfish Project (an internet-driven discussion forum and think tank) brought their first project, a pledge called the Recognition of Responsibility, to the 2002 World Summit in Johannesburg.

She still lectures and writes about sustainability and the environment. Her activities as a child, and her commitment since, have acted as a guiding light to her peers, her generation and to many whose job it is to consider how best to act on environmental issues.

Clarence Darrow

If it was reversed and eleven white men had shot and killed a black while protecting their home and their lives against a mob of blacks, nobody would have dreamed of having them indicted … They would have been given medals instead."

Closing trial speech in defence of Henry Sweet, Detroit, USA, Tuesday 11 May 1926

Clarence Seward Darrow was born on 18 April 1857 and died on 13 March 1938. He was an American lawyer and a leading member of the American Civil Liberties Union. In the mid-1920s Darrow was, without doubt, the most famous trial lawyer in the United States. His famous cases included the murder trial of Nathan Leopold and Richard Loeb in 1924 (in which two teenage sons from wealthy families were accused of murdering a fourteen-year-old boy) and the now extraordinary 1925 "Monkey Trial" of John Scopes, a teacher stopped from teaching evolution. In a number of his cases, Darrow was up against another superb orator, William Jennings Bryan who, in the Scopes trial, expounded his fundamentalist interpretation of the Bible. Darrow actually lost this case, although it was claimed that he had out-talked and out-argued Bryan, whose views were eventually held in ridicule by many.

In 1926 a white mob in Detroit had attempted to drive an African-American family out of the home they had purchased in a predominantly white neighborhood. In the ensuing struggle, a white man was killed, and eleven African-Americans in the house were promptly arrested and charged with murder. In one case, Dr Ossian Sweet and three members of his family were put on trial during the course of which Darrow famously argued to the (all-white) jury: "I insist that there is nothing but prejudice in this case; that if it was reversed and eleven white men had shot and killed a black while protecting their home and their lives against a mob of blacks, nobody would have dreamed of having them indicted. They would have been given medals instead ..."

Following the mis-trials of the eleven, it was agreed that each of them would be tried individually. Darrow first defended Dr Ossian Sweet's brother Henry, who had confessed to firing the shot on Garland Street that, it was assumed and proved, had killed the white man. Henry was found not guilty on grounds of self-defence and the prosecution promptly dropped the charges on the remaining ten.

Darrow's closing defence argument in Henry Sweet's trial for murder took seven hours. This was quite normal for Darrow. His reputation stood on the fact that he carefully built up his cases by firstly demolishing every single opposing argument. This is a commonly used speech device: knock down, with dignity or with wrath, the opposite view. In the Henry Sweet case, Darrow's arguments were many, although he readily played openly on the accurate observation that prejudice was rife. He did this, not in a hectoring way, but by carefully painting a real picture, a detailed scenario, peppered with strong images, utilizing language that could not be misunderstood. You can almost see the jurors' embarrassment: "Gentlemen, does anybody need to argue to you as to why those people were there? ... A neighbourly crowd? A man who comes to your home and puts a razor across your windpipe, or who meets you on the street and puts a dagger through your heart is as much a neighbour as these conspirators and rioters were who drove these black people from their home. Neighbours, eh? Visiting? Bringing them greetings and good cheer! Our people were newcomers. They might have needed their larder stocked. It was a hot night. The crowd probably brought them ice cream and soda and possibly other cold drinks. Neighbours? Gentlemen – neighbours? They were neighbours in the same sense that a nest of rattlesnakes are neighbours when you accidentally put your foot upon them … And every man who knows anything about this case knows it. You know what the purpose was …"

Lessons from Clarence Darrow

Let people anticipate and relish the thought process of your speeches. Darrow gained notoriety for his moving closing arguments presented without notes. He made his cases important by tying the fate of one lonely and persecuted outcast into the entire notion of humanity and freedom. He viewed (many) criminals as people led by circumstance into committing antisocial acts, rather than as free-willing monsters. For this reason he was a bitter opponent of capital punishment, viewing it as a barbaric practice. His language is invariably conversational, rarely using legalese. He begins his defence with: "Now, let's see; I am going to try to be as fair as I can with you gentlemen; still I don't mind being watched at that. I just want you to give such consideration to what I say as you think it is worth."

Skill and practice are invaluable. In his trial speeches, Darrow demonstrated his superb qualities as a lawyer. His arguments were crystal-clear, simple and often stark. He knew how to take his audiences (juries) with him in constructing a notion, a thought, an idea. He built up a case slowly but carefully and entertainingly. His language was measured and strong; his dramatic instincts and persuasive abilities extraordinary. Darrow argued, for example, that the Henry Sweet case was about racism not murder: "Take the hatred away and you have nothing left." In this speech he carefully laid the grounds upon which he would set out his defence.

A Legacy

In the pre-television, newspaper world of Darrow, words clearly mattered more than images. Much more. Oratorical skills were truly valued; whole speeches were heard and were also then read widely. In Darrow's time, there was a general belief that intellectual battles could be won, not just fought. It was the only way, through rhetoric, that change in all manner of things could be brought about.

Power has shifted in the American courtroom since Darrow ended his career. There are more constraints operating on lawyers today and trials are more scripted. Few modern judges would, for example, let a defence lawyer call a prosecutor as a witness. The personal stories, the natural, conversational language, the biting sarcasm and the ever-present poetry that we find in Darrow's summations would likely be met today with strong moral disapproval.

Darrow did set a moral tone, a tone for defending people's rights and for the defence of the innocent against the bullying and prejudicial masses. As he says towards the close of the Henry Sweet trial speech: "I know the Negro race has a long road to go … The law has made him equal, but man has not …"

Darrow was regarded as sensational. Despite the fact his formal education was limited, his persuasive powers and grasp of argument were exceptional. One aspect of his legacy is his use of vibrant, colourful and focused phrases. Unsurprisingly, he also became a champion against racial discrimination. Unfortunately, his character was occasionally called into question; he was charged with bribery and he was vilified for his humiliation of Williams Jennings Bryan. Nonetheless, he holds a reputation for being one who fought for the weak, as one who drew on morality and as one who could convince courts that the powerful in the land would not always win, by any means.

Demosthenes

You had nothing to say then; very well, show us our duty now."

The Judicial Oration "On the Crown", Athens, Greece, 330 BC

Demosthenes (384–322 BC) was an Athenian statesman and orator. It was at the age of twenty that he delivered his first judicial speeches, when he successfully argued to get back from his guardians what was left of his inheritance. He then made his living as a professional speechwriter and a lawyer, writing speeches for use in private cases. In Ancient Greece it was the audience that decided on an issue, not the speaker. Then, a politician had to more or less follow the views of the population, as a consequence of which oratory was regarded as a crucial art and was taught as such. A speaker could lose a political or legal decision by poor speaking, lazy delivery or wretched and insufficient argument. Demosthenes became known as a great practitioner of oratory and also a great teacher of the skill.

Demosthenes's passion was Athens and, in defence of the city, he attempted to motivate citizens against Philip II of Macedon. In 351 BC, Demosthenes began his famous Philippics speeches which primarily warned Athens of the threatening danger of a fast-expanding Macedon. The First Philippic was succeeded by three Olynthiacs in which Demosthenes begged that Athens should send forces to defend Olynthus (the strongest northern city) against Philip, but his pleas were largely ignored. In 348 BC Olynthus fell. Demosthenes led armed opposition against Philip's growing military and political ambition, but the result was Philip of Macedon's greatest victory at Chaeronea in 338 BC.

After the wars with Philip, Ctesiphon, a great supporter of Demosthenes, offered the reward of a golden crown to the orator. Five years later, when Demosthenes's policies had again met with little success, his enemy, Aeschines, indicted Ctesiphon, claiming that his offer of a crown was illegal and that Demosthenes had no right to such an award. Aeschines was probably right. But, as with the trial of Socrates, cases in Athens were not always tried on the legal technicalities. In the end, Aeschines received less than one fifth of the trial vote and lost the case. Prosecutors who achieved less than a fifth of the vote were heavily fined in Athens, to prevent frivolous lawsuits. The fine was so heavy that Aeschines was forced to go into exile on the grounds that he couldn't pay it.

After Philip's death, Demosthenes took part in the uprising against the new King of Macedon, Alexander the Great, but to no avail. To prevent a similar revolt against his own rule, Alexander's successor in the region, Antipater, sent his forces to arrest Demosthenes, but instead the orator committed suicide.

Lessons from Demosthenes

Focus and prepare, however difficult this may be. It is said that, as a boy, Demosthenes had poor pronunciation and a stammer. It seems his preparation for all his speeches was elaborate and meticulous and it has been claimed that he practised making speeches with pebbles in his mouth. Legend also has it that he rehearsed by the seashore so that he would have to project against the noise of the wind and the waves. It would be heartening to believe that these things were so.

Carefully plan your argument so that you take your audience with you. Watch out for any possible holes in your argument. Small holes often lead to minor damage below the speech's Plimsoll line, but from that small amount of damage, it and you may sink. The "On the Crown" speech is a strong political plea. Demosthenes's entire political career was at stake, but he repudiated nothing of what he had done. What he did was to reinforce all of the positives in his life and, in particular, what he had achieved for Athens and what his opponent had not. He began with a general view of Greece and described the phases of his struggle against Philip. He also launched a personal attack against Aeschines, whom he ridiculed. To this he added charges of corruption and treason. In essence, he carefully destroyed Aeschines's character: "For this contemptible fellow, I have a short, plain and sufficient answer. Aeschines, if the future was revealed to you and to nobody else, you should have given us the benefit of your predictions when we were deliberating; if you had no foreknowledge, you are open to the charge of ignorance just like the rest of us. Then what better right have you to denounce me than I to denounce you …?"

Demosthenes also emphasized that he alone promoted a coalition with Thebes. Although Athens had been defeated, asserted the orator, it was better to be defeated in a glorious struggle for independence than to simply surrender liberty: "But then, if Athens, after claiming to be the greatest of nations, had abandoned her position, she would have been held guilty of betraying Greece to Philip. If, without striking a blow, she had abandoned the cause for which our forefathers flinched from no peril, is there a man who would not have spat in your face? In your face, Aeschines: not at Athens, not at me …"

The speech attacks with probing detail, even though some of the facts are likely to have been exaggerated. He defends his own position as a loyal, brave Athenian – again with probable exaggeration. Nonetheless, the speech is passionately earnest, expressed through anger, pity and irony. He is unwilling ever to ease up in his demolition of Aeschines's character: "You stand revealed in your life and conduct, in your public performances and also in your public appearances. A project approved by the people is going forward. Aeschines is speechless. A regrettable incident is reported. Aeschines is in evidence. He reminds one of an old sprain or fracture: the moment you are out of health it begins to be active."

Humour is in short supply, but that's just as likely to have been the oratorical order of the day. In most of the speeches that remain there is clear indication of extensive preparation, although it is likely (as is the case today) that Demosthenes went to some trouble to hide the fact. Short, sharp sentences give the impression of spontaneity.

A Legacy

Demosthenes published many of his orations, around sixty of which survive. Romans studied his art as part of their own oratorical training. Juvenal praised him as "largus et exundans ingenii fons" (a large and overflowing fountain of genius) and he inspired Cicero's speeches (also called the Philippics) against Mark Antony. Cicero praised Demosthenes as "the perfect orator".

His speeches are superb examples of how to attack and defend argument. His advice was always given with consideration of how the city-state (Athens) might benefit, although he was perhaps not far-sighted enough to see that the Athenian city-state was coming to an end.

During the Renaissance, Demosthenes's eloquence was venerated and he was widely read, second only perhaps to Cicero. In modern times, Demosthenes's style has been much copied, along with his principles. Those drawing up the Constitution of the United States were inspired by him as were the orators of the French Revolution and French Resistance fighters in World War II; thereafter Demosthenes's name became a symbol of independence and resistance.

Deng Xiaoping

In carrying out our modernization programme, we must proceed from Chinese realities. Both in revolution and in construction we should also learn from foreign countries and draw on their experience, but mechanical application of foreign experience and copying of foreign models will get us nowhere ... China's affairs should be run according to China's specific conditions and by the Chinese people themselves."

Opening speech at the Twelfth National Congress of the Communist Party of China, Beijing, China, Tuesday 1 September 1982

Deng Xiaoping was born in Sichuan, China. He was a Chinese revolutionary and reformer, as well as the leader of the Communist Party of China (CPC). Deng never held office as the head of state or the head of government, but from 1978 to the early 1990s he did serve as the de facto leader of the People's Republic of China. He was born on 22 August 1904 and died on 19 February 1997.

Deng Xiaoping is widely recognized as being a political innovator and introducing a new brand of socialism to China. It would be fair to say that he led the transformation of China into one of the fastest-growing economies in the world. Under his leadership, the Chinese people's standard of living grew markedly.

Lessons from Deng Xiaoping

Provide direction. Deng Xiaoping said in this 1982 speech: "China's affairs should be run according to China's specific conditions and by the Chinese people themselves. Independence and self-reliance have always been and will always be their basic stand. While the Chinese people value their friendship and cooperation with other countries and other peoples, they value even more their hard-won independence and sovereign rights." Deng never claimed to be a great speaker and he found the process difficult. A shy man for the most part, he preferred argument and discussion in small groups; for him, the value of oratory was to guide, focus and provide direction. Nonetheless, he practised fervently and prepared well, no matter what or how big his audiences might be. The challenge he faced was to match the content of his words – the need to develop, modernize and avoid staying wedded to the past – with the reality of the highly structured, rigid and often fearful system that existed in communist China in the early 1980s.

Be very clear in what you are asking your audience to believe. There are speeches, seemingly good speeches, where those in the audience leave thinking that the speech meant something other than that which the speaker intended. Deng Xiaoping was not guilty of this in his speech. His solution to pushing China towards modernization was to use a formal system to create and then regulate a modern, freer economy. This is brilliantly and consistently shown in his speeches. To us they may at times appear formal and dry, but his audiences responded well to that type of delivery. What they sought was authority, knowledge and absolutely focused direction.

Deng Xiaoping used the authority that the system provided to encourage, reassure and, most importantly, direct people. He spoke openly and provided a clear set of priorities in which he demanded that his audiences believe. In some respects, perhaps, he resembled a CEO setting out a bold new strategy or vision for his business and then helping people to move in the right direction in adopting it. Crucially, this meant keeping the best of the past, maintaining current stability and creating, and taking, new opportunities.

Adopt the right style. It wasn't simply what Deng Xiaoping said, but how he said it, that inspired people to change. He was keen to place China on a highly individual footing. He knew that China had to manage its economy in its own way whilst at the same time drawing on the experience of other nations: "In carrying out our modernization programme we must proceed from Chinese realities. Both in revolution and in construction we should also learn from foreign countries and draw on their experience, but mechanical application of foreign experience and copying of foreign models will get us nowhere." He took a classical Chinese approach when delivering his speeches. Metaphors were sometimes used but more often his style was analytical, logical and straightforward. Sadly, much of this progress was set back by the fearful repression that followed protests in Beijing's Tiananmen Square in 1989 – a situation that might have been avoided with better communication at the time and a closer understanding of the government's messages.

A Legacy

Deng Xiaoping may be remembered as a leader who understood that authoritarian China required economic reform to rescue itself from socialist oblivion. Mao called him "a needle wrapped in cotton" and indeed he had a reputation for seeming to be mild and equitable when in actual fact he was ready to strike at those who would oppose his plans. With China likely to be a driving, if not dominant, force in the world economy for much of the 21st century, it's fitting that one of China's greatest leaders should have resembled a quiet, thoughtful business leader much more than an extrovert politician. Late in life, he commented: "We felt that China was weak and we wanted to make it strong." As was usual in his methodology, he expressed things simply: "So we went to the West to learn."

Since 1979, and possibly as a result of Deng's policies, China has enjoyed exemplary GDP growth. It is now one of the world's largest economies and the largest emerging market. Deng Xiaoping introduced a professional, but specifically Chinese, style of economic management and leadership to China after decades of strife, revolution and violence. His policies transformed China, but it is the example of his seemingly mild, but firm and authoritative approach that has provided a blueprint for his successors to follow.

After Deng Xiaoping, under the leadership of Jiang Zemin, government policies reinforced Deng's ideas, thoughts, methods, and direction. His emphasis on light industry, small units that were managed locally, suited China's large population and created a large, cheap labour market which became significant on the global stage. Favouring joint ventures over home-grown domestic industry, Deng encouraged foreign capital and it came in vast quantities.

Charles Dickens

It would be worse than idle – for it would be hypocritical and unfeeling – if I were to disguise that I close this episode in my life with feelings of very considerable pain."

Speech made after The Farewell Reading, St James's Hall, London, UK, Tuesday 15 March 1870

Charles John Huffam Dickens was born on 7 February 1812 and died on June 9 1870. Dickens was one of the most popular English novelists in Victorian times (some say the greatest). Less well known perhaps was that he was a social campaigner and spent much of his time arguing passionately for change to improve the circumstances of the poor, particularly in London.

Written under the pen-name "Boz", Dickens's novels frequently appeared in periodicals and magazines in serialized form, a popular format for fiction in Victorian times. It was common for authors to complete entire novels before any serial production began. However, in Dickens's case, his works were often composed in parts, each part written shortly before it was published. The result was very similar to the style of popular television serial dramas of today where the characters are exaggerations of good and bad. Similarly, the stories had a particular flow and rhythm, punctuated by one shock or cliffhanger after another, with the public looking forward with bated breath to the next instalment.

Dickens's speeches, too, were beautifully written and he went to great lengths to ensure that each sounded like a tale. His speeches were a series of stories which gave colour to his argument. He went to great trouble to ensure that all aspects of the speech were interesting, that there should be no dips in the narrative. His presentation technique was to keep his audiences focused and his skill was to create anticipation. In this he was the consummate storyteller too. His voice would rise and fall, sometimes to a whisper. He would imitate accents and take the part of characters with gusto to make a point. Any speech of his was theatrical and dramatic. Audiences were spellbound. People would listen for hours, often in tears as he related some aspect of London slums or roaring with laughter at his description of a factory owner or politician. Dickens was exemplary and skilled in the art of satire and was able to pinpoint with great accuracy the problems in society and their resolutions.

Lessons from Charles Dickens

If you are popular and your audience knows you, seize the day and use these things to great effect. However, don't squander the opportunity on vainglory. A speech is an opportunity to move your strategy, message or plan forward, a chance to reinforce argument and to persuade your listeners that your views are worthwhile. On 15 March 1870, Dickens read extracts from *A Christmas Carol* and *The Pickwick Papers* and brought to a brilliant close the memorable series of public readings which had for sixteen years proved a source of enormous enjoyment to huge audiences throughout Britain and, of course, America, where Dickens became enormously popular. He completed this particular evening with a farewell speech. His lecturing and performances had exhausted him.

The building, St James's Hall, was packed. Word had spread that this was perhaps the last chance to hear the distinguished novelist interpret his own characters and to say goodbye. Dickens was already very ill when he made this particular speech and many will have known this. People are said to have wept at the end of the evening. One can understand why.

Amidst repeated acclamations and wild applause, with hats and handkerchiefs waving in every part of the hall, Dickens retired, withdrawing with him one of the greatest intellectual treats the public ever enjoyed: "It would be worse than idle – for it would be hypocritical and unfeeling – if I were to disguise that I close this episode in my life with feelings of very considerable pain. For some fifteen years, in this hall and in many kindred places, I have had the honour of presenting my own cherished ideas before you for your recognition and, in closely observing your reception of them, have enjoyed an amount of artistic delight and instruction which, perhaps, is given to few men to know."

Whether or not people have paid money to see you, they *have* paid with their time. This means that you owe them, never the other way round. Speakers should always put on their best performance and effort – or why bother? That evening, Dickens apparently read with more spirit and energy than he had ever done before. But then, he always made a point of preparing properly and of understanding what his audiences liked, what made them laugh, gasp or cry. His voice, to the end, retained its distinctive clarity, excellent projection and great expression. Each character in each passage came alive by a simple transition of tone, a pause or a specific, stressed word, an inflection here and a hoarse whisper there. People could all but see the vividly painted characters before them.

Good stories can be repeated and, if told well (and that's the key),

people will look forward to the retelling. In the packed room, people (who most assuredly would know the stories by heart) waited impatiently for the beginning of each passage. Not a single syllable was lost and the listeners adored the moments of humour and deep pathos. Wherever Dickens went, the most popular readings were those from *Oliver Twist, Little Dorrit* and *A Christmas Carol.* With the last, audiences particularly delighted in the description of Bob Cratchit's Christmas Day and the episodes with Tiny Tim. This particular evening was clearly no different. The general delight at hearing of Ebenezer Scrooge's reformation was only halted by the sad thought that with it the very last of the tale was dying away. Dickens ended his presentation that evening by saying "... I vanish now for evermore, with a heartfelt, grateful, respectful and affectionate farewell."

Remember that when you are making a speech, no matter how large or small the audience, you are on stage. The applause of the audience rang for several minutes through the hall and when it had subsided, Dickens, with strong emotion but in his usual expressive manner, made his speech, which was polished and moving. The speech is short but beautifully crafted and you can see his clear enjoyment of the words. Great writing, clever writing, goes a long way to the delivery of a great speech, of course. In Dickens's case, he used few or no notes.

A Legacy

Dickens was a regular and fiery critic of the poverty and social dysfunction of Victorian society. Readers were often surprised and astonished by revelations of what went on in society outside their immediate sphere of understanding or experience. Dickens's second novel, *Oliver Twist* (1839), shocked readers with its images of poverty and crime and was responsible for the clearing of the actual London slum that was the basis of the story. There were other instances where Dickens's words led to public and political focus on the extreme conditions in which people worked and lived. In particular, he brought attention to issues such as sanitation, sewage and the workhouse and would walk the streets of London sometimes for hours on end, both to gain inspiration but also to see first-hand what went on in the downtrodden parts of society. He condemned those in power and the petty officials who managed the institutions and who benefited (certainly financially) from the misery of others. His description of English prisons in *The Pickwick Papers* and *Little Dorrit* was without question a factor in the closing down of a number of London jails.

Some might argue that Dickens's language was convoluted – and perhaps it was – but overall, critics agree that his choice of words and his expression were superb. His ability to describe a situation, a person and a relationship was unique. Above all, he set a bar for storytelling and the ability to tell stories well is a factor most important in the skill of speech-making. Dickens's public oratory was also powerful and direct. He knew how to amuse or to inform any audience in person or through his writing.

In March 1870 the ailing Dickens was received by Queen Victoria, who later said: "He had a large, loving mind and the strongest sympathy with the poorer classes."

Benjamin Disraeli

… Because they believe that it will secure to us a highway to our Indian Empire and our dependencies, the people of England have from the first recognized the propriety and the wisdom of the step which we shall sanction tonight."

Disraeli's speech on the acquisition of the Suez Canal Shares, House of Commons, London, UK, Monday 21 February 1876

Benjamin Disraeli, Earl of Beaconsfield, was born on 21 December 1804 and died on 19 April 1881. He was a British politician who served twice as Britain's prime minister. For over thirty years his influence on British and indeed international politics was great and he is certainly regarded as a great orator of Victorian times. Before politics, Disraeli began writing novels primarily to pay off his debts and this ability to write reasonable (but not great) novels did make his speeches colourful and succinct. He made language work.

In 1875 the Khedive of Egypt had gone bankrupt and quickly needed to sell shares in the Suez Canal, shipping through which was predominantly British. It was clear that Britain somehow had to purchase the Egyptian shares. This Disraeli promptly did. He organized the purchase of 176,602 shares in the Canal in order to stop the French blocking Britain's trade lifeline to India and Australia.

Disraeli personally persuaded MP and financier Lionel de Rothschild to lend the British government the £4m needed to buy the shares. It was, as it happens, a good deal. By 1914 the shares were worth over £40m. The purchase of the shares was not a foregone conclusion, however. Disraeli declared to the House: "Sir, although, according to the noble Lord, we are going to give a unanimous vote, it cannot be denied that the discussion of this evening at least has proved one result. It has shown, in a manner about which neither the House of Commons nor the country can make any mistake, that had the right honourable Gentleman the Member for Greenwich (Mr W. Gladstone) been the Prime Minister of this country, the shares in the Suez Canal would not have been purchased ... the people of England have from the first recognized the propriety and the wisdom of the step which we shall sanction tonight."

Lessons from Benjamin Disraeli

Not all great speakers start well. If your first few speeches don't work, it doesn't mean you can't be a great speaker. Disraeli's first speech in the House of Commons was anticipated with much interest. Since he had become famous as a writer and had made numerous and perhaps ill-advised accusations against leaders of the opposition, politicians expected a contest in parliament and the rise of a formidable speechmaker. Yet he began his speech (rather nervously and then pompously) to shouts of derisive laughter and glee from the opposition. It was a disaster. Hurt and somewhat dismayed, Disraeli took his seat with the prophetic statement: "I have begun several times many things and have often succeeded at last. I shall sit down now, but the time will come when you will hear me." Gradually, Disraeli grew in confidence and, with considerable effort and practice, he did indeed become a great maker of great speeches.

Consider your turn of phrase. These days it's often the case that extracts from speeches, even ones made at modest occasions, are used in intranets, on blogs, in websites, in magazines, on television programmes and so on. Ensure that your speech has some quotable remarks. Once you have your theme and your argument, make some bold statements (never without being able to substantiate them of course). Memorable lines are important and convoluted material is both unkind on your audiences and point-less. Disraeli was certainly adept at creating lines that were memorable and quotable. For example: "I repeat ... that all power is a trust; that we are accountable for its exercise; that from the people, and for the people all springs, and all must exist." Another of Disraeli's famous lines is this: "In a progressive country change is constant ... change ... is inevita-ble." Another: "A consistent soul believes in destiny, a capricious one in chance." And one which we very much like: "A man may speak very well in the House of Commons and fail very completely in the House of Lords. There are two distinct styles requisite: I intend, in the course of my career, if I have time, to give a specimen of both."

A Legacy

Disraeli's most lasting achievement was probably the establishment of what became the modern Conservative party. Throughout his career, Disraeli was noted for powerful epithets, strong phrases that contained truisms and which struck chords with listeners and readers. Some of the phrases, such as "Never take anything for granted" from his speech on 5 October 1864 and "Justice is truth in action" from a speech on 11 February 1851, are ones we still use today. Some were simply powerful and unforgettable: "The most dangerous strategy is to jump a chasm in two leaps." He was patient and formal with his colleagues, but was a powerful debater and seldom relinquished his objective. His speeches were apposite and his argument always clever. He used verbal devices such as the rule of three, much used by many in this book. For instance: "There are three kinds of lies: lies, damned lies and statistics." And: "I never deny. I never contradict. I sometimes forget."

In the business of saving Britain's interest in the Suez Canal, to which our chosen speech relates, Disraeli was accused by Gladstone of undermining Britain's constitutional system due to his total lack of consent from parliament when buying the shares with private funding. Admittedly it was unusual, but in retrospect it was a good job that Disraeli did what he did. When he heard that the French were negotiating for purchase of the shares, he had to move quickly and there was little or no time to convene the Commons. As he could not wait for parliamentary allocation of funds, he sent his private secretary, Montagu Corry, to Lord Rothschild to ensure a loan. Apparently, when Corry told Rothschild that the prime minister wanted £4m the next day, Rothschild ate a grape, and asked "What is your security?" "The British government," said Corry. "You shall have it," replied Rothschild.

Disraeli made Victorian society fairer and, while it is thought that Gladstone was possibly the greater British statesman of the nineteenth century, Disraeli was certainly a colourful leader and a great orator. His foreign policies were regarded as brave and strong, defending Britain at all costs, not only by clever strategy but also by clever rhetoric and well-presented argument.

Frederick Douglass

"What to the Slave is the Fourth of July?"

Address to the Rochester Ladies and Slavery Society, Rochester, New York, USA, Monday 5 July 1852

Frederick Douglass, originally named Frederick Augustus Washington Bailey, was born on 14 February 1818 and died on 20 February 1895. Douglass was a women's suffragist, a brave and superb orator, an abolitionist, author, reformer and statesman. Among his famous phrases are "I could, as a free man, look across the bay toward the Eastern Shore where I was born a slave" and "One and God make a majority".

Without question, America holds him as one of its most prominent African-American figures. Possibly the most prominent. Douglass was born into slavery but escaped in 1838. Extraordinarily, by 1872 he became the first African-American to be nominated as a vice-presidential candidate. Douglass ran with the first woman to run for president, Equal Rights Party nominee Victoria Woodhull. Pretty extraordinary in those days, and with interesting parallels today. Douglass is remembered for his ability to persuade and his forceful rhetoric. Indeed, many current politicians, mostly in the United States, quote Douglass and honour him with rightful reverence. Here was a brave man, a good man and one who, more than many, helped to eradicate slavery.

Lessons from Frederick Douglass

Prepare, prepare, prepare. Douglass is thought to have spent the best part of three weeks preparing this particular address. Six hundred people, mostly abolitionist women, had been invited to the Corinthian Hall on 5 July 1852. Douglass had been invited to speak by the Rochester Ladies and Slavery Society and his address is arguably the most famous and strongest anti-slavery speech ever made. It is simply brilliant in its construction and deliberation. Its craft is wonderful and just from reading it you marvel at the cleverness of argument, the wit, the anger, the humour and the sheer power of it. The presentation must have been superb, too, because by all accounts Douglass spoke well and had a great delivery. On this occasion, it was reported that the applause at the end (and often throughout) was tremendous.

If you have an innate skill, improve it. Douglass's skill on stage ranked him alongside the greatest of the nineteenth-century orators. He was eloquent, commanding attention and respect when he spoke. He also had the ability to present essential facts with precision while clearly expressing ideas. Merely being able to speak well doesn't necessarily make you a great orator. There's more. Douglass possessed broader qualities held by all reform orators: bravery, absolute will, nerve, concentration and perseverance.

His speeches illustrated and condemned the inhumanity shown by the strong to the weak. He condemned violence, cruelty, poverty and the destructiveness of alcohol, but not as a preacher – more as a patient teacher. He had innate ability, despite all the horrors and inequalities that he'd experienced and those that he knew befell African-Americans, women, immigrants and the poor. And yet, despite the gravity of his topics, what stands out in Douglass's speeches, albeit not this one, is his ability to make his audiences laugh. Flashes of humour – not queasy, sterile attempts at poor jokes but self-deprecating and relevant stories which make audiences smile because you *know* what will make them smile – are the nuggets of great speechcrafting.

Build your case, develop your argument. Be clever. As was the tradition in the black communities of New York State, Douglass insisted on speaking on the 5th, not the 4th of July. He put his audience at ease by offering plaudits to America's founding fathers. He acknowledges the importance of the Fourth of July, which he terms an American "Passover". He also recognizes that there is huge hope in the young country which he says is "still impressible". He understands that, given its youth, the country could be open to change. The audience is drawn in – comfortably and safely.

Then Douglass calls the Declaration of Independence the "ringbolt" of the nation's destiny and urges his listeners to "cling to this day … and to its principles, with the grasp of a storm-tossed mariner to a spar at midnight".

Without much warning, we find there's a barrage of pronouns presaging what's to follow. The nation is "your nation", the fathers "your fathers". The nation's story is taught in "your common schools, narrated at your firesides, unfolded from your pulpits". Douglass, without much mercy, directs his white audience to consider the corruption within America's politicians, its people and its morals. Now we see the theme – the hypocrisy of slavery and racism in a growing republic, in a modern nation state, in a land supposedly for and of the free. Then, with power that undoubtedly caused a wave of invective to fly from the pulpit, hitting the good women as if they had been cudgelled, Douglass says: "Pardon me …what have I … to do with your national independence?" His anger must have astonished his audience: "I am not included within the pale of this glorious anniversary! Your high independence only reveals the immeasurable distance between us. The blessings in which you this day rejoice are not enjoyed in common. The rich inheritance of justice, liberty, prosperity and independence bequeathed by your fathers is shared by you, not by me. The sunlight that brought life and healing to you has brought stripes and death to me. This Fourth of July is yours, not mine. You may rejoice, I must mourn."

Then Douglass takes his audience on a journey that helps them eventually see America as a world of slavery, of hatred, of brutality, of sales at auction, of utter humiliation. He damns this new, fresh country and, more, the Church in whose name much of the damage is perpetrated. This is a tirade, a frightening list of the terror done by Americans to Americans. He finishes with a reference that this audience would have understood well: "... be warned! A horrible reptile is coiled up in your nation's bosom; the venomous creature is nursing at the tender breast of your youthful republic; for the love of God, tear away ..."

But, after the storm, Douglass is gentle and offers hope. Again, one can all but hear the sigh of relief from the gentle audience. Here was hope, here was a possible opportunity for a new day, here was a man with fervour and in whom the audience had collective belief. As one, they rose and clapped and cheered. Oh, to have witnessed that.

A Legacy

It is in the context of the extraordinary popularity of Harriet Beecher Stowe's novel *Uncle Tom's Cabin* in 1852 that Douglass delivered this incredible speech. If *Uncle Tom's Cabin* is the fictional masterpiece of American abolitionism, then there is no doubt whatsoever that Douglass's speech is the rhetorical, oratorical masterpiece of slavery abolition in the United States. There was no nineteenth-century American to have offered a more poignant, powerful critique of the nation's racial condition.

Douglass's fame as a journalist grew and he became as well known for his writing as he did for his oratory. He not only championed the rights of African-Americans, but was also a staunch supporter of the burgeoning women's rights movement.

From 1877 to 1881 Douglass was the US Marshal of the District of Columbia; from 1881 to 1886 he was recorder of deeds for Columbia; and from 1889 to 1891 he was minister to Haiti.

Douglass had respect for, as well as doubts about, Abraham Lincoln. At Lincoln's funeral Douglass was surprisingly called upon by the mourners to speak. He did so, without notes or preparation, in such a way that all were both moved and uplifted. His biggest thanks came from Lincoln's widow. A few years after the Rochester Ladies' address, slavery had all but disappeared in America, but soon the true replacement, segregation, was the new law and a sickening, gut-wrenching racist practice.

Elizabeth I

I know I have the body of a weak and feeble woman; but I have the heart of a king, and of a king of England, too."

Speech to troops preparing to repel a Spanish invasion, Tilbury, Essex, England, Monday 8 August 1588

Queen Elizabeth I lived from 7 September 1533 until 24 March 1603 and was Queen of England and Ireland from 17 November 1558 until her death. The daughter of King Henry VIII and Anne Boleyn, Elizabeth was born a princess, but was declared illegitimate. Her brother, Edward VI, removed her from the succession, but his will was set aside and in 1558 she succeeded her half-sister, the Catholic Mary, during whose reign Elizabeth had been imprisoned on suspicion of supporting Protestant rebels. As a result of these hardships, she was already, by the age of 25, experienced and ready for the pressures that undeniably lay ahead.

Possibly the greatest of these challenges was the ongoing rivalry between England and Spain over control of trade in the New World. Elizabeth's former brother-in-law, King Philip II of Spain, decided to end English attacks on his ships and claim the throne of England – and by conquering it, return the country to Catholicism. He assembled a large invasion force and fleet (the Spanish Armada) and in July 1588 sailed into the English Channel. The armada was repelled during a nine-day battle with a combination of superior naval vessels (British ships were more manoeuvrable with a lower centre of gravity), better tactics and favourable weather, which was unseasonably stormy. The weather caused the Spanish to take refuge in port, where they presented a simple target for British fireships. When they came out of port the Spanish ships were then scattered by storms. The British commanders were also bolder and it was during this uncertain, fearful time that Queen Elizabeth gave her most stirring speech: rousing, resolute and inspirational.

Lessons from Elizabeth I

Act thoughtfully. History is full of stories of monarchs who ran from a challenge or simply ignored reality. Elizabeth rarely did; she was calm and quite prepared to be patient and tolerant – at least, she was by the standards of the day. For example, she refused for several years to execute her cousin, Mary Queen of Scots, until evidence of Mary's threat became overwhelming. When she spoke at Tilbury in 1588 she struck the right note at the right time, realizing the need to mobilize hearts and minds as well as providing encouragement and inspiration. She was also very much aware that news of the speech's content would spread.

Recognize concerns and project confidence. Elizabeth understood that English people were uncertain about being led by a woman and were fearful about their enemies: the Catholic Church and the King of Spain in equal measure. The necessary reassurance was provided by her presence, her attire (resembling a 16th-century warrior Queen with white charger and silver breastplate) and her words. Her words recognized the need to put steel into the heart of fearful soldiers and instil belief: "By your valour in the field, we shall shortly have a famous victory over the enemies of my God, of my kingdom and of my people."

A Legacy

Throughout her life, Elizabeth moved carefully from one challenge or difficult situation to another, yet by the end of her long reign she had laid the foundations for the British Empire and, just as significantly, given her country a greater self-confidence and sense of identity than it had ever had before.

Perhaps her greatest legacy, captured perfectly in her speech at Tilbury, is the development of the calm, determined aspect of the British national character: "I have always so behaved myself that, under God, I have placed my strength and safeguard in the loyal hearts and good will of my subjects. And therefore I am come amongst you at this time, not as for my recreation or sport, but being resolved, in the midst and heat of the battle, to live or die amongst you all; to lay down, for my God, and for my kingdom, and for my people, my honour and my blood, even in the dust."

Ralph Waldo Emerson

We will walk on our own feet; we will work with our own hands, we will speak our own minds."

Oration, later titled "The American Scholar", delivered at the Phi Beta Kappa Society, Harvard University, Cambridge, Massachusetts, USA, Thursday 31 August 1837

Ralph Waldo Emerson was born on 25 May 1803 and died on 27 April 1882. He was an American academic, philosopher and poet. Despite his reputation for being socially shy and mild-mannered, he was regarded as one of the greatest, stirring orators of the time. His audiences found his lectures, talks or speeches educational, learned and enthusiastic. He, in turn, had enormous respect for his audiences and cared deeply about people's views of what he said.

The culture of the United States was influenced by European writers, artists and philosphers long after the nation had declared independence. Emerson took it upon himself to help explain to people what an American cultural identity might be like. This was both an exciting and frustrating opportunity. Emerson thought unequivocally that the development of intellect needed a belief : "The study of letters shall be no longer a name for pity ... A nation of men will for the first time exist, because each believes himself inspired by the Divine Soul which also inspires all men."

He was certainly of the view that to promote a scholarly approach to culture, slavery had no part to play. Freedom was all. His belief in the abolition of slavery was at odds with the views of many of his peers, and thus controversial. But Emerson thrived on controversial themes. By the middle of the nineteenth century, he was (almost) as well known as Daniel Webster – and for exactly the same attributes. If Webster was seen as one who shaped American politics, then Emerson was one who shaped American culture.

Emerson had poise. His voice was resonant and his manner appealed to everyone who met him. It is alleged that a reporter once asked a cleaner, who always attended his lectures when Emerson was in her location, whether she had understood anything of what he said. "Not a word," she apparently replied, "but I like to go and see him stand up there and look as though he thought everyone was as good as he is."

Lessons from Ralph Waldo Emerson

Belief will always command attention, provided that the case is strong and delivered to suit the audience. Once established as a regular "circuit" speaker, Emerson often used his oratory in the cause of abolishing slavery. After the civil war had begun, he continued to make the case for the emancipation of the slaves. It's important to contextualize this. The predominant view among many strata of society was that slavery was both acceptable and apposite. Belief in the necessity and right to hold slaves was common and feelings towards any "liberal" change to the status quo were, in the minds of many, virulent. Emerson proved that antagonistic audiences can be turned round.

Be inspirational and aspirational. Emerson had a learned warmth along with a genuine and passionate focus which audiences liked and about which they felt very comfortable. His speech was determined but never hectoring. His language and the structure of his sentences were both pleasing and added great logic to his arguments. He was, observers said, charming. He used voice modulations carefully and sometimes would stop for a moment, as if to consider or frame his next sentence or thought. Whether deliberate or not, we can't say, but that too added value to his appeal.

Emerson used notes and, more often than not, wrote out his speeches in full. That's to our benefit because they were published and circulated widely at the time. In front of an audience, he did not necessarily read word for word that which he had prepared. But the lectern was his base, his rock, to which he would return if he became lost, which he rarely did.

A Legacy

Emerson travelled around America lecturing and speaking to societies, universities and institutions. People to whom he spoke were enthused and the themes of social betterment were picked up by many with the influence and power to effect change. Arguably, there was no one then in the United States who came close to matching his eloquence or authority.

A generation became far more aware of the power of education, mostly from listening to and reading the works of the likes of Emerson.

For America, his voice was that which shaped the country's thirst for culture. In "The American Scholar" he says: "The first in time and the first in importance of the influences upon the mind is that of Nature. Every day, the sun; and, after sunset, Night and her stars. Ever the winds blow; ever the grass grows. Every day, men and women, conversing, beholding and beholden. The scholar is he of all men whom this spectacle most engages. He must settle its value in his mind … Therein it resembles his own spirit, whose beginning, whose ending, he never can find – so entire, so boundless …" It is a beautifully written passage, typical of the man's ability to make a complex issue simple and relevant.

Benjamin Franklin

I confess that there are several parts of this Constitution which I do not at present approve, but I am not sure I shall never approve them. For having lived long, I have experienced many instances of being obliged by better information, or fuller consideration, to change opinions even on important subjects, which I once thought right, but found to be otherwise."

Short speech to the Constitutional Convention before the signing of the Constitution's final draft, Philadelphia, Pennsylvania, USA, Monday 17 September 1787

Benjamin Franklin was born on 17 January 1706 and died on 17 April 1790. He was one of America's founding fathers. He was also a writer, a politician, a scientist with an admirable list of inventions to his name, a diplomat who was lauded by many of the world's nations and, without doubt, a statesman. The very first public lending library in America was established by Franklin, as was Pennsylvania's first fire department. Most of all, he can be said to have established the notion and practice of the American nation.

It was while Franklin was a diplomat during the American Revolution that he achieved the all-important French alliance, thereby helping to make independence possible. In his short 1787 Constitutional Convention speech he says: "Mr President, I confess that there are several parts of this constitution which I do not at present approve, but I am not sure I shall never approve them: For having lived long, I have experienced many instances of being obliged by better information, or fuller consideration, to change opinions even on important subjects, which I once thought right, but found to be otherwise. It is therefore that the older I grow, the more apt I am to doubt my own judgment and to pay more respect to the judgment of others … But though many private persons think almost as highly of their own infallibility as of that of their sect, few express it so naturally as a certain French lady, who in a dispute with her sister, said 'I don't know how it happens, Sister, but I meet with no body but myself who's always in the right' (Il n'y a que moi qui a toujours raison)."

Interestingly, Franklin was the only statesman to have signed all four documents that created the new country: The Declaration of Independence (1776), the Treaty of Alliance with France (1778), the Treaty of Paris establishing peace with Britain (1783) and The Constitution (1787).

Lessons from Benjamin Franklin

If necessary, your well-crafted speech can be read or given by someone else, but only if your reputation precedes you. Benjamin Franklin, Pennsylvania's delegate to the Constitutional Convention of September 1787, and one of the few Americans then with a truly international reputation, asked to give a short speech to the Convention before the Constitution was signed. However, he was unwell and could not attend to deliver the speech. He asked fellow Pennsylvanian James Wilson to deliver it. We don't know how well Wilson gave the speech, although it is thought that he did so with power and deliberation. Franklin's reputation was huge and all will have listened with care.

The speech is considered a masterpiece. Franklin wanted to unite the Convention's delegates and he knew that his argument would need to be strong. In the speech he admits that he has had strong reservations about the viability or necessity of the Constitution in its given form. But he then says that if he could doubt his own infallibility and still support the Constitution, so should, so must, everyone.

A Legacy

In his speech, Franklin, as in all things, is honest and certainly direct: "Thus I consent, Sir, to this Constitution because I expect no better, and because I am not sure that it is not the best. The opinions I have had of its errors, I sacrifice to the public good. I have never whispered a syllable of them abroad. Within these walls they were born, and here they shall die ... I hope therefore that for our own sakes as a part of the people, and for the sake of posterity, we shall act heartily and unanimously in recommending this Constitution ... On the whole, Sir, I cannot help expressing a wish that every member of the Convention who may still have objections to it, would with me, on this occasion doubt a little of his own infallibility, and to make manifest our unanimity, put his name to this instrument."

The Constitution of the United States of America is the basis of the country's supreme law. It is the law. The document makes clear the three main branches of the government: The legislative branch with a bicameral congress (that is, one with two chambers), an executive branch led by the president and a judicial branch headed by the Supreme Court. It is the shortest and oldest written constitution of any major sovereign state. The American Constitution was completed in Philadelphia at the Federal Convention, followed by the speech written by Benjamin Franklin who urged unanimity. He got it and the Constitution was agreed and signed.

Countless buildings and institutions across America are named after Franklin or built in his honour and his name is spoken with reverence. His reputation as a polymath and a great statesman is without parallel in the USA, to the point that many refer to him as the first "American".

Galileo Galilei

I must altogether abandon the false opinion that the sun is the centre of the world and immovable and that the earth is not the centre of the world and moves and that I must not hold, defend or teach in any way whatsoever, verbally or in writing, the said false doctrine."

Galileo's *Recantation* at his trial, Convent della Minerva, Rome, Italy, Wednesday 22 June 1633

Galileo Galilei was born in Italy on 15 February 1564 and died on 8 January 1642. He discovered the isochron of the pendulum at the age of nineteen. By the time he was 22, he had invented the hydrostatic balance and, at the age of 25, he was offered his first lectureship at the University of Pisa. He is possibly best remembered now as the inventor of the astronomical telescope, but Galileo in his time earned an enviable reputation throughout Europe as an inventor, a physicist and as an excellent teacher.

In 1633 Galileo Galilei's views and, particularly, his writings on astronomy and philosophy flew in the face of established religion and resulted in his trial for suspected heresy. Because he believed that the planets revolved around the sun and not the earth, Galileo was denounced as a heretic by the church in Rome. As he points out in his recantation of his (alleged) crime: "I wrote and printed a book in which I discuss this new doctrine already condemned and adduce arguments of great cogency in its favour, without presenting any solution of these and for this reason I have been pronounced by the Holy Office to be vehemently suspected of heresy, that is to say, of having held and believed that the Sun is the centre of the world and immovable and that the earth is not the centre and moves." He faced the Roman Inquisition, undoubtedly not a pleasant experience, and was obliged to renounce his beliefs publicly though, of course, his theories were eventually proved to be quite correct.

Lessons from Galileo Galilei

Maintain dignity, even in the most challenging circumstances. Galileo was required to publicly recant his opinions, something which must have been anathema for him. In return, his sentence of imprisonment was commuted to house arrest for life – still extremely hard on someone who was used to travelling to pursue his teaching and studies. His offending *Dialogue on the Two Chief World Systems*, published in 1630, was banned and publication of any of his works was forbidden, including any he might write in the future.

The striking point about Galileo Galilei's words is the dignity with which they were delivered. He spoke clearly, recognizing that while the Church had left him with no other option, history and science would vindicate his views. He understood that he had to live in the moment, in 1633, and he did so with gravitas and honour:

A Legacy

Galileo's trial marks a monumental point at which religion and science went their separate ways. An investigation into Galileo's conviction, calling for its reversal, was opened in 1979 by Pope John Paul II. In October 1992, a papal commission finally admitted that Vatican records showed Galileo had not been restrained from teaching or writing about Copernicanism in 1616, as was maintained at his trial. The commission admitted the Vatican's error. In 2000 Pope John Paul II issued a formal apology for all the errors of the Church over the previous 2000 years, including Galileo's trial.

In physics, Galileo is remembered for discovering the laws of falling bodies and the movement of projectiles; in astronomy, he is best known for pioneering telescopic observation and, through this, discovering sunspots, the irregular surface of the Moon, the satellites of Jupiter and the phases of Venus. He is perhaps remembered most of all for supporting and reinforcing Copernicus's sun-centred universe in which the earth and other planets revolve. Importantly, he helped loosen scientific learning and knowledge from the restrictions of spiritual belief. The first spacecraft to orbit Jupiter and the proposed global satellite navigation system bear Galileo's name.

Legend has it that, as Galileo got up from his probably painful knees at the end of his recantation, he said under his breath (and we hope that he did): "Eppur, si muove," meaning "And yet it does move," referring to the earth.

Indira Gandhi

While there is bondage anywhere, we ourselves cannot be fully free. While there is oppression anywhere, we ourselves cannot soar high."

Presentation of the Jawaharlal Nehru Award for International Understanding to Coretta Scott King, New Delhi, India, Friday 24 January 1969

Indira Priyadarshini Gandhi was born on 19 November 1917. She was prime minister of the Republic of India for three consecutive terms between 1966 and 1977 and also served a fourth term from 1980 until her assassination on 31 October 1984. She was unrelated to Mahatma Gandhi, but India's first prime minister, Jawaharlal Nehru, was her father. The Gandhi name she held by marriage.

Indira Gandhi was a passionate orator although she found public speaking very hard and had much training and tuition. She was regarded as a tough leader, certainly in the early years of her administration. Her strength came to the fore particularly when India faced significant difficulties. For instance, despite very heavy international pressure during India's war with Pakistan in 1971, Gandhi refused to back off or retreat. Her political instinct is what drove her decisions and it mattered to her (and her position) that she was seen to be the people's leader. This was always difficult given India's political divisions, religious partitions and factions.

Gandhi's speeches drew people to her cause and her arguments – though less so towards the end of her leadership. Her language was the language of the audience, her references those of her audience, her understanding of pain in tune with that of her audience.

In this 1969 speech she made an analogy between the loss of Martin Luther King Jr and losses in India. It's a theme to which she returned many times: "This is a poignant moment for all of us. We remember vividly your [King's widow's] last visit to our country. We had hoped that on this occasion, Dr King and you would be standing side by side on this platform. That was not to be. He is not with us, but we feel his spirit ... We thought of the great men in your own country who fell to the assassin's bullet and of Mahatma Gandhi's martyrdom here in this city, this very month, twenty-one years ago. Such events remain as wounds in the human consciousness, reminding us of battles yet to be fought and tasks still to be accomplished."

Lessons from Indira Gandhi

Facts matter and are necessary – not as a shopping list but to support your case. Indira Gandhi's speeches were always to the point and were factually open and direct, but they contained emotional elements too, which helped to create a sense of belonging in the audience. She was acutely aware of the sacrifice that many made around the world for their beliefs and she was equally aware of the effect that such sacrifice had upon ordinary people. Many in India considered her radical rhetoric, her political decisions and extremely tough political management too much, the result often being negative. But observers comment that people from all political hues and classes believed that she cared deeply about India's troubled economic and social issues. The morality of worth was top of her agenda. As she says in this speech: "It is ironical that there should still be people in this world who judge men not by their moral worth and intellectual merit but by the pigment of their skin or other physical characteristics ... Our *own* battle is not yet over ... While there is oppression anywhere, we ourselves cannot soar high ..."

Be confident – but justify your confidence. Gandhi eventually became a forceful speaker even though, throughout her life, she disliked large social occasions. She used subtle techniques to help make her audiences feel comfortable towards her and to respond positively to her words. For example, she would dress in clothing common to the women in a particular audience and she spoke to audiences, not at them. People also liked her quiet, public persona, her seemingly modest manner and her courtesy.

A Legacy

In 1999 Indira Gandhi was voted the greatest woman of the past 1000 years in a poll carried out by BBC News.

While her early leadership in India is regarded as solid, when she delivered many changes that the country needed, her last years in power were filled with political struggles, scandal, and political differences that led to violence. She is best remembered for her earlier leadership, and some argue that the India of today could not have happened without her.

After the war with Pakistan in 1971, Indira Gandhi was adored by the nation. She could do no wrong. People saw her as a warrior leader. She certainly kept the country united. However, in the late 1970s and early 1980s, terrorism and a general malaise among factions caused huge ructions and social deterioration on a massive scale. It seemed that the nation was a ship out of control and Gandhi appeared not to know how mend the rudder.

Yet many remember her as the saviour of India and the protector of a country that might otherwise have faced another partition or general disintegration. While her administration ended in violence and acrimony, she is held up as having changed India, keeping it on a strongly democratic and economic course.

Mohandas K. Gandhi

In the democracy which I have envisaged, a democracy established by non-violence, there will be equal freedom for all. Everybody will be his own master. It is to join a struggle for such democracy that I invite you today ... Our quarrel is not with the British people; we fight their imperialism ... At a time when I may have to launch the biggest struggle of my life, I may not harbour hatred against anybody."

The "Quit India" speech, The All India Congress Committee, Bombay, India, Saturday 8 August 1942

Mohandas Karamchand (Mahatma) Gandhi was born on 2 October 1869 and was assassinated on 30 January 1948. He is India's most famous political and spiritual leader, as well as the inspiration behind the Indian independence movement. His resistance to British occupation and his demand for freedom led him to establish Satyagraha, a non-violent foundation which promulgated mass civil disobedience. It was Gandhi's leadership of a largely peaceful revolution which eventually led India to independence.

"Mahatma" means "Great Soul" in Sanskrit. Gandhi was also known by other affectionate names, such as "Bapu" ("Father" in Gujarati). India honoured him as the Father of the Nation and his birthday, 2 October, is a national holiday. The "Quit India" speech was given in Hindustani, not English.

Gandhi was an intelligent lawyer, but he was not a particularly good scholar and neither was he a great warrior. It also took a long time for him to find his voice. Crucially, he considered himself an average person with average abilities. As a young man he found it difficult to muster the courage to speak in public and his first attempt at legal practice failed miserably. He was, however, a man with exceptional sincerity and honesty. He believed passionately in freedom and self-determination for the Indian people in a country where they could release themselves from poverty, starvation and hatred. He was an intensely practical person and, once a principle appealed to him, he immediately began to translate it into action. He did not flinch from taking risks and didn't mind confessing mistakes. He was not worried or troubled by opposition, scorn or ridicule, of which he had more than his fair share. Truth, for him, was all-important.

Lessons from Mohandas K. Gandhi

Be self-deprecating, but not excessively so. Gandhi knew precisely how to engender huge support and to gauge an audience's mood. His was an oratory that had to be learned, not least because he was, certainly in early days, painfully shy.

In this speech, he reinforces a major point by being self-deprecating. He says: "Let me, however, hasten to assure that I am the same Gandhi as I was in 1920. I have not changed in any fundamental respect. I attach the same importance to non-violence that I did then. If at all, my emphasis on it has grown stronger. There is no real contradiction between the present resolution and my previous writings and utterances. Occasions like the present do not occur in everybody's and but rarely in anybody's life ..."

Avoid ego, think not of yourself but of your audience and inspire people with a clear, compelling message. Gandhi's message was clear, simple and precise. He wanted to make sure his audience was motivated, encouraged and empowered. Simplicity, not stupidity, was important to him. His focus was always clear. He wanted the British to leave, but he did not want violence, despite the hatred of the British felt by the majority of the Indian people. In this speech he says: "Ours is not a drive for power, but purely a non-violent fight for India's independence."

Almost any speech by Mahatma Gandhi can be described as a motivational, persuasive and inspirational experience. This well-known speech, distinguished by its eloquence, power and humanity, makes excellent use of language and imagery. Like most great speeches, its construction is superb.

A Legacy

The British government's response to this speech was to arrest Gandhi. In fact, virtually the entire Congress leadership was to find itself in prison. It's hard to say which aspect of his legacy is greater. It could be the stirring example of non-violent protest that has encouraged what *Time* magazine referred to as "the children of Gandhi" (like The Dalai Lama, Lech Walesa, Martin Luther King Jr, Aung San Suu Kyi, Benigno Aquino and Desmond Tutu). Equally, it could be (and most probably is) a free, secular and democratic Indian Republic. What is not in doubt is that Gandhi's words remain an indispensable part of his legacy.

Bill Gates

I hope you will judge yourselves not on your professional accomplishments alone, but also on how well you have addressed the world's deepest inequities … on how well you treated people a world away who have nothing in common with you but their humanity."

Commencement address, Harvard University, Cambridge, Massachusetts, USA, Thursday 7 June 2007

William Henry (Bill) Gates III was born on 28 October 1955. He is most famous, of course, for his founding (along with Paul Allen) of Microsoft and for being one of the world's richest men. Although he is admired by many for putting a computer in almost every home, some commentators and regulators have criticized his and Microsoft's tactics, which were considered anti-competitive. More recently, Gates and his wife Melinda have engaged in a number of philanthropic activities; through their Foundation, established in 2000, they have donated large amounts of money to various charities and scientific research initiatives.

Gates gives many speeches. He enjoys them. His speeches tend to be genial, focused and relatively slow. The slowness of delivery is not a negative or a distraction, but actually allows the listener to absorb the all-important ideas and thinking. The ideas are what people want to hear; they know that Gates is a pioneer and, as with Steve Jobs of Apple, there is a guru-like status attached to him. He does not have the best speaking voice in the business, but when he does speak we hear and see a sincere man, with total belief in his topic of the day and one who readily engages our interest. And people listen to a mild-mannered Gates who has achieved huge success and wealth. His success and his story are legendary – and people respond to that success. They want to learn from it.

Lessons from Bill Gates

If your presentation style is relaxed, you will need more practice. Bill Gates's speaking style is notably relaxed and casual. From time to time, he uses PowerPoint (there is something of an obligation, after all), but he does so sparingly. He does his homework and understands his audiences. He's laid back, but shows focus – an approach that has the effect of relaxing and engaging his audience.

Establish rapport quickly. Bill Gates's speeches quickly establish a bond with the audience. They are well structured and highly personal, with a valuable emotional pull. Usually they include moments of fun and audiences enjoy the fact that this person has taken time out to address them, to share some of his insights. This is important communication practice from which many executives could learn.

Be comfortable and create your own personal style. Gates does not stand behind a lectern; instead he faces the audience unobstructed. This suits his style and makes him seem friendly, approachable and confident. He favours a steady, conversational tone where one line of thought leads smoothly, comfortably and seamlessly to the next.

You can be a "gentle" speaker and still display deep emotion. In his speeches, Gates is able to show his anger – for example, at the state of the world, where children are allowed to die of curable diseases: "One disease I had never even heard of, rotavirus, was killing half a million kids each year – none of them in the United States. We were shocked. We had just assumed that if millions of children were dying and they could be saved, the world would make it a priority to discover and deliver the medicines to save them. But it did not. For under a dollar, there were interventions that could save lives that just weren't being delivered. If you believe that every life has equal value, it's revolting to learn that some lives are seen as worth saving and others are not ... So we began our work in the same way anyone here would begin it. We asked: How could the world let these children die?"

Gates is speaking to Harvard graduates, people who will (eventually, if not yet) have influence, money and, one supposes, power. He knows that these are people who must care and begin to act if those in the world who have little hope are to be helped. There is passion, quietly expressed, and there is persuasion: "The barrier to change is not too little caring; it is too much complexity ... The media covers what's new – and millions of people dying is nothing new. So it stays in the background, where it's easier to ignore ... And so we look away ..."

A Legacy

Time magazine has frequently named Bill Gates one of the 100 people who have most influenced the last century and Microsoft's co-founder certainly belongs among the world's greatest drivers of new ideas. Was much of his success down to luck? Possibly, but to help build and sustain a business with the size and influence of Microsoft cannot be down to luck alone. Most would agree that his vision and his company have shaped how we communicate and the methods we use to do so. As he moves beyond Microsoft to throw his energies into philanthropy, Gates will be remembered as an inspiring technologist who really invented the commercial software market and populated the world with around half a billion PCs. The legacy is a strong one, no matter what may happen in the next age of computing, computing software and applications.

But Microsoft is not the prime focus now for Gates. The Bill and Melinda Gates Foundation is designed to improve people's health in developing countries. In the USA it also helps those with the least resources to improve their lives through predominantly educational initiatives.

Many observers think that Gates's greatest contributions to society are in the future – helping to fight disease, to improve health and to reduce poverty. At the end of his Harvard Commencement speech he says simply: "You have more than we had; you must start sooner, and carry on longer. Knowing what you know, how could you not?"

Charles de Gaulle

… Has the last word been said? Must we abandon all hope? Is our defeat final and irremediable? To those questions I answer – No! … Whatever happens, the flame of French resistance must not and shall not die."

"The Flame of French Resistance" speech, broadcast by the BBC from London, UK, Tuesday 18 June 1940

Charles André Joseph Marie de Gaulle was the first president of the French Fifth Republic and, before that, the leader of the Free French Forces during World War II. He was born on 22 November 1890 and died on 9 November 1970. His series of radio addresses from England in June 1940 rallied the French people, in particular exiled French army officers, encouraging them to carry on fighting Nazi Germany. These addresses were broadcast on 18, 19 and 22 June 1940. It is history that has called the broadcasts "The Flame of French Resistance" speeches.

The Nazis overtook France quickly and met little resistance since there was a general (and quite understandable) lack of preparation. The French Resistance was to play a very important part in destroying some of the Nazi fabric and organization. It was also crucial in helping the Allies fight the war on several fronts.

Lessons from Charles de Gaulle

Provide leadership in adversity by being firm and by offering a crystal-clear sense of direction and action. In May 1940, France capitulated – only six weeks after the German invasion. France's sense of despair was deep. De Gaulle quickly took command and developed plans on how the enemy should be fought. Clearly this was not ever going to be on open battlefields. De Gaulle's words and delivery strengthened and uplifted the French who were despondent and confused at the speed at which their country had been overrun. His speeches became a rallying call and people responded. The French Resistance was born and it was to be a thorn in the side of the occupying forces until the liberation of France some years later.

As a result of the de Gaulle broadcasts, the French people knew that there was hope and the response was dramatic. As de Gaulle said on 18 June, "Speaking in full knowledge of the facts, I ask you to believe me when I say that the cause of France is not lost. The very factors that brought about our defeat may one day lead us to victory. For, remember this, France does not stand alone. She is not isolated. Behind her is a vast empire, and she can make common cause with the British empire, which commands the seas and is continuing the struggle."

Find the right platform and gain support for your speech. Maybe you need to stream it on video through your company's intranet; maybe the location would add value to your message. De Gaulle found his stage. As soon as he arrived in the UK, after the fall of France in June 1940, he went to see Churchill and asked for the prime minister's help in using the BBC to broadcast to France and to the French in Britain. Churchill agreed immediately, giving de Gaulle a valuable platform from which to rally support.

Project authority with a calm, measured tone, with confidence and with the facts. When de Gaulle spoke, his voice was strong, firm and clear. His military training and combat experience meant he knew how to address frightened and confused people in hard and embattled times. His tone was commanding, personal and direct. His language was rhythmic and steady and, rather than displaying rage against the Frenchmen who had readily given in to the advancing Germans, he simply presented the facts, gradually increasing his defiant rhetoric. He knew that his people would find the challenge difficult so his language and voice displayed understanding and then strength and a challenge: "But has the last word been said? Must we abandon all hope? Is our defeat final and irremediable? To those questions I answer – No!"

Persuade people with powerful metaphors. "The flame of French resistance" is a terrific metaphor: simple, powerful and enduring. The proof is that de Gaulle's words, and this phrase, lived long in the memory and inspired many people – in Britain as well as France.

A Legacy

De Gaulle's legacy is significant, wide-ranging and enduring; it's also both obvious and subtle at the same time. The character and structure of the current French political system, the constitution of today's French Fifth Republic, the French independent nuclear deterrent and much of the policy and institutions of the European Union were organized or directly influenced by de Gaulle.

Alongside this legacy is a powerful self-belief given back to the French and a reaffirmation of the distinctive nature of French national life and culture. This was critical in the war and in the development of Europe that followed. De Gaulle's words rallied and then directed France, in much the same way as did those of Winston Churchill and Franklin Roosevelt for their democracies. Even after his death, de Gaulle's words have continued to give energy and clear expression to a strong, long-lasting sense of French nationalism.

Rudy Giuliani

This is not a time for further study or vague directives. We are right and they are wrong. It is as simple as that."

Opening remarks to the UN General Assembly Special Session on Terrorism, UN, New York, USA, Monday 1 October 2001

Rudolph William Louis (Rudy) Giuliani was born on 28 May 1944 and became mayor of New York City in 1994, a post he held until 2001. Giuliani became internationally famous during and after the 11 September 2001 (9/11) attacks on the World Trade Center. He was already known widely for his tough stance on crime and social order in New York City and for substantially cutting the numbers receiving welfare.

Rudy Giuliani ran for the Republican Party nomination in the 2008 US presidential election but, after leading in national polls for much of 2007, his candidacy faltered; in early 2008, he did poorly in both the caucuses and the primaries and withdrew from the race.

On the morning of 9/11, Islamist terrorists, with an al-Qaeda affiliation, hijacked four scheduled passenger aircraft. The hijackers intentionally crashed two of the airliners into the Twin Towers of the World Trade Center, shocking a watching world and killing everyone on board along with many who had started their day's work in the Towers, both of which collapsed within two hours, causing further deaths and injuries.

The hijackers flew the third plane directly into the Pentagon and the fourth crashed into a field near Shanksville, Pennsylvania, after some of its passengers and flight crew had tried to retake control of the plane, which the hijackers had wanted to fly to Washington DC. There were no survivors from any of the flights.

Lessons from Rudy Giuliani

Make your passion contagious. If you're passionate about something and if you want the audience to share that passion, then your speech has to be delivered in a passionate way. Obvious, but not easy. In this speech at the UN, when the disaster was fresh in everyone's minds, Giuliani passionately urged the General Assembly to face down any country that supported terrorism. He wanted those nations out on a limb – and so too did most opinion-formers. Giuliani's was the first address by a New York mayor to the United Nations for over fifty years and he was aware of the honour and the opportunity. The speech was part of a special five-day assembly to debate a treaty on combating terrorism, attended by representatives from over 150 countries.

Be fiery, but also be controlled. Giuliani's delivery was forceful and emotive. He was angry: "This was the deadliest terrorist attack in history. It claimed more lives than Pearl Harbor or D-Day." But he was the master of his material and managed his emotions well, using justified and careful bursts when it suited the narrative: "This was not just an attack on the City of New York or on the United States of America. It was an attack on the very idea of a free, inclusive, and civil society." His main thesis was that if countries didn't stand shoulder to shoulder in the fight against terrorism – whatever that might mean in the future – then terrorists would succeed in destroying freedom, democracy and the underlying principles on which the United Nations had been built.

His voice was powerful and strong, his language pointed and his images real. He made no apology for being blunt. The speech was also at times gentle and poignant. But it is primarily a persuasive piece and encapsulates a strident mood: "Our beliefs in religious freedom, political freedom and economic freedom – that's what makes an American. Our belief in democracy, the rule of law and respect for human life – that's how you become an American. It is these very principles – and the opportunities these principles give to so many to create a better life for themselves and their families – that make America ..." He was determined that people should not be cowed by this event: "This is not a dispute between religions or ethnic groups. All religions, all decent people, are united in their desire to achieve peace, and understand that we have to eliminate terrorism. We're not divided about this ... Freedom from fear is a basic human right."

A Legacy

After the 9/11 attacks it was Giuliani, not President George W. Bush, who was the immediate voice of authority on American television. His response was hailed internationally and earned him the nickname of "America's Mayor", a title given to him first by Oprah Winfrey at a Yankee Stadium 9/11 memorial service on 23 September 2001.

Also in 2001, *Time* magazine named Giuliani "Person of the Year" and from that point onwards he was much in demand for his stand against terrorism and as a proponent of freedom from fear.

In his public statements, Giuliani was a mouthpiece for what Americans, and particularly New Yorkers, felt after 9/11. He was seen as a point of safety: capable, understanding, driven, sharing in their anger and despair. He said: "Tomorrow New York is going to be here", and he went to great lengths to explain and show how New York would develop, literally, from the ashes of the disaster.

Shortly after the attacks, which were something that America had not experienced before, certainly not in peace time or since Pearl Harbor, The Security Council, the supposed real power in the United Nations, passed a resolution providing a qualified mandate for action against those responsible. It was a resolution without much bite. A further resolution called for all nations to crack down on terrorism and to implement measures that were agreed in time, but which came to very little.

Giuliani was seen as a leader and a man of action, someone upon whom people could rely at a time when shock and grieving pervaded the country. He helped bring people together and enabled a spirit of good will to reign between citizens. There are some who would gainsay Giuliani's contribution and actions following 9/11, but it is generally held that the job he did and the results of what he did were necessary and excellent. One result of this fervour has been the development of American Homeland Security and a increased awareness by Americans of the world outside America.

Patrick Henry

Give me Liberty, or give me Death!"

Speech at the Second Virginia Convention to ensure that Virginia joined the American Revolution, The House of Burgesses, St John's Church, Richmond, USA, Thursday 23 March 1775

Patrick Henry was born on 29 May 1736 and died on 6 June 1799. He was one of America's founding fathers. Despite his education and wild, youthful spirit, or because of it, he became an immediate success as a young lawyer, helping locals with a number of high-profile and successful cases. Henry did not, in his younger days, behave much like the gentleman he was and could regularly be found in taverns playing his fiddle. This made him extremely popular and trusted, something that benefited his local legal practice.

Henry became a great advocate of, and participant in, the American Revolution, at the beginning of which he gave the famous "Give me Liberty, or give me Death!" speech.

Lessons from Patrick Henry

Always speak with conviction. While Patrick Henry may not have known the law as well as other attorneys, he had a reputation of convincing juries. His style of speech was not the usual, traditional legal oratory, often heavy with quotations from the Classics and which frequently baffled juries. His delivery was much more like that of a town preacher, using biblical references (readily understood by all in court). He appealed much more to emotion and passion and this was gratefully welcomed by those who had to struggle with reason and legal jargon.

The "Give me Liberty, or give me Death!" speech was made at a meeting of Virginia's delegates at the House of Burgess, the legislative body of the Virginia colony. The delegates were undecided as to whether they should prepare for military action against the fast-approaching and well-armed British military force. Henry argued in favour of gathering arms and meeting the British head-on. The speech is urgent and determined. He makes it clear that the time for delay has passed: "This is no time for ceremony. The question before the House is one of awful moment to this country. For my own part I consider it as nothing less than a question of freedom or slavery ..." The resolutions presented by Henry put the colony of Virginia "into a posture of defence ... embodying, arming and disciplining such a number of men as may be sufficient for that purpose".

If the message is vital and urgent, be radical or bold in your delivery. Few people knew of Henry's personal difficulties. In 1772, following the birth of her sixth child, his wife Sarah suffered from severe and often violent depression. She was kept in a basement room of the family home and was forced to wear a straitjacket in order to prevent her from taking her own life. The son of Sarah's doctor later wrote that while Henry was trying to get his countrymen to fight the British, "his soul was bowed down and bleeding under the heaviest sorrows and personal distress".

Despite his personal worries, Henry spoke on 23 March 1775 without notes and in a firm and stout voice that grew in stature and in confidence, ending thus: "Why stand we here idle? What is it that gentlemen wish? What would they have? Is life so dear, or peace so sweet, as to be purchased at the price of chains and slavery? Forbid it, Almighty God! I know not what course others may take; but as for me, give me liberty, or give me death!"

Following his speech, the vote was taken and his resolutions were passed by a very narrow margin. Virginia had joined the American Revolution.

A Legacy

Research indicates that the wording that we know as Henry's speech is less than accurate. Argument still rails back and forth as to which words are correct and which not. It doesn't matter. Patrick Henry is considered to be the voice of the American Revolution. Certainly he is inextricably linked with the eventual defeat of the British and his ability as an orator was what stirred Americans to take action. He was an idealist and would rarely back down when argument went against him.

More than anything, he is seen as a great patriot. After the Revolution, Henry was an outspoken critic of the United States Constitution and argued against its adoption, maintaining that, should it be so adopted, then the federal government would have far too much power. He didn't give up and eventually ensured that the Bill of Rights was adopted to amend the new Constitution.

In 1795 President George Washington offered Henry the post of secretary of state, which Henry declined. And in 1798 President John Adams nominated him as special emissary to France, which Henry also had to decline because of failing health. He was elected to the House of Delegates but died three months before he was due to take his seat.

Adolf Hitler

" We shall not shy away from any sacrifice if it is ever necessary. Let the world understand that!"

Reichstag speech, Berlin, Germany, Friday 6 October 1939

Adolf Hitler was born on 20 April 1889 and committed suicide on 30 April 1945. He is rightly despised as one of the most evil men in history. Here was a man whose actions and beliefs resulted in suffering on an unprecedented scale and the most destructive war ever witnessed. Why, then, include him as a great communicator? The answer is simple: his first weapon was his oratory and it was this that enabled him to move a country from peace to war. Our understanding of the threat posed by dictators and extremists is enhanced if we recognize the cold menace posed by Hitler's words and communication techniques.

In 1919 Hitler became a spy and was assigned to infiltrate a small and seemingly ineffective political organization – the German Workers' Party (DAP). He was impressed with founder Anton Drexler's anti-semitic, nationalist, anti-capitalist and anti-Marxist ideas. Drexler in turn liked Hitler's oratory and invited him to join the DAP. Hitler left the army in March 1920 and, by early 1921, was becoming effective at speaking in front of large crowds.

Oratory was certainly what kick-started Hitler's political career and, while he had shown few leadership skills, he was still able to impress and influence people. These skills were developed during the 1920s and by the time he manoeuvred himself and his Nazi party into power in 1933, his oratory was awe-inspiring and, as we know, devastating.

Lessons from Adolf Hitler

Describe current dilemmas and explain them to suit your argument. This is odd advice perhaps, particularly given the man and his history, but it's a well-known truth that if a speech shows how a dilemma might be solved and people understand the solution, then they will support it – particularly if they are given someone or something to hate. In the case of Hitler's cause, of course, that very sentence is chilling. He was skilled at telling the German people precisely what they wanted to hear and then apportioning blame for their plight. For example, he emphasized and championed the "stab-in-the-back" theory that Germans had been betrayed by the armistice of November 1918 and the Versailles treaty. He drew people to his side with the promise that "We are all facing the same foe, so unite with me and I will protect your interests." In 1930 unemployment in Germany was around four million. Hitler's sentiments and extremism were supported by the fact that Germany was in economic meltdown. Minorities could be blamed with ease and they were – with terrible consequences.

Accentuate tribalism if you want to get people onside. It is an interesting and rarely discussed fact of life that people are essentially tribal. It is a huge generalization, of course, but one with an essential truth – that people typically like others who display similar characteristics to them and are unsure of those who don't. Hitler understood that tribalism gives us teamwork, loyalty and engagement. Sadly, it also leads to sectarianism, rivalry, fear and, inevitably, violence. In terms of speechmaking, getting people on side is relatively easy: telling your audiences things with which you know they will be comfortable; creating humour directed at parties, objects, things outside the room; reinforcing characteristics – personal, organizational, political, financial – that you know they will support.

Present a past that nobody wants any more. It's a platform on which to build. In this speech Hitler spells out the positioning statement from which he will, time after time, declare that he alone can lead the German people towards a brilliant future: "More than fourteen years have passed since the unhappy day when the German people, blinded by promises from foes at home and abroad, lost touch with honour and freedom, thereby losing all. Since that day of treachery, the Almighty has withheld his blessing from our people. Dissension and hatred descended upon us … We never received the equality and fraternity we had been promised, and we lost our liberty to boot. For when our nation lost its political place in the world, it soon lost its unity of spirit and will …" For any speech, damning the past on its own is never a good thing; it's far too easy to say that the previous incumbent or the previous government or the previous actions by others, were simply wrong, bad, dangerous or stupid. There needs to be a build-up of a case, a careful rationale so that it becomes very clear to the listener why the past was, in some very big way, wrong or, more likely, unfair. The key of course is to present a future which makes up for the past's doom or errors. This is a fine line and only the very best speechmakers can do this. Spit on the past with great care.

Paint a picture of a brighter, better future. If you claim that the past was poor, you have to make a watertight case for the future. But always make it a detailed picture which audiences can imagine and visualize very clearly.

Hitler's speeches moved from describing the woes his audience faced and the causes of their problems to his solutions: a vision of a bright, modern utopia. He painted beautiful word pictures that enabled his audiences to see what he saw. The fact that he never received a parliamentary majority or a majority of the popular vote suggests that his vision was not quite as compelling as he hoped, but it was sufficient.

The risk with painting pictures of the future is that it can only be done once and, when people know that the message and the argument have been duplicitous or false, it's hard to repeat the process. False promises are usually visible from a distance.

Appeal to the values of your audience. Hitler understood his audiences, perhaps best described as the German lower middle class, people who, precisely because they did not have much, had something to fiercely protect and someone to fear. They also wanted more. He built this group into a core following before moving to the next phase: a cult of personality that emphasized the Führer (leader) as their protector.

Use rhetorical techniques. Hitler developed his delivery by rehearsing in front of mirrors and carefully choreographing his display of emotions. He was coached in public speaking and was taught how best to use gestures. Munitions minister and architect, Albert Speer, helped produce and manage Hitler's massive Nuremberg rallies and believed that Hitler was, above all else, an actor. The theatre of each public speaking engagement was paramount. Techniques included manipulation of his settings (such as the rallies and the 1936 Olympics) as well as silence and pauses (he would often wait for silence before quietly starting a speech). Gradually he would become animated, raising his tone and using other techniques, such as rhetorical questions, as his speeches built to an orchestrated crescendo. Audiences loved the passion and the theatrical power of the whole ensemble. They liked what he said too.

Hitler's favourite composer was the German nationalist Richard Wagner and it can be argued that many of Hitler's speeches resemble a Wagnerian composition: dramatic, martial, often lengthy and bombastic, with dark, shifting tones and powerful, climactic movements.

A Legacy

Among the many lessons from Hitler's Germany is an understanding of the potential offered by charismatic oratory combined with the new, mass media of radio and cinema that were expanding during the 1930s. Massive rallies, propaganda, leaflets, promotional films, spin and party political broadcasts were not invented by Hitler, but his use of them showed just how devastatingly effective they could be in getting across a policy, changing minds or establishing a political point of view. In Hitler's case, of course, he had the addition of might and force on his side, which changed many minds quite quickly. Propaganda can be used to lead people to believe whatever the proponents want. Hitler proved that if a lie is repeated often enough then people will believe it to be truth.

After World War II, Germany was in the depths of despond. It was a broken nation. Over a relatively short period of time, however, it became prosperous and a leading light in what was to become a collective Europe. However, the shadow of Hitler still exists in the form of German guilt and, indeed, in the form of the growing number of extremists who support his principles worldwide.

Ho Chi Minh

All the peoples on the earth are equal from birth, all the peoples have a right to live and to be happy and free."

Declaration of Independence of the Democratic Republic of Vietnam, Ba Dinh Square, Hanoi, Vietnam, Sunday 2 September 1945

Ho Chi Minh was born on 19 May 1890 and was a revolutionary and statesman who later became prime minister of the Democratic Republic of Vietnam (North Vietnam) from 1946 to 1955 and president from 1946 to 1969.

From the early 1940s Ho led the Vietnamese independence movement, establishing the communist-governed Democratic Republic of Vietnam in 1945 and then defeating the French Union in 1954 at Dien Bien Phu and forcing the French to leave the country. In the late 1950s Ho lost political power, but he remained as the figurehead president until his death on 2 September 1969.

Lessons from Ho Chi Minh

Quote from other speeches and literature to support your point. A pithy and apposite quotation can always add value to a speech. In his 1945 address, Ho proclaims the independence of the Democratic Republic of

Vietnam from France and Japan following the regional chaos that marked the end of World War II.

The speech is broadly based on the American Declaration of Independence and the Declaration of the Rights of Man. It begins: "My fellow countrymen. All people are created equal. They are given by their creator certain rights that nobody is able to take away. Among these are the rights of life, liberty and the pursuit of happiness." By the end of the speech, the massive Saigon crowd was cheering wildly but most people knew that there were new struggles in front of them. Ho Chi Minh's voice was not particularly strong, but the quiet fervour and passion he expressed most certainly was.

Build a case against the past only if you can justify it and you know that the audience will support your argument. Ho focused heavily in his speech on the French and then the Japanese as enemies of Vietnam. About France's reputation he says: "They have weakened our race with opium and alcohol. In the field of economics, they have sucked us dry, driven our people to destitution and devastated our land. They have robbed us of our rice fields, our mines, our forests and our raw materials. They have monopolized the issuing of banknotes and the import and export trade. They have invented numerous unjustifiable taxes and reduced our people, especially our peasantry, to extreme poverty ..." By repeating "they have" he builds an undeniable case against the alleged enemies of the fledgling state. It's a common device and one which invariably works if the speaker knows with certainty that the audience will agree with what's being said.

On freedom he speaks with panache and fiery language about the enemies of the new state departing in shame, leaving a people freed of the chains of occupation: "The French have fled, the Japanese have capitulated, Emperor Bao Dai has abdicated. Our people have broken the chains which have fettered them for nearly a century and have won independence for Vietnam."

A Legacy

Ho closed his speech of independence with: "The entire Vietnamese people are determined to mobilize all their physical and mental strength, to sacrifice their lives and property in order to safeguard their freedom and independence." By and large this pulled people towards him and made him the North Vietnamese hero for a long time. However, Ho was not remembered fondly by all Vietnamese. During a terrible land reform after he had claimed the country's presidency, an estimated 50,000 North Vietnam citizens lost their lives, between 50,000 and 100,000 were imprisoned and freedom of speech was heavily restricted. Fear was predominant. Some Vietnamese who lived through Ho Chi Minh's leadership detested him for bringing chaos to the country.

As president of North Vietnam, Ho led the armed struggle against the South – and its American ally – ostensibly to unite the country. The Vietnam War was one of the most brutal in history, made worse to the West by fast delivery of shocking television and film footage of terrible human damage and soldiers returning to the USA in body bags. Public opinion, heavily influenced by what appeared on news programmes each day, ensured that the United States had to withdraw from the conflict. It was humiliating for America.

With few resources, poverty rife and an army that was risible, but with substantial help from Peking and Moscow, Ho and his people had withstood the enormous firepower of the world's most powerful nation. In that defiance, he helped force one American president out of office and dimmed the memory of another. He had caused the US to reassess itself and that process resulted in discoveries that were not all good.

In Vietnam today, Ho Chi Minh is regarded reverentially by the communist government, even though it has long since abandoned most of his economic policies, many of which are (and possibly were) regarded as dubious. His image appears on the front of every Vietnamese currency note and his portrait is featured in many of Vietnam's public buildings.

Ho's personal qualities of simplicity, integrity and determination were widely admired, even by the many who strongly disagreed with his political beliefs. His successors rely heavily on his memory to keep alive the spirit of revolution.

Although America opposed the North Vietnamese leader partly because he was a communist, Ho once explained: "It was patriotism, not communism, that inspired me."

He was named by *Time* magazine as one of the 100 most influential people of the twentieth century, while the former capital of South Vietnam, Saigon, was renamed Ho Chi Minh City in his memory and honour.

General Sir Mike Jackson

We should not ignore, also, the grim prospect of future conflict over access to sources of energy and water."

"Defence of the Realm" lecture, the 2006 Richard Dimbleby Lecture, BBC, London, UK, Thursday 7 December 2006

General **Sir Michael David Jackson**, born on 21 March 1944, was formerly Chief of the General Staff of the British Army. Jackson delivered the prestigious annual Richard Dimbleby Lecture in London, in which he criticized the British Ministry of Defence's management of the armed forces. He told his audience: "One's loyalty must be from the bottom. Sadly, I did not find this fundamental proposition shared by the MoD."

Lessons from General Sir Mike Jackson

Make emphasis count. Jackson, in this speech, said: "What we cannot do is cut and run on these strategic campaigns before it is right to do so. And that 'it is right to do so' means careful and calculated strategic judgement – a judgement which, I repeat, should not be seen through the prism of political popularity, or otherwise … I think it was Machiavelli who said that 'wars begin when you will, but they do not end when you please'."

Jackson was adamant that a wider audience should know of the way that British soldiers, fighting for their country, were poorly supplied, poorly housed, badly paid and not cared for sufficiently well after they had been wounded or discharged for health reasons: "The defence of the realm requires that when you will the ends – the political objectives which require the use of force – you must will the military means. And if you will the military means, you must also will the financial means …"

He was, he said, ashamed of the way the government was managing its troops in a nation that once could hold its head high militarily. In essence, he also demanded that soldiers should be treated with respect.

Talk about teamwork working. It galvanizes audiences and gives listeners a sense of belonging. Teamwork is invariably appropriate as a theme for a speech. General Jackson told the live audience and radio listeners: "It's a sense of shared endeavour, a sense of being a member of the team. Unless you have that glue which keeps the army together … you will not have an army worth the name."

He was passionate about soldiers' rights. More than anything, Jackson made his views clear, explained why he thought what he did and expressed the whole with passion and zeal. Any listener (this was a broadcast after all) would have been mesmerized by a senior soldier with an extraordinary track record defending the basic needs of the ordinary soldier. They would have heard him claim that in order to fight, to win wars, to defend a nation, teamwork, in all its meanings and references, was a basic need.

A Legacy

After the fall of Saddam Hussein and the plaudits that then ran around the world, General Jackson was critical of the United States in its management of Iraq, post-Saddam. He said that the approach was "intellectually bankrupt". He pointed particularly at US defence secretary Donald Rumsfeld's unrealistic approach to the management of the social structure of postwar Iraq. He was concerned that the United States was concentrating upon a military build-up rather than planning to restructure the country and help govern it. General Jackson's comments, quite naturally, were treated with angry disdain in America. However, many in the international media applauded him and commended the bravery of his stand. Whatever the truth of who was right or wrong, he did point to the fact that invading armies needed to plan the peace as much as wage the war.

Jackson's criticism of the UK government in its treatment of British soldiers and his concern at the lack of funds for the army to manage and do its job properly struck a chord in the UK and awareness of the pressures on the ordinary soldier has since widened considerably. Many believe that the British government has still not allocated sufficient funding to support operations in Iraq or Afghanistan, or indeed elsewhere in the world. Commentators say that soldiers' care, equipment and support are still lacking, to the point that they, the soldiers, are still at some risk. It is also pointed out that if anything has harmed the special relationship with the United States, it might well be the fact that the British were unable to do more than act as a support function in theatres of war – predominantly because of the lack of supplies, equipment and logistical support.

Thomas Jefferson

A wise and frugal Government, which shall restrain men from injuring one another, shall leave them otherwise free to regulate their own pursuits of industry and improvement, and shall not take from the mouth of labor the bread it has earned. This is the sum of good government ..."

First inaugural address, Washington DC, USA, Wednesday 4 March 1801

Thomas Jefferson (born 13 April 1743 and died 4 July 1826) was the third president of the United States, from 1801 to 1809. Notably, he was also a principal author of the Declaration of Independence in 1776 and one of the United States' founding fathers.

A republican through and through, Jefferson achieved distinction as a horticulturist, architect, archaeologist, inventor and founder of the University of Virginia. He was also a credible dancer and a decent violinist. In 1962 President Kennedy welcomed 49 Nobel Prize-winners to the White House. He said: "I think this is the most extraordinary collection of talent and of human knowledge that has ever been gathered together at the White House – with the possible exception of when Thomas Jefferson dined alone".

Lessons from Thomas Jefferson

Make your speech powerful. Jefferson's inaugural was a powerful speech and was a welcome opportunity, as it is today, to set out the incomer's stall. Jefferson establishes how he means to govern: "... Every difference of opinion is not a difference of principle. We have called by different names brethren of the same principle. We are all Republicans, we are all Federalists ... If there be any among us who would wish to dissolve this Union or to change its republican form, let them stand undisturbed as monuments of the safety with which error of opinion may be tolerated where reason is left free to combat it ..." And at the close of the address, he admits softly to human frailty, but he puts this in a way that actually makes him seem strong and, more pertinently, reasonable: "I shall often go wrong through defect of judgment. When right, I shall often be thought wrong by those whose positions will not command a view of the whole ground. I ask your indulgence for my own errors, which will never be intentional, and your support against the errors of others, who may condemn what they would not if seen in all its parts ..."

Even if you don't write your own speech, improve your writing skills and read the speeches of others. Some of the best speeches are written by their speaker. Jefferson could write. He was the principal author of the United States' Declaration of Independence. He also wrote powerful and inspiring speeches which shaped the course of American history. Initially, he was not a great public speaker and he preferred writing instead. With time and much private practice, however, his eloquence and oratory became as one with his ability to write.

Understand that the best speeches contain facts and passion, argument and emotion, belief and direction. In 1800 Jefferson became president after a tight election. The election deepened a great rift between federalists, who wanted stronger power for the fledgling United States government, and republicans, like Jefferson, who saw centralized government as a necessary evil that had to be controlled. Above all, thought Jefferson, central government should never be allowed to be more than the rights of individual states.

A Legacy

The preamble to the Declaration of Independence is possibly the most famous of Jefferson's (and indeed American) writings and continues to evoke the original spirit of the American nation, much copied and much admired by the world: "We hold these truths to be self-evident, that all men are created equal, that they are endowed, by their Creator, with certain unalienable Rights, that among these are Life, Liberty, and the pursuit of Happiness ..." One phrase in particular rings with eloquence and beauty: "We hold these truths to be self-evident ..." It has a great cadence and phraseology such as this will add verve and power to any speech.

Jefferson is held in huge regard. As well as serving two terms as president, he also held a wide range of posts in the burgeoning United States: vice-president, secretary of state, minister to France, congressman and governor of Virginia. He also founded the University of Virginia and was president of the American Philosophical Society. He championed human rights and, in 1803, managed the purchase of Louisiana from France. In 1815 Jefferson's substantial library was sold to Congress and forms the basis of the current Library of Congress.

Muhammad Ali Jinnah

You may belong to any religion or caste or creed; that has nothing to do with the business of the State ...”

Presidential Address to the Constituent Assembly of Pakistan, Karachi, Pakistan, Monday 11 August 1947

Muhammad Ali Jinnah, who was born on 25 December 1876 and who died on 11 September 1948, is generally regarded as the father of Pakistan. He was the Muslim League's leader and Pakistan's first governor-general. His practice of peaceful change was in contrast to the civil disobedience led by Mohandas Gandhi and, in the 1920s, Jinnah broke from the Indian National Congress to focus on an independent Muslim state.

In 1940 he demanded a separate nation. After bitter and often violent struggles, despite Jinnah's wish for peaceful transition, Pakistan became a state in 1947. In the first presidential address he said: "The first and the foremost thing that I would like to emphasize is this – remember that you are now a sovereign legislative body ... It, therefore, places on you the gravest responsibility as to how you should take your decisions ... You will no doubt agree with me that the first duty of a government is to maintain law and order, so that the life, property and religious beliefs of its subjects are fully protected by the State."

Lessons from Muhammad Ali Jinnah

Some speeches require conciliation – rarely an easy task. Jinnah recognized the need to look for some good in, or benefit from, all of the different factions in an audience and Pakistan as a whole contained many such factions. Inaugurating the Pakistan Assembly on 11 August 1947, he spoke of an inclusive and pluralist democracy. He wanted the country to know that all citizens would have equal rights regardless of religious beliefs or social standing.

He spoke slowly, deliberately, and was careful to look at his audience. He was also at pains to ensure that what he said was inclusive: "If you change your past and work together in a spirit that everyone of you, no matter to what community he belongs, no matter what relations he had with you in the past, no matter what is his colour, caste or creed, is first, second and last a citizen of this State with equal rights, privileges and obligations, there will be no end to the progress you will make ... You are free; you are free to go to your temples, you are free to go to your mosques or to any other place of worship in this State of Pakistan. You may belong to any religion or caste or creed – that has nothing to do with the business of the State ..."

Balance head and heart – and recognize that usually most speeches have only one chance of working. This speech remains a controversial one in Pakistan and elsewhere in the Muslim world, since some claim that Jinnah wanted a secular state, while supporters of Islamic Pakistan are insistent that the speech is being taken out of context (other speeches by Jinnah are far more supportive of Islam and the Islamic way of life). But, whatever the slant, this was a speech that had one chance of working. It would rise or fall by its persuasion and logic. The country, while being brand-new, was a cauldron of factions and disagreements. Jinnah's words had to soothe and explain, reveal a vision and show how it would become reality.

A Legacy

Mass migrations and massacres accompanied the Punjab's partition. Jinnah was, at the time of this speech and partition, unwell and frail. It remains doubtful, however, had he lived longer than 1948, whether Pakistan could have avoided its growing crisis. His vision was clear, as was the soaring freedom that he knew people wanted: "We are starting with this fundamental principle that we are all citizens and equal citizens of one State ..."

Jinnah is still revered as Pakistan's founding father. His birthday is a national holiday in Pakistan and his memory is held as sacrosanct. Professor Stanley Wolpert, in his book *Jinnah of Pakistan*, wrote: "Few individuals significantly alter the course of history. Fewer still modify the map of the world. Hardly anyone can be credited with creating a nation-state. Mohammad Ali Jinnah did all three."

Steve Jobs

"Your time is limited, so don't waste it living someone else's life ... Don't let the noise of others' opinions drown out your own inner voice. And most important, have the courage to follow your heart and intuition."

Commencement address, Stanford University, California, USA, Sunday 12 June 2005

Steven Paul Jobs was born on 24 February 1955. He is the co-founder of Apple Inc. and former CEO of Pixar Animation Studios, which he also founded. He is viewed as a leader of the technology revolution and one of the Silicon Valley entrepreneurial greats. Apple has developed products that are functional, superbly designed and elegant, earning the company and Jobs a devoted and very large worldwide following. He has superstar status and whenever he appears at an Apple or industry forum, there is not an empty seat. Many believe that the two are inextricably linked: Jobs is Apple. That of course is less than healthy from a business point of view but it shows the regard in which he is held.

Lessons from Steve Jobs

Be yourself. When Jobs spoke at the Stanford University commencement in 2005 his address was simple, frank and open, with opinions expressed about entrepreneurship, work and life. He reflected on what kept him going through challenging times. He understood that people wanted to hear what made him tick. It's the stories of what makes the person that mesmerize. People want to know why – and how – you're up there speaking to them. So tell them.

Wearing jeans and sandals under his black university robe, Steve Jobs delivered an address that spanned his adoption at birth to his insights into mortality. His speech struck a balance between the obstacles he encountered during his very public life and the lessons he learned along the way.

Be honest. People like honesty even if it's painful (to you or them) and they warm to it. Jobs said: "Your time is limited, so don't waste it living someone else's life. Don't be trapped by dogma – which is living with the results of other people's thinking. Don't let the noise of others' opinions drown out your own inner voice. And most important, have the courage to follow your heart and intuition. They somehow already know what you truly want to become. Everything else is secondary ..."

Be modest – but recognize that there's little room for false or excessive modesty. People often want to learn from your achievements (possibly why you're making a speech) and they will value a connection, insight or source of inspiration. People in audiences want ideas, thoughts that help their thinking – thinking that supports theirs.

At the Stanford University Commencement, University President John Hennessy welcomed the estimated 23,000 students, academics and families by saying that Jobs embodied the university's spirit and its "willingness to be bold and strike out in new directions".

Jobs was modest in his address about his achievements and his advice was uncomplicated: "Don't lose faith ... And the only way to do great work is to love what you do ... So keep looking until you find it. Don't settle."

A Legacy

Jobs believes that customers don't know what they want until they see it. The "it" has to look good, be easy to use and have great applications. His view is similar to that of Henry Ford who said: "If I'd asked my customers what they wanted, they'd have said a faster horse."

A strong Jobs legacy is that of making design work with function. Apple design has influenced the shape and look of a myriad of household products as well as influencing aspects of cars, mobile telephones, music, aircraft and computer software. When asked about his business on the American television show *60 Minutes*, Jobs replied: "My model for business is The Beatles. They were four guys who kept each other's negative tendencies in check; they balanced each other. And the total was greater than the sum of the parts. Great things in business are not done by one person; they are done by a team of people."

Barbara Jordan

" We have made mistakes. In our haste to do all things for all
people, we did not foresee the full consequences of our actions.
And when the people raised their voices, we didn't hear. But our
deafness was only a temporary condition and not an irreversible
condition ..."

Keynote address: "Who Then Will Speak for the Common Good?" Democratic
Convention, New York, USA, Monday 12 July 1976

Barbara Charline Jordan was born on 21 February 1936 and died on 17
January 1996. She served as a congresswoman in the United States House
of Representatives from 1973 to 1979.

There were still very few African-American women serving in the
House in the 1970s. Jordan was the first from a southern state (Texas) and
was known there and on television for her passionate rhetoric, beautifully
constructed speeches and powerful oratory. Notably, in 1974, she made an
influential speech before the House Judiciary Committee supporting the
impeachment of President Nixon.

Jordan was at one point thought a likely running mate with Jimmy
Carter in 1976. (Some say that the multiple sclerosis that she had suffered
since 1973 put her out of contention.) Also in 1976, she became the first
African-American woman to deliver the Democratic National Convention
keynote address and it's this speech that was, and is, considered by a large
number of American politicians to be superb. As a convention speech in
modern times, most agree it held top spot until Barack Obama gave his
Convention address in 2004.

Lessons from Barbara Jordan

Consider language all the time, not just when you're making a speech.
Jordan was aware that her audiences listened carefully to what she said
when she was making a speech but also when she was interviewed. She
always considered her words very carefully. People regarded her as honest.
She is famous for some excellent social commentary: "The American
dream is not dead. It is gasping for breath, but it is not dead." And: "We
the people – it is a very eloquent beginning. But when the Constitution of
the United States was completed on the 17th of September in 1787, I was
not included in that 'We the people'. I felt for many years that somehow
George Washington and Alexander Hamilton just left me out by mistake.

But through the process of amendment, interpretation, and court decision, I have finally been included in 'We the People'." Here's another: "What the people want is very simple. They want an America as good as its promise."

Speech structure is critical. Speakers owe it to their audiences to shape an argument, explain their reasoning and attempt to win hearts and minds. This takes time. As a lawyer, Jordan was always keen to promote clarity of presentation along with, in her view, an understanding of constitutional law. Her "Common Good" speech is carefully constructed and flows melodically. It has emotion, logic and strength. The early refrain of "but I don't choose to do that" is an excellent way to heighten expectation: "I could easily spend this time praising the accomplishments of this party and attacking the Republicans, but I don't choose to do that. I could list the many problems which Americans have. I could list the problems which cause people to feel cynical, angry, frustrated: problems which include lack of integrity in government; the feeling that the individual no longer counts; the reality of material and spiritual poverty; the feeling that the grand American experiment is failing or has failed. I could recite these problems and then I could sit down and offer no solutions. But I don't choose to do that either. The citizens of America expect more ..." It's not a list, but a device by which she covers much more than simply telling us what she is going to say. Equally, her repetition of the phrase "We are a people" encourages us to feel confident and optimistic: "We are a people in a quandary about the present. We are a people in search of our future. We are a people in search of a national community ..." The speech reels us in and we are happy to be caught.

A Legacy

Jordan's speech was remembered by many, not least for this: "But this is the great danger America faces. That we will cease to be one nation and become instead a collection of interest groups: city against suburb, region against region, individual against individual. Each seeking to satisfy private wants. If that happens, who then will speak for America? Who then will speak for the common good?"

In 1979 Jordan returned to America's south as a professor at the University of Texas teaching political values and ethics. Her classes, emphasizing public service as the highest purpose of government work, became so popular that a lottery was needed to manage the numbers of students wanting to attend them. In 1985 she was awarded the extraordinary honour of being named Best Living Orator.

Jordan was once again a keynote speaker at the Democratic National Convention in 1992, the one at which Bill Clinton was nominated. In 1994 Clinton appointed her to the Commission on Immigration Reform and in the same year presented her with the Medal of Freedom.

Jordan became a champion for African-Americans or women seeking office. She loved politics because it meant she could make a difference and was wedded to the idea and the words of the Constitution. She felt strongly that politicians were but public servants in the very real sense.

Jordan remains an inspiration to many people. She was born poor, female and black but broke barriers to succeed. Her modesty was genuine while her oratory soared.

John F. Kennedy

And so, my fellow Americans: ask not what your country can do for you – ask what you can do for your country."

Inaugural address, Washington DC, USA, Friday 20 January 1961

John Fitzgerald Kennedy, America's 35th president, was born on 29 May 1917 and was assassinated on 22 November 1963. He was one of the most gifted orators of modern times – for several reasons. First, he was appealing partly because of his youth, education, good looks and wealth. He was also a master at tapping into the optimistic spirit of the age. He understood the times in which he lived, the nature of his audiences and, above all, how to connect with people.

Lessons from John F. Kennedy

Make the most of your own qualities, experience and advantages. Kennedy's relative youth (and inexperience) meant that he was seen as someone who would be optimistic, fresh and able to make changes. He had a deep knowledge of and interest in foreign affairs and so made issues of national security and global concerns a hallmark of many of his speeches. He had also served heroically during the Pacific War, commanding a patrol boat that was sunk near the Solomon Islands. Despite an injury to his back, he saved the life of one man by hauling him through the water to an island before gathering together his crew and ensuring that they were safe. When Kennedy spoke of patriotism, freedom and public service, which he frequently did, people listened.

Inspire your audience with a clear vision and a challenge. Kennedy begins his inaugural with a dramatic and powerful opening which makes it very clear that he is a progressive: "We dare not forget today that we are the heirs of that first revolution. Let the word go forth from this time and place, to friend and foe alike, that the torch has been passed to a new generation of Americans – born in this century, tempered by war, disciplined by a hard and bitter peace, proud of our ancient heritage – and unwilling to witness or permit the slow undoing of those human rights to which this nation has always been committed, and to which we are committed today at home and around the world." And consider these words from Kennedy's speech at Rice University on 12 September 1962: "We choose to go to the moon in this decade and do the other things – not because they are easy, but because they are hard. Because that goal will serve to organize and measure the best of our abilities and skills, because that challenge is one that we are willing to accept, one we are unwilling to postpone, and one which we intend to win." Many of Kennedy's speeches are littered with stirring calls to action and challenges, all with a lasting and profound impact. Bold, audacious goals set at the right time and in the right way undeniably cause excitement, enthusiasm and fire the imagination.

Use technology and the most appropriate tools to best effect, but not just because they are there. People really don't much care for PowerPoint, unless there's a precise purpose. If there is a purpose, keep it minimal. Kennedy understood the need to use the relatively new medium of television to reach a wide audience. For example, in September 1960, during the campaign for the presidency, Kennedy debated with Republican candidate and vice president Richard Nixon in the first televised presidential debate in US history. Radio listeners thought that Nixon had won, but the huge television audience considered Kennedy the winner because he was seen to be more relaxed and more comfortable with the occasion than his rival. He was also better-looking, something that shouldn't matter of course but invariably does. The debates are now regarded as the point at which the medium of television began to play a dominant role in US national politics.

Empathize and show support. "Ich bin ein Berliner" in German actually means: "I am a chocolate-covered doughnut". What Kennedy should have said when addressing a crowd of over 80 per cent of the population of West Berlin on 26 June 1963 was: "Ich bin Berliner". It didn't matter whatsoever. He travelled a long way to show understanding and support to the beleaguered population of West Germany and this overcame any shortcomings he may have had with the German language. In fact, it was seen as endearing.

Work with talented people. If you can't write great speeches, get someone on board who can. Kennedy was a great speaker, but he was supported by a brilliant team of writers, foremost of whom was Ted Sorensen, Kennedy's close advisor. It was Sorensen's phrases that ignited the imagination of a generation and his book, *Counselor*, highlights some of Kennedy's attributes as a communicator.

Do something memorable. Kennedy's life was littered with memorable moments: from being the son of one of America's wealthiest men to being a war hero, senator and the youngest president. His stirring speeches helped his audience feel that it knew him already or was, at the very least, interested in what he was doing. In a sense, the audience was already warmed up and favourably disposed (at least, as far as is possible in the partisan world of politics) before he even said a word. Barack Obama has a similar gift.

A Legacy

Interestingly, there were relatively few legislative accomplishments during Kennedy's presidency. Much of the landmark legislation that he initiated (such as action on civil rights) was carried through after his death. Uniquely, Kennedy's legacy is his aspiration, his spirit and challenge, his sentiments and his perceived strength and nobility. These continue to inspire modern politicians across the political spectrum and, perhaps more significantly, people across the world.

Politicians and business leaders across the world today listen carefully to John F. Kennedy's speech structures and delivery.

Robert F. Kennedy

What we need in the United States is not division; what we need in the United States is not hatred; what we need in the United States is not violence and lawlessness, but love and wisdom and compassion ..."

Robert F. Kennedy's speech on the assassination of Martin Luther King Jr, Indianapolis, USA, Thursday 4 April 1968

Robert (Bobby) Francis Kennedy was born on 20 November 1925. He was the younger brother of President John F. Kennedy. He was a politician in his own right and was probably destined for high places, perhaps the highest office in America. It was during the campaign for the 1968 Democratic presidential nomination that he gave his speech on the assassination of Martin Luther King Jr. Bobby Kennedy's speech was simple and strong. The language was clear, the vocabulary apposite, the whole moving. He was assassinated on 6 June 1968, only two months after making this speech.

Lessons from Robert F. Kennedy

For experienced speakers, the power of immediate, stark information can often produce the best rhetoric. Robert Kennedy prepared a few notes just before his speech. His preparation was short but his experience in speaking in public was long. He was well aware of King's reputation and the strength he gave to African-Americans (and indeed others). His speech was given from a truck's trailer. It was a short speech – five minutes flat.

Simple, poetic rhetoric is effective. Robert Kennedy was the first to inform the audience (and, indirectly, much of the world, because his speech was televised) of the death of Martin Luther King Jr. The immediate result was that people screamed and then wept. This was a loss of a leader and, in many people's minds, a friend. The police were concerned that a riot might ensue.

Kennedy knew (and said) that people would be angry, a view shared by Kennedy's team and the police, given that the assassin was thought to be white. Kennedy was able to empathize with this anger and was not afraid to say so. He had of course felt, he told the crowd, the same anger and desperate despair when his own brother had been killed in cold blood.

The speech was from the heart and on the level, never condescending or obsequious. He speaks as if he were one of the crowd – a clever tactic from a skilled speechmaker.

Understatement, when you know that the audience comprehends the reality of a situation, is a good technique. Kennedy said that evening: "For those of you who are black and are tempted to be filled with hatred and mistrust of the injustice of such an act, against all white people, I would only say that I can also feel in my own heart the same kind of feeling. I had a member of my family killed, but he was killed by a white man. But we have to make an effort in the United States. We have to make an effort to understand, to get beyond, or go beyond these rather difficult times …"

Some commentators have described the speech as one of the greatest in American history and, while it is short, it is unassuming but has relevance beyond that evening: "What we need in the United States is not hatred; what we need in the United States is not violence and lawlessness, but love, and wisdom and compassion toward one another, and a feeling of justice toward those who still suffer within our country, whether they be white or whether they be black."

A Legacy

Throughout the speech, Kennedy was calm. He was also able to engage the audience and establish a rapport almost immediately. He was aware of the absolute seriousness of the occasion. The speech revolves around the themes of equality, injustice and the country's divisions and Kennedy is at pains to pay tribute to everything for which King stood. He shows that he shares King's aims and hopes. The speech set in train an awareness in America that a politician, a white politician, could be fair, could understand and could champion the same goals as an African-American, and an African-American of massive standing at that.

Later, in his road towards the presidency, blocked so tragically, Kennedy made racial justice a mainstay of his argument. Part of his attraction to the public was his ability to communicate with young people – a vital target audience and one which was beginning to see the need for racial integration.

Senator Edward Kennedy concluded his eulogy about his dead brother Robert by quoting George Bernard Shaw: "Some men see things as they are and say 'Why?' I dream things that never were and say, 'Why not?'"

Muhtar Kent

I believe that for every headwind we confront, there's an equally powerful tailwind to be ridden. The trick is finding it."

Remarks at Wharton Business School, Philadelphia, USA, Thursday 20 November 2008

Muhtar Kent was born in the USA on 1 December 1952. He is a business-man of Turkish descent, currently The Coca-Cola Company's president and CEO, and has spent most of his working life at the company. Coca-Cola drinks are sold in more than 200 countries and it is one of the world's most recognizable and valuable brands.

Economists estimate that emerging markets around the world will add half a billion new middle-class consumers over the next five years. To attract these new customers, Coca-Cola has an expansionist develop-ment programme to introduce new products, not only in the carbonated drinks sector. In order to attract the growing number of consumers in the health and wellness market, Coca-Cola intends to innovate in healthier soft drinks. It is predicted that this market will grow by US$38 billion over the next year and by 2014 will be worth an estimated US$480 billion.

The future for Coca-Cola in the 21st century remains bright – and intensely competitive – a theme highlighted in this Wharton Business School speech.

Lessons from Muhtar Kent

Business speeches work best when they display genuine enthusiasm. We can't stress this enough because many corporate speeches manage to show no passion about anything. It's hard to understand why these people are making a speech at all, unless of course they own the business or are in an inalienable position. The fact is, we shouldn't be obliged to listen to those who can't be bothered to deliver a decent speech, properly prepared with the audience in mind. Equally, if the speaker isn't enthusiastic, how can we be?

Muhtar Kent's address to students was largely about belief and enthu-siasm, belief in the good that can come out of the global economic crisis that took root in 2008 and enthusiasm in the future and its opportunities. The speech explores the theme of "opportunities". Kent acknowledges the economic downturn but his comments are vital and positive. He regards turbulence, for example, as a positive: "Rest assured, though, that whether it's a financial crisis, or a geopolitical crisis, or an energy crisis, or an environmental crisis – turbulence will be the new norm in the years ahead. And that's not necessarily a bad thing, either."

Adopt a strong, recurring theme. Kent argues that four massive global trends are unfolding: rising demand for (and cost of) energy; rising food prices; a growing middle class; and rapid urbanization. The first two, of course, are not positive. Higher energy and food costs require companies like his to manage in an economy of constant scarcity and financial pressure: "the new normal", Kent calls it. But, by 2020, a billion new people will enter the middle class, he explains. Most will reside in urban areas – to such an extent that within the next twelve years China, India and the southern hemisphere will be more urban than North America, Europe and Japan. Increasingly urban and mobile consumers across the world should mean growth for a company that already derives four-fifths of its profits internationally.

A Legacy

It's hard, one could argue, to see how a company like Coca-Cola might fail. Yet big brands do sometimes fail. We have only to look at America's motor industry (e.g. General Motors) to see the huge changes there. And Coca-Cola has had its bleaker moments, some through its own carelessness. Big brands can be sneered at or lauded. They are important to a country's business success and observers see them as a barometer of what's happening, particularly on the wider economic scale.

Coca-Cola and the United States are held as synonymous; it's considered the quintessential American brand. Many look to Coca-Cola management for a long view on the business environment and Muhtar Kent is sought out for his opinions on where the markets are going. He has a reputation for being direct, clever, outspoken and ever keen to develop new markets. He knows that, because of the brand's might, where Coca-Cola succeeds in new markets, other American businesses tend to follow.

Leadership is always a key issue, a constant theme in any major speech, particularly in business. Kent's definition of leadership is not abnormal or unusual, but it is recalled and repeated in many of the speeches he makes, not least this one: "As the CEO, my job is to create a climate of success for our people and inspire them to achieve the vision we have created for our business. That's really the true essence of leadership."

Nikita Khrushchev

When we pause to consider everything which Stalin perpetrated, we must be convinced that Lenin's fears were justified. The negative characteristics of Stalin, which, in Lenin's time, were only incipient, transformed themselves into a grave abuse of power by Stalin, which caused untold harm to our party."

"On the Cult of Personality" or "Secret Speech" to the Twentieth Party Congress of the Communist Party of the Soviet Union, Moscow, Union of Soviet Socialist Republics, Wednesday 25 February 1956

Nikita Sergeyevich Khrushchev was born on 17 April 1894 and died on 11 September 1971. He served as general secretary of the Communist Party of the Soviet Union from 1953 to 1964, following the death of Joseph Stalin, and also as chairman of the Council of Ministers from 1958 to 1964. He was famously responsible for the de-Stalinization of the USSR, as well as the implementation of wide liberal reforms.

Lessons from Nikita Khrushchev

Occasionally, do the unexpected. A surprise decision, idea or message in a speech is a powerful tool. Surprises command attention (and sometimes respect) and can force people to examine and alter their views or beliefs. Surprise can go even further, setting a tone and energizing an organization's culture, for example, by showing that it is acceptable to question and challenge ideas and sometimes the status quo. This is the legacy of Khrushchev's startling and earth-shattering speech to the Soviet Communist Party Congress in 1956, denouncing Stalin: "Fearing the future fate of the party and of the Soviet nation, V. I. Lenin made a completely correct characterization of Stalin, pointing out that it was necessary to consider the question of transferring Stalin from the position of Secretary General because of the fact that Stalin is excessively rude, that he does not have a proper attitude toward his comrades, that he is capricious, and abuses his power ..."

The element of surprise, a huge risk in this case, actually helped Khrushchev establish his authority over the Communist Party and Soviet leadership. By criticizing his predecessor (not a trick we would readily recommend, unless you know that the audience feels the same way and that you know you can unequivocally do better), Khrushchev was going further than anyone else had dared: "It is clear that here Stalin showed in a whole series of cases his intolerance, his brutality, and his abuse of power."

If you're going to launch a surprise message, balance the broader points with specific detail and construct a thorough and compelling case. Khrushchev didn't just wax rueful about a few of Stalin's shortcomings. He utterly demolished every aspect of Stalin's behaviour, character, decisions and rule. It was very important to create a clean sweep and people needed permission to think what Krushchev was actually saying. He did this with an over-arching analysis, a clear, point-by-point structured criticism, the use of highly revealing and specific examples and by invoking the might of Lenin, the father of the revolution. Never mind the fact that Stalin (and his ruthless methods) may have contributed to ultimate Soviet success against Nazi Germany, the establishment of an empire in Eastern Europe and the development of a nuclear deterrent. For Khrushchev, Stalin's failure was total and absolute: "Stalin acted not through persuasion, explanation and patient cooperation with people, but by imposing his concepts and demanding absolute submission to his opinion … Stalin originated the concept enemy of the people …" For the people of Russia, the response to Khrushchev was, by and large, huge relief.

Fresh ideas and creative staging are to be encouraged, but craziness rarely works. This is particularly true if you have no idea as to the audience's reaction. Be warned. Unfortunately, Khrushchev was to go too far with this technique. Surprise is one thing, but when he kept behaving in a surprising way – for example, banging his shoe in protest at a meeting of the United Nations General Assembly – he was making it clear to his colleagues that he was simply too unpredictable and chaotic to continue as leader. Khrushchev's party colleagues removed him from power in 1964, replacing him with Leonid Brezhnev.

A Legacy

People often feel a need to be respectful or polite about an individual, especially if they are dead or otherwise unable to respond. Khrushchev had no such qualms. On reading Khrushchev's speech, two clichés come to mind: the pen is mightier than the sword (although Stalin's sword was certainly mighty) and those who live by the sword, die by it. Khrushchev's words tore apart any consensus in Russia about Stalin's legacy and this absence of consensus remains today. He opened the door (a little) to a country that was used to having all doors shut. Having demolished Stalin in this speech, Khrushchev concluded with: "We are absolutely certain that our party, armed with the historical resolutions of the 20th Congress, will lead the Soviet people along the Leninist path to new successes, to new victories ... Long live the victorious banner of our party – Leninism."

Martin Luther King Jr

We will not be satisfied until justice rolls down like waters and righteousness like a mighty stream ... I have a dream today."

"I Have a Dream" speech, Lincoln Memorial, Washington DC, USA, Wednesday 28 August 1963

Martin Luther King Jr was born on 15 January 1929. He was an American clergyman and (possibly *the*) prominent leader of the African-American civil rights movement. In 1964 he became the youngest person to receive the Nobel Peace Prize for his work to end racial segregation and discrimination. By the time of his assassination on 4 April 1968, he had refocused his efforts on ending poverty and opposing the Vietnam War. In 1986 Martin Luther King Day was established as a US national holiday. At the start of this famous "I Have a Dream" speech, King, like many fighting for the cause of fairness in society, stated his case boldly and for all levels of society to hear and understand. He highlighted the fact that America's founding fathers "were signing a promissory note to which every American was to fall heir". He pointed out that this note guaranteed that *all* men would be granted the inalienable rights of life, liberty and the pursuit of happiness and that America had defaulted on this promise.

Lessons from Martin Luther King Jr

Whatever your stage skills (and we all have some), hone them. Martin Luther King Jr had a physically commanding presence. Strong, energetic, tall and broad, he possessed a deep, sonorous voice that had the power to project his message with clarity and authority across America. He was well placed to do this as he regularly (if inadvertently) honed his rhetorical skills as part of his work as a Southern Baptist preacher. He looked and sounded inspiring and very much in charge on stage and also on television. He sounded (and still sounds) excellent on radio and recordings.

Build a powerful rhythm and cadence, using tone and language. King's speeches had a strong, driving rhythm that was almost musical. It drew the listener in. It comforted and then excited. This came from his speeches' structure, the tone and use of language. For example, "I have a dream today" is one of several sentences that are repeated at regular intervals in the speech. Like a chorus in a song, it becomes a familiar refrain that people can, and want to, repeat and remember.

Repetition is useful as a device. Martin Luther King Jr, like other great speakers, knew the reinforcing power of repetition. "I have a dream", "Now is the time", "We cannot be satisfied", "Go back", "Free at last" – these are all phrases that are repeated in bursts throughout the speech. Perhaps because they become familiar and understood, they seem to result in energy and expectation – even participation – from the audience, much as would happen in a Baptist church. King turned a speech into a participative event – no mean feat.

Provide a specific, compelling, exciting but truthful vision of the future. King was inclusive – with a message that had an appeal as wide as it was deep. The images and vision of the future invoked by him were powerful and universal.

Know and respect your audience. King understood that his audience passionately wanted progress and change and that they were peaceful, ordinary people. He projected this normality as a stirring and virtuous stand – for example, by saying: "Let us not seek to satisfy our thirst for freedom by drinking from the cup of bitterness and hatred".

Use metaphors and familiar, appealing images. King dipped into the natural world as well as the Bible to find stirring, evocative popular images. For example: "Now is the time to rise from the dark and desolate valley of segregation to the sunlit path of racial justice" and "We will not be satisfied until justice rolls down like waters and righteousness like a mighty stream". The images express power: the energy of the sun, the force of a torrent. The point he is making is that his ideas are both natural and inexorable. The language is superb and soaring.

A Legacy

King's legacy has several elements. In practical terms, he hastened the civil rights legislation passed during President Lyndon Johnson's administration; this finally signalled an end to institutional racial discrimination in the United States. Perhaps even more significantly, he inspired people and encouraged them, through his actions and his words, to fight subsequent battles against injustice and discrimination.

A less widely recognized legacy is what he did for the art of rhetoric and communication. He showed that millions of people could be moved in peacetime to fight for social causes and social justice; he highlighted the power of public opinion when it is on the march.

King was honoured in his lifetime and even more so afterwards. His words still bring heart to many.

Junichiro Koizumi

Today, I would like to share with you a vision of a new United Nations … We need an effective United Nations that reflects our aspirations and the standards of today's world, not those of sixty years ago."

"Turning Words Into Action" speech to the Plenary Session of the United Nations General Assembly, New York, USA, Thursday 15 September 2005

Junichiro Koizumi was born on 8 January 1942. He served as Japan's prime minister from 2001 to 2006. Viewed as a maverick, but highly popular, leader of the Liberal Democratic Party (LDP), he became known as an economic reformer. In 2005 Koizumi led his party to win one of the largest parliamentary majorities in modern Japanese history.

Japanese culture is distinctive and, since the nineteenth century, has often been misunderstood by westerners. It was Koizumi who helped the United States in particular to better understand Japan and vice versa. His speeches may not be seen as groundbreaking classics, but his style – and that of the Japanese generally – deserves recognition. His speeches are powerful and determined. They work with audiences that want those two attributes. Quite apart from anything else, guiding and developing a fast-moving and complex country like Japan requires specific skills in communication. These are the same skills used by Japanese executives to drive firms such as Toyota, Nissan and Sony to the top of their industries (in Japan and outside it) within a single generation.

Lessons from Junichiro Koizumi

Use the authority accumulated from your achievements and experience to develop your own personal style. Koizumi's speeches are thoughtful, clear and accessible, delivered by a modern, energetic and engaging politician. While he may be known for his long hair, guitar-playing and love of Elvis Presley (once accompanying President George W. Bush on a tour of Presley's home at Graceland), his words and style consistently convey energy, authority, a maturity and an enviable charisma. He successfully fuses his own experience and personality with the authority of the office, with the result that his style is highly personal and interesting. Koizumi is many things, but they do not include being bland or easy to ignore.

Show respect and thoughtful humility. Koizumi's speeches tend to be simple, pragmatic, thoughtful and well structured, much as his audience would expect. No soaring rhetoric, just a compelling case clearly expressed and passionately delivered. His speech to the United Nations General Assembly is a typical example: respectful but progressive.

Emphasize unity and a common purpose. Japanese culture tends to give great importance to a sense of belonging and unity. This has useful implications for western executives (or politicians) looking to build teamwork or collaboration. The key is to identify a common purpose or shared goal and then explain what it is, why it matters and what it means, in practice, for each individual. Other useful actions, such as acknowledging potential problems or unexpressed concerns, are then made easier. For example, speaking at the United Nations, Koizumi commented: "Reform is always a challenge, as it requires us to confront the status quo. But that is no justification for inaction. Let us all unite in an endeavour to make this session of the General Assembly the session for action."

A Legacy

Koizumi's legacy is clear: a progressive, positive Japan that is ready and willing to contribute to the community of nations. This contribution is being achieved in a functional but thorough and highly effective way – the Japanese way. Koizumi's UN speech was innovative in many ways, not least in his emphasis on nation-building after conflict: "Peace does not prevail automatically when a conflict ends. The new, strong United Nations, with the proposed Peacebuilding Commission in place, must show initiative in ensuring a smooth transition from ceasefire to nation-building, and to reconciliation, justice and reconstruction. Japan is ready to play its part in this challenging but vital undertaking ..."

Koizumi was regarded by Japan and the United States, for example, as an agent for change. His impact on Japan's domestic politics, on its economic policy, and on the international community will be long-felt. Before he took charge of the country in 2001, Japan had seen ten leaders in twelve years. Its economy was tiring and its foreign policy was regarded as weak, certainly with little regional or international influence. Koizumi ruled with a firm hand and a vision from which he rarely wavered. He is said to have put Japan on the world map and to have managed an economic revival envied by many.

Unlike many leaders of nations, Koizumi supported America by sending to Iraq a small number of troops – an important moment for Japan, for obvious reasons.

James Lavenson

Now frankly I think that the hotel business is ... antique. There has been practically no change in the attitude of room clerks at hotels since Joseph and Mary arrived at that inn in Bethlehem and that clerk told them that he'd lost their reservation."

"Think Strawberries" speech to the American Marketing Association, Plaza Hotel, New York, USA, 1973

James Lavenson (who was born in 1919 and died on 19 September 1998) was president and chief executive officer of the Plaza Hotel in New York from 1972 to 1975. In that time, he initiated radical changes and turned around the fortunes of the hotel, making it highly profitable. His (then) novel attitudes towards selling, and empowering staff to sell, was refreshing and pioneering. He was also regarded by employees as an extraordinary manager who made work collaborative and fun.

Lessons from James Lavenson

Stories are a valuable part of speeches. James Lavenson's famous "Think Strawberries" speech started out as an article that tells the entertaining story of how he turned more than 1,100 employees of the Plaza into a highly motivated and successful customer-focused sales force. The entire speech is comprised of anecdotes. Every factor in the sales success story is supported by a brief story, charmingly and amusingly told and taken mostly from his own experience. It's the sharing of that experience in a fun way that audiences liked. All audiences like stories and good ones, well related, are remembered. Lavenson had a naturally easy style, perfectly suited to speeches about selling. He didn't need to hector an audience; his simple stories and his positive "can-do" attitude made him enormously popular.

Self-deprecating humour works – but you *have* to know your audience. Lavenson used old-fashioned humour and exaggeration in his speech: "… One day early in my career there … I heard the phone ring at the bell captain's desk and no one was answering it. So to give a demonstration to my staff that there was no job too demeaning for me, I went over and I picked up the phone and said, 'Bell captain's desk. May I help you?' The voice came on the other end. 'Pass it on, Lavenson's in the Lobby.'"

Lavenson steered away from clichés and delighted in tales about his experience. That enabled him to share what worked and what didn't. He was honest (and very entertaining) about his mistakes and gave listeners tacit permission to make errors as long as they learned from the experience. The self-deprecation of this speech works because he establishes a rapport with the audience and there is an intimacy, a kind of warm, momentary friendship. His achievements went before him and audiences were fascinated to know exactly how this man had achieved. The speech doesn't make anything sound complicated or difficult and he doesn't aim to baffle. He is a great proponent of common sense.

Sincerity and genuine concern matter. Lavenson was of the view that, if his staff knew more about the hotel as a whole, then they could offer that information to clients and prospective clients. He made sure that his employees were more knowledgeable and he put into practice simple changes that made a big difference. For example, he got them to remember their guests' names.

Lavenson established an excellent induction programme – rare in those days. And he "walked the walk", again long before that became fashionable for business leaders, although it seems that many still don't stray from the safety of their offices or executive floors. James Lavenson was one of the first CEOs to understand what employee communication was about – for example, recognizing that one-third of the hotel's staff were Hispanic and spoke no English. One third of the staff also therefore had no understanding of any printed materials in the hotel for guests or for training. Lavenson promptly ensured that all internal communications were in both English and Spanish. He also ensured that English lessons were available. When he made speeches, Lavenson told audiences what he did – simply and with the added element of fun.

A simple idea can become a strategy. "Think Strawberries" was James Lavenson's way of saying that all staff in the hotel had to "ask for the order" and not wait until customers demanded a service. The strawberry issue was nothing to do with buying the fruit out of season. It was about selling strawberries. He was perturbed to learn that when people in the dining room were offered dessert, those on diets would refuse. Lavenson's point was that staff should make a small effort and suggest strawberries as an option. What started as an effort to sell a particular dessert became a strategy for the up-selling of *all* hotel services.

End your speech quickly and sweetly. The endings of speeches can often be over-long. Lavenson doesn't thank anyone for listening to him, he doesn't thank people for their time or even for their attention. Tied to the main theme of the speech, the ending is elegant and charming. And short. And sweet.

A Legacy

Lavenson was instrumental in selling The Plaza to Western International Hotels: "Everybody sells, and that includes me. I made sales calls with the Plaza salesman, and I have only one regret. I got so worked up myself over the strawberry programme that I was indiscriminate about whom I called on. And one day I called on Western International Hotels, and sold them the whole place."

Lavenson's legacy is that he changed the way a hotel group operated. He also established a sales philosophy still used today in businesses around the world. It wasn't an easy philosophy to sell to his own staff. As he says in this speech, "But ... they were very quick to point out the negative: 'Nobody eats dessert any more,' they said, 'everybody is on a diet ...' 'So sell them strawberries,' we said, 'but sell them!'"

The problems that Lavenson faced in the 1970s are still evident to some extent in all service industries. Yet his approach contributed a fresh focus on issues of customer service (ideas that were further developed by management writers such as Tom Peters and Robert Waterman in their book *In Search of Excellence*).

The Plaza flourished under Lavenson's management and was sold at a profit. His management ideas hit the textbooks and he was asked many times to consider a business school career. He did become a speaker in much demand for entertaining audiences with his refreshing ideas of how to motivate people and how to get everyone in an organization to sell. His employers were delighted.

Lee Kuan Yew

Democracy should not be made an alibi for inertia ... The real issue is whether any country's political system, irrespective of whether it is democratic or authoritarian, can forge a consensus on the policies needed for the economy to grow and create jobs for all, and can ensure that these basic policies are implemented consistently."

Jawaharlal Nehru Memorial Lecture, "India in an Asian Renaissance", New Delhi, India, Monday 21 November 2005

Lee Kuan Yew was born on 16 September 1923. He was leader of the People's Action Party (PAP) and the first prime minister of the Repub-lic of Singapore, remaining in office from 1959 to 1990. Commentators have it that it was Lee who led Singapore's (much admired) development to become a world-class and burgeoning economy. His and Singapore's success have been regarded as an excellent example of shrewd investment and a fresh understanding of world economies. Certainly, Lee's influence has been one of the most powerful in South- East Asia.

Lessons from Lee Kuan Yew

Share your analysis. Lee Kuan Yew provided an intelligent leadership to a country that forty years ago counted for little in the region. At the outset of his administration, he showed himself to be far-sighted and created a compelling case for businesses and other countries outside the region to invest in Singapore. In speeches, he had a reputation for superb logic and excellent reasoning, which helped him and his government to effect change, sometimes draconian social change. His ability to use facts and information was recognized as first-class. For example, speaking in New Delhi in 2005, at the age of 82, on the subject of an Asian renaissance, Lee marshalled a wealth of facts and data to support his central argument that India and China were leading an Asian renaissance and beginning to fulfil their potential. He explained how Singapore had fulfilled its own potential and how expectations could be beaten.

Communicate simply and simply explain. Lee Kuan Yew's 1955 election address to the people of the Tanjong Pagar electoral district and his 2005 address at the Jawaharlal Nehru Memorial Lecture share several valuable qualities. Both are direct and set programmes in context, both provide interest to a wider audience and both are at some pains to carefully explain issues. What they lack in soaring rhetoric (since this is not what audiences expected from the delivery) is compensated for by simplicity: Lee takes time to explain his views, ensuring that people followed his argument and stayed with the speech's progression. He succinctly puts forward his case for building Singapore: "I soon realized that before distributing the pie I had first to bake it. So I departed from welfarism because it sapped a people's self-reliance and their desire to excel and succeed ... When most of the Third World was deeply suspicious of exploitation by western MNCs [multinational corporations], Singapore invited them in. They helped us grow, brought in technology and know-how and raised productivity levels faster than any alternative strategy could."

Connect with your audience by emphasizing shared experience. During this memorial lecture speech, Lee Kuan Yew showed his audience that he understood and respected Jawaharlal Nehru's situation, complimenting Nehru and the Indian people and explaining that they had shared similar struggles – for example, both overcoming discrimination. This not only established Lee's credibility with his listeners but also helped them to relate to him through a shared experience and gave them an insight into the challenges they all faced together.

A Legacy

During his long tenure as prime minister, Lee Kuan Yew led a huge surge in Singapore's fortunes and development. He guided the country from being a poor, struggling nation to one of the most developed economies in Asia. This was achieved despite a small population, limited space and lack of natural resources. Lee's view was that Singapore's only real natural resource was its people, along with a strong work ethic. He is credited with being the architect of Singapore's development and prosperity, not least in the shaping of law and order, behaviour and civic pride, each the envy of many countries. His style was known to be autocratic, but it can be said that the approach made a difference in a short space of time and commanded the respect of Singaporeans. Lee Kuan Yew showed what can be achieved by a people led by a determined but fair leader who imparts self-belief, discipline, a clear vision and a commitment to action. As Lee said in this speech when considering India's growth and then that of Singapore: "... democracy should not be made an alibi for inertia".

Abraham Lincoln

We here highly resolve that these dead shall not have died in vain – that this nation, under God, shall have a new birth of freedom – and that government of the people, by the people, for the people, shall not perish from the earth."

"The Gettysburg Address", The Soldiers' National Cemetery in Gettysburg, Pennsylvania, USA, Thursday 19 November 1863

Abraham Lincoln was the 16th president of the United States of America. He was born on 12 February 1809 and died on 15 April 1865, assassinated at a theatre by John Wilkes Booth. Lincoln is regarded by most Americans and others as one of the greatest contributors to the strength, identity and growth of the nation. During his lifetime, America grew rapidly and expanded westward – a situation that paved the way for unparalleled US economic and political growth during the twentieth century and an expansion that also resulted in the turmoil of the American civil war from 1861 to 1865, with over 600,000 battlefield deaths.

In the presidential election of 1860, the Republican Party, led by Lincoln, campaigned against the expansion of slavery beyond the states in which it already existed. The Republican victory resulted in seven Southern states seceding from the Union even before Lincoln took office on 4 March 1861. Maintaining the Union, winning the civil war and resolving the issue of slavery were the unprecedented challenges faced by Lincoln.

Lessons from Abraham Lincoln

Deliver a message that is clear and, when necessary, uncompromising. Lincoln was not a natural orator. He had to work at it and he did. When he delivered the Gettysburg Address, one of the most popular speeches in United States (and possibly world) history, at the dedication of the

Soldiers' National Cemetery in Gettysburg, Pennsylvania, he was speaking during one of the bloodiest wars in history. Not only that, it was but four months after the Union armies had resolutely defeated the Confederacy at the Battle of Gettysburg. His powerful message was simple and clear: democracy was yet worth fighting for. It was valid. This was conveyed in a mere 268 words (although historians differ slightly in their description of the total as there are no less than five recorded versions of the speech). It doesn't really matter. Reading it quietly or aloud and no matter how good or bad a speaker you are, this speech will give you a shiver of sheer delight.

Talk of universal values, values to which the majority of your audiences can readily adhere. During the Gettysburg Address, Lincoln invoked the principles of human equality that were a notable, popular part of the Declaration of Independence. For the first time since he became president, he reaffirmed Thomas Jefferson's words that should have been American bedrock: "All men are created equal". Lincoln's outwardly calm words were bold and unmistakeable: there was no room for slavery in America's future.

Make the most of powerful settings. Your surroundings, your backdrop can make a difference. Today we are all highly visual and are used to seeing dramatic material on television, in theatre, opera and in movies. Think Olympic opening ceremonies. Think Academy Awards. Think Broadway, Bollywood and the great theatres of the world's cities. Think communication. Whether speaking in the Illinois senate or the Gettysburg battlefield, Lincoln had a strong awareness of his surroundings that he utilized to full effect. For example, he used the powerful symbolism of his speech at Gettysburg to redefine the civil war as a struggle, not merely for the Union, but as "a new birth of freedom" that would bring equality and create a unified nation in which states' rights were no longer dominant. Furthermore, Lincoln saw an opportunity not only to consecrate the cemetery, but also to dedicate the living to the struggle, ensuring that "government of the people, by the people, for the people, shall not perish from the earth".

Pay attention to cadences, rhythm and phrases. If you know this is hard for you, then get some mentoring or training. There really is no embarrassment attached to that. And just listen to how great speakers talk; see how great speeches are written. Lincoln's Gettysburg Address begins with the phrase "Four score and seven years ago", an authoritative device that gives his words a powerful, timeless rhythm and an almost biblical quality – a simple, but brilliant technique. Unlike a number of other presidents,

Lincoln had a thin voice which didn't carry. It resulted in a lukewarm reception for his speeches – even the Gettysburg Address – at the time they were delivered. That didn't matter. People read the speech. That's what happened then; speeches were printed and circulated or put in newspapers. And, in this case, other (better) orators quoted Lincoln in their own speeches. They still do, of course.

News of this speech and its words spread. The power and the gentle flow of his words must have caused men and women to weep as they read these lines: "But, in a larger sense, we cannot dedicate – we cannot consecrate – we cannot hallow – this ground. The brave men, living and dead, who struggled here, have consecrated it, far above our poor power to add or detract. The world will little note, nor long remember what we say here, but it can never forget what they did here. It is for us the living, rather, to be dedicated here to the unfinished work which they who fought here have thus far so nobly advanced." Superb and moving rhetoric. Just read it aloud. And remember, this was a country battered and bruised; it needed these words.

When they work for your intent and message, quote the words of others. Accepting the Republican Party nomination in 1858, Lincoln delivered another famous speech that contains the quotation, "A house divided against itself cannot stand", which is taken from the New Testament, Matthew 12:25: "Every kingdom divided against itself is brought to desolation; and every city or house divided against itself shall not stand." When he spoke, Lincoln was referring to the division of the country between slave and free states. The "house divided" phrase had been used eight years before Lincoln, during the Senate debate on the Compromise of 1850, when Sam Houston had proclaimed: "A nation divided against itself cannot stand." Appropriate, vibrant quotes will add value to your speech.

A Legacy

History records Lincoln's greatest attributes as wisdom, integrity, humanity and determination. His ability to project these qualities and inspire people through his words formed a vital legacy. The words of the Gettysburg Address are carved into the south wall of the interior of the Lincoln Memorial and have continued to inspire other leaders through the generations, most notably Martin Luther King Jr and, more recently, Nelson Mandela and Barack Obama.

Standing on the steps of the Lincoln Memorial in August 1963, Martin Luther King Jr delivered his "I Have a Dream" speech, beginning with the enduring words: "Five score years ago, a great American, in whose symbolic shadow we stand today, signed the Emancipation Proclamation. This momentous decree came as a great beacon light of hope to millions of Negro slaves who had been seared in the flames of withering injustice." The Constitution of the French Fifth Republic states that the principle of the Republic of France is "gouvernement du peuple, par le peuple et pour le people" ("government of the people, by the people, and for the people"), a literal translation of Lincoln's words.

David Lloyd George

If Britain is treated badly where her interests are vitally affected, as if she is of no account in the cabinet of nations, then I say emphatically that peace at that price would be a humiliation intolerable for a great country like ours to endure."

Chancellor of the Exchequer's annual Lord Mayor of London address, Mansion House, London, UK, Friday 21 July 1911

David Lloyd George was prime minister of the United Kingdom from 1916 to 1922. He was born on 17 January 1863 and died on 26 March 1945. According to Winston Churchill, Lloyd George "was the greatest Welshman which that unconquerable race has produced since the age of the Tudors" – despite the fact that Lloyd George was actually born in Manchester. For all intents and purposes, given that he was brought up in Wales, history has regarded him as Welsh, a language that he spoke fluently.

On 21 July 1911, at the Mansion House in London, Lloyd George delivered the customary annual address given by Britain's chancellor of the exchequer. In it, he warned Germany that Britain would not tolerate interference with its international interests. It was a surprising demand that Germany should back off; the unveiled threat of action if it did not was patently clear.

This speech came in the wake of the Second Moroccan Crisis, a clash between the main European powers that began on 21 May 1911 when French troops occupied the city of Fez in Morocco at the appeal of the sultan, to restore order after rebel tribes threatened the city. On 1 July 1911 Germany sent its gunboat *Panther* to the port of Agadir as a strong protest against growing French influence in Morocco and the Congo. Germany considered that Britain would keep out of the conflict and that, once isolated, France would give way and give up. But this was not the case. It was expected that Lloyd George would use his annual speech as an opportunity to talk about pacifism and disengagement from the conflict between France (Britain's ally, along with Russia, in the Triple Entente) and an aggressive and gung-ho Germany. His audience was very surprised when Lloyd George used the occasion to stress that Britain would not stand down in any circumstances against anyone who attacked either its own interests or those of its partners and allies.

Lessons from David Lloyd George

Make your speeches rousing. Let your language soar. This speech was certainly a rousing one, according to those who heard it. Once into his stride in any of his speeches, Lloyd George became passionate and, on this occasion, he implied (leaving very little to the imagination) that war might be the price of continued threats to the security of his country and its friends. It was brave, but coolly calculated rhetoric: "I would make great sacrifices to preserve peace. I conceive that nothing would justify a disturbance of international goodwill except questions of the greatest national moment. But if a situation were to be forced upon us in which peace could only be preserved by the surrender of the great and beneficent position Britain has won by centuries of heroism and achievement, by allowing Britain to be treated where her interests were vitally affected as if she were of no account in the Cabinet of nations, then I say emphatically that peace at that price would be a humiliation intolerable for a great country like ours to endure."

Enjoy speaking. Funnily enough, many speakers don't. This is an obvious point, but if you're going to make speeches you must love language. Lloyd George's talented oratory and public-speaking styles led to a series of government posts. He was a great speaker, but also a great listener – an important quality in any orator. The two attributes are connected: great speakers have to be ever sensitive to the moods and motivations of their audiences. Lloyd George spent time practising his speaking styles (which varied enormously, depending upon his audiences) and found it relatively easy to find a suitable turn of phrase to suit a point or argument. In the case of this particular speech, he was at his most resolute.

A Legacy

This issue was all about the building and protection of empires. It was about jealousies and the showing of muscle. The battle lines of the future World War became increasingly clear. Britain and Russia would stand firm with France in any future conflict that threatened its security. And an isolated Germany began to build its own alliances specifically with the Austro-Hungarian Empire – and also built up its own strength in order to be prepared for the war that most in Europe felt inevitable.

The Mansion House speech made it clear to Germany that France was not isolated. Kaiser Wilhelm, reluctant from the beginning to make such an aggressive move, ensured that his foreign office withdrew. In an agreement concluded in November 1911, France received German recognition of its protectorate over Morocco, which it added to its North African holdings of Algeria and Tunisia. Germany was awarded some compensation in other areas of Africa, which it considered inadequate.

Lloyd George's premiership was noted for its determined approach and this was particularly evident at the post-World War Versailles peace conference. By the time of the 1918 UK general election, Lloyd George's popularity had reached its peak and his appeal was simple and direct: in his view, Britain needed to be, as he put it, "a nation fit for heroes".

Huey P. Long

It is necessary to save the Government of the country, but is much more necessary to save the people of America."

"Every Man a King" address, broadcast over the NBC radio network, Friday 23 February 1934

Huey Pierce Long Jr, born on 30 August 1893, was an American Democrat politician and senator from Louisiana, the state for which he became governor. His radical policies met with huge public approval, but his life was cut short. He was assassinated on 10 September 1935.

Long was passionate about helping ordinary working people to share in the country's wealth. In 1934 he created the Share Our Wealth programme, which had as its motto "Every Man a King". The initiative called for wealth distribution measures to be put in place so that the country's economic wealth could be distributed fairly after the Great Depression, which had left the USA with high levels of crime and crippling poverty.

The public liked Long's enthusiasm and realistic view of what could be. His charisma was infectious and his popularity grew fast, specifically for his social reform ideas and his willingness to take forceful action. He was regarded as a champion of the common man. He thought that every American was entitled to a home, to proper education, a car and a job that paid a proper wage. By the mid-1930s he had reached almost film-star status. Long was said to have been shot by a Dr Weiss who apparently had a political grievance against the Louisiana governor. Long died at the age of 42. Allegedly, his last words were: "God, don't let me die. I have so much left to do."

Lessons from Huey P. Long

Adapt to your platform. Huey Long used a national radio broadcast to spread his ideas about the redistribution of wealth. He knew that the floor was his. The language of the address was powerful and Long's rhetoric a mix of humour and invective. He used quotations from the scriptures as well as offering profanities; there were stark facts, challenging statements and rhetorical questions. He spoke in a way that everyone would understand and he used language with which all listeners would identify. People felt that he was one of them. One news reporter commented: "Better than any other politician I've known, Huey knew what his audiences wanted to hear."

Use memorable, well-known phrases. Speak in a way that your listeners will understand. That doesn't mean being untrue to yourself; it means being true to communication. Share Our Wealth, the campaign for redistribution of opportunity and fortune (and also the title of Long's 1933 autobiography, which incidentally was priced so that the poor could buy a copy), was from a speech given by Democratic presidential candidate William Jennings Bryan, an orator greatly admired by Long and indeed many across the length and breadth of the United States.

At the beginning of the broadcast, Long set out his stall in simple, repetitive phrases. He appeared confident and focused: "Share Our Wealth societies are now being organized and people have it within their power to relieve themselves from this terrible situation." In truth, at that time there were very few Share Our Wealth societies in action.

The language he used was bright and energetic: "How many of you remember the first thing that the Declaration of Independence said? It said, 'We hold these truths to be self-evident, that there are certain inalienable rights of the people, and among them are life, liberty, and the pursuit of happiness'; and it said, further, 'We hold the view that all men are created equal.' Now, what did they mean by that? Did they mean, my friends, to say that all men were created equal and that meant that any one man was born to inherit $10,000,000,000 and that another child was to be born to inherit nothing?"

A Legacy

Long was one of the first politicians to appreciate the power of radio as a brilliant medium. He made many broadcasts and people liked his positive style and his confident and fervent manner. He closed his "Every Man a King" broadcast with the powerful use of phraseology: "Now, we have organized a society, and we call it the Share Our Wealth society, a society with the motto 'Every Man a King'. Every man a king, so there would be no such thing as a man or woman who did not have the necessities of life … We propose to limit poverty that we will allow to be inflicted upon any man's family … Every man a king. Every man to eat when there is something to eat; all to wear something when there is something to wear. That makes us all sovereign …"

By the spring of 1935 over 7 million Americans had formed local Share Our Wealth societies and this success acted as a formidable base for Long's anticipated presidential bid. However, Long was assassinated and his proposals were never adopted. Nevertheless, the Share Our Wealth ideas directly influenced President Franklin Roosevelt's administration.

As governor of Louisiana, Long achieved a great deal including vast increases in new road mileage, many new bridges, free books for schools, new schools, evening classes particularly to assist in adult literacy, new hospitals, airports and a new and fairer state voting system. Interestingly, views today on Long are divided. Some recall him as a man of and for the people, while others see him as a power-crazy bully. Whatever the view, after his death, there were many politicians who emulated (or tried to emulate) his speaking style and adhered to his programme of social change.

General Douglas MacArthur

> The shadows are lengthening for me … In my dreams I hear again the crash of guns, the rattle of musketry, the strange, mournful mutter of the battlefield. But in the evening of my memory I come back to West Point. Always there echoes and re-echoes: 'Duty, Honor, Country …'"

"Duty, Honor, Country" speech, United States Military Academy, West Point, New York, USA, Saturday 12 May 1962

Douglas MacArthur (born 26 January 1880; died 5 April 1964) was a greatly honoured American general. He was enormously instrumental in American victories fought in the Pacific during, and towards the end of, World War II. On 2 September 1945 he accepted Japan's surrender.

The general was charged with managing the American occupation of Japan after the war but, while he governed well, he was heavily criticized for protecting the Japanese imperial family from any war crimes' prosecution, a prosecution which the world at large felt was appropriate and just.

In 1950 and 1951 MacArthur led the United Nations Command forces which defended South Korea against the North Korean invasion. However, MacArthur openly disagreed with President Truman about America's policy towards Korea and, despite MacArthur's popularity, the president had no alternative but to remove him from his command.

Lessons from Douglas MacArthur

Your speeches should, where appropriate, reflect achievement. Achievement can be presented in many ways – arrogance, hubris, modesty, lists. Whatever device is used (and arrogance is not good), consider once again what the audience would value knowing and how people are likely to view your comments. Many regard MacArthur's "Duty, Honor, Country" speech as ranking with President Lincoln's Gettysburg Address – one of the most moving, reflective speeches about public service, selflessness and sacrifice. The speech is not overtly sentimental but it does focus on what these three words mean to both the soldier and the public served: "The code which those words perpetuate embraces the highest moral laws and will stand the test of any ethics or philosophies ever promulgated for the uplift of mankind. Its requirements are for the things that are right, and its restraints are from the things that are wrong …"

Modesty works. The speech opens with a warm, simple and gentle story which says much about the man who is speaking. It gives the audience tacit permission to feel good about the moment and extraordinarily warm towards the soldier they have gathered to honour: "... As I was leaving the hotel this morning, a doorman asked me, 'Where are you bound for, General?' and when I replied, 'West Point', he remarked, 'Beautiful place. Have you ever been there before?'" He then does another very clever thing – a good device for any speechmaker. Without protesting too much, he claims not to be worthy. Cleverly done (and only possible if your track record is known and is indeed genuinely sound), this can ensure that the audience reaffirms a belief in you. That reflects well on the audience and people like the feeling it promotes. As MacArthur says: "'Duty', 'Honor', 'Country' – those three hallowed words reverently affirm or reaffirm what you hold dear, what you can be, what you will be. They are your rallying point to build courage when courage seems to fail, to regain faith when there seems to be little cause for faith, to create hope when hope becomes forlorn. Unhappily, I possess neither that eloquence of diction, that poetry of imagination, nor that brilliance of metaphor to tell you all that they mean."

Keep your theme in mind – always. Too many speeches or presentations wander off, take twists and turns or go completely off-piste. That's laziness or self-indulgence. We've all listened to speeches that begin well enough and then follow long and winding roads on which we become lost, with no signposts to get us back to the safe lanes that we might recognize. This doesn't mean that a speech should trudge along in a straight line with no scenery or fresh air to breathe. That analogy aside, your theme, your argument and your message must be there – in one way or another – throughout what you say. In this case, MacArthur's speech soars with rhetoric, with stories and with moments of truth – always reverting back to its core theme of the three words which were the essence of the man and his reputation as a soldier. In any speech, for any purpose, it's vital to keep your main theme uppermost in your, and your audience's, mind. That focus will drive what you say.

A Legacy

After being dismissed by President Truman, MacArthur returned to Washington, D.C. where, on 19 April 1951, he made his last official appearance in a farewell address to the US Congress. The speech was interrupted by thirty ovations. He recalled: "Old soldiers never die; they just fade away ... And like the old soldier of that ballad, I now close my military career and just fade away – an old soldier who tried to do his duty as God gave him the light to see that duty. Goodbye." One of his last public appearances was when he gave the 1962 West Point "Duty, Honor, Country" speech. MacArthur was 82 years old then and he spoke without notes for 34 minutes to more than 2000 cadets.

The drama of the occasion and its setting was appropriate: rows upon rows of finely turned out cadets and officers, an auditorium full of history, a historical occasion. And everyone knew it. MacArthur finished his speech with a moving, powerful close which, perhaps embarrassing but nonetheless pleasing for him, caused the whole of the 2000 in the audience to rise as one and cheer: "The shadows are lengthening for me. The twilight is here. My days of old have vanished – tone and tints. They have gone glimmering through the dreams of things that were … In my dreams I hear again the crash of guns, the rattle of musketry, the strange, mournful mutter of the battlefield. But in the evening of my memory I come back to West Point. Always there echoes and re-echoes: 'Duty, Honor, Country …' I bid you farewell." Not a dry eye in the house.

Malcolm X

A ballot is like a bullet. You don't throw your ballots until you see a target and, if that target is not within your reach, keep your ballot in your pocket."

"The Ballot or the Bullet" speech, Cory Methodist Church, Cleveland, USA, Friday 3 April 1964

Malcolm X was born Malcolm Little on 19 May 1925. He was an African-American Muslim minister and human rights activist, assassinated on 21 February 1965 while giving a speech in New York. To his admirers, he was a brave voice for the rights of African-Americans, a man who indicted white Americans for crimes against black Americans. His opposition and the authorities accused him of preaching violence and racism. He has been described as one of the most influential African-Americans of the twentieth century.

Lessons from Malcolm X

Speeches benefit from fervour and belief. "The Ballot or the Bullet" was a vivid public address delivered by Malcolm X in which he urged his audience, predominantly African-Americans, to exercise their right to vote. But, using violent language, he warned the audience that should the United States government continue to put barriers in the way of African-Americans from attaining full equality, then it would be necessary for them to take up arms – and use them. This is a shocking speech, even now.

Language can be scary. What Malcolm X does in this and other speeches is to utilize the language of the street. Some of the analogies are extremely anguished and harsh; all of the expression is direct. This is not a cosy fire-side chat but a provocative address meant to push white people, the police and politicians to anger and to pull supporters in to join a struggle that Malcolm X wanted to be highly combative. He was critical of the African-American communities that allegedly just gave up any hope of rights: "The white man is too intelligent to let someone else come and gain control of the economy of his community. But you will let anybody come in and take control of the economy of your community, control the housing, control the education, control the jobs, control the businesses, under the pretext that you want to integrate. No, you're out of your mind ..."

Malcolm X becomes more provocative and his language spikier and more of the street; he senses the crowd becoming uneasy in some quarters and knows that he is urged on in others: "Anytime you have to rely upon your enemy for a job, you're in bad shape ... Let me tell you, you wouldn't be in this country if some enemy hadn't kidnapped you and brought you here. On the other hand, some of you think you came here on the *May-flower* ... The government has failed us; you can't deny that." The speech is clever and the anecdotes entertaining. The whole piece promotes a sense of fascination in the listener; it's gripping and few turned away.

Make your speech relevant. Malcolm X noted that 1964 was an election year, a time: "When all of the white political crooks will be right back in your and my community ...with their false promises which they don't intend to keep." He said that President Johnson and the Democratic Party supposedly supported the civil rights bill but there was very little evidence of genuine interest. He maintained that, even though the Democrats controlled both the House of Representatives and the Senate, politicians hadn't taken genuine action to pass the bill. He said that African-Americans were becoming "politically mature" and should begin to think for themselves, take a stance. More than that, he made it plain that African-Americans could provide the swing vote in the coming election. He made it clear that they could elect candidates who would be interested in them. This was a clever device, gradually informing the audience of what they could have and what they would lose if they did nothing.

Invective is powerful, but it has to be managed. Malcolm X described how potent a weapon the ballot could be if exercised with care: "A ballot is like a bullet. You don't throw your ballots until you see a target and if that target is not within your reach, keep your ballot in your pocket." His language was emotive and powerful and his meaning absolutely crystal-clear. The government, he said, "has failed the Negro".

A Legacy

"The Ballot or the Bullet" speech was intended to reach out to moderate civil rights leaders. The intention was also to incite some action on the basis that to do nothing would be pitiful and result in no change, no hope. He said: "It'll be liberty or it'll be death". The speech also supported black nationalism and self-defence – at the very least. Deliberately the speech makes no mention of religion but cleverly prefers to accommodate African-Americans from all backgrounds.

This speech and the work of Malcolm X heightened the awareness of black issues and helped reconnect African-Americans with their heritage. It was time, he said on many occasions, that black people abandoned any shame. There was, he asserted, nothing to be ashamed about.

Many African-Americans, and certainly many who lived in large cities, considered that Malcolm X spoke up for them about inequalities where they dared not. He did more, many thought, than the mainstream civil rights activists, although his call for inevitable violence was too dangerous for some.

It is said that the Black Power movement owed its origins to Malcolm X, along with the slogan used across America and beyond: "Black is Beautiful".

Nelson Mandela

I have cherished the ideal of a democratic and free society in which all persons live together in harmony and with equal opportunities. It is an ideal which I hope to live for and to achieve. But if needs be, it is an ideal for which I am prepared to die."

"An Ideal for which I am Prepared to Die" speech, delivered from the dock at the opening of Nelson Mandela's trial on charges of sabotage, Supreme Court of South Africa, Pretoria, 20 April 1964

After qualifying as a lawyer, **Nelson Mandela** (born 18 July 1918) became a political activist with the African National Congress (ANC), which was banned for its opposition to apartheid – the South African government's policy of racial segregation. In 1960 Mandela was leader of Umkhonto we Sizwe (Spear of the Nation), the armed wing of the ANC. In April 1964 he stood trial and was imprisoned for life for sabotage and plotting violent revolution. As a result of his powerful and memorable defence speech at this trial, Mandela became a worldwide symbol for the anti-apartheid movement.

In 1989 President Frederik W. de Klerk began dismantling the apartheid system and, in 1990, the ban on the ANC was lifted. Mandela was freed on 11 February 1990, after 26 years in prison. On the day of his release, Mandela made a careful speech explaining that his main focus was to bring peace to the black majority and give them the right to vote. Although he declared his commitment to peace and reconciliation with the white minority, he made it clear that the armed struggle was not over.

In 1993 Mandela was jointly awarded the Nobel Peace Prize with President de Klerk and on 27 April 1994 the ANC won South Africa's first multi-racial elections, with Mandela elected as president. His policies and example, but mostly his words, steered the country away from the institutional violence that had blighted the country for generations.

Lessons from Nelson Mandela

Inspire trust. Trust is important, but hard to achieve. And how can you build trust with a hostile group of people? Research suggests that several qualities promote trust, qualities evident in Mandela's speeches: showing bravery (but not stupidity) and openness; behaving unselfishly; valuing fairness; showing compassion; displaying empathy; being supportive; offering respect; giving credit to others; and providing a vision of the future with which audiences can identify. All desperately easy to deliver, of course! However, Mandela managed it.

His bold vision was shown in this 1964 trial speech when he said: "I have cherished the ideal of a democratic and free society in which all persons live together in harmony and with equal opportunities." His courage is clear: "It is an ideal which I hope to live for and to achieve. But if needs be, it is an ideal for which I am prepared to die." Mandela frequently gave credit to others, as his "Free at Last" speech in May 1994 demonstrates: "South Africa's heroes are legend across the generations. But it is you, the people, who are our true heroes."

Be honest, clear and succinct. At his trial Mandela said: "This is what the ANC is fighting. Their struggle is a truly national one. It is a struggle of the African people, inspired by their own suffering and their own experience. It is a struggle for the right to live." Mandela recognized that he was being branded a communist, which was used as an excuse for apartheid. Mandela dealt with this point honestly, clearly and cleverly: "There has often been close cooperation between the ANC and the Communist Party. But cooperation is merely proof of a common goal ... The history of the world is full of similar examples. Perhaps the most striking illustration is to be found in the cooperation between Great Britain, the United States of America and the Soviet Union in the fight against Hitler."

Reassure people and never ignore your audience's likely state of mind. When he was elected president of a multi-racial South Africa, Mandela understood that triumph could give rise to uncertainty and trepidation, particularly among those who had lost. Rather than dismiss these views, he provided reassurance – a message he had given constantly – by saying: "I hold out a hand of friendship to the leaders of all parties and their members – and ask all of them to join us in working together to tackle the problems we face as a nation."

Engage people through your personal experiences or situation. Mandela was never afraid of discussing his own experiences and views, as he did in his autobiography *Long Walk to Freedom*. In his speeches, Mandela's persona is engaging precisely because he speaks from the heart. It helps that audiences know what he's been through. That doesn't mean that every speaker has to have suffered – all people have experiences that make them what and who they are. Share some of these. Commentators have remarked that Mandela is an ordinary individual who became successful and revered by maintaining his decency, integrity, humanity and purpose, despite exceptional obstacles and injustice.

A Legacy

Nelson Mandela was the first black president of South Africa. That's a legacy in itself.

Mandela's legacy is two-fold. Most obvious is the democratic and multi-racial Republic of South Africa for which he fought. His other legacy is the inspiration he has instilled in others. Mandela's achievements relied on his skill in engaging and persuading people with his openness, tenacity, empathy and vision, powerfully expressed through his words.

There have been occasions when not all of the world has agreed with Mandela's views, such as his tacit support for what some would call revolutionary governments heavily involved in terrorism. Notable commentators have said that he could have done even more in his time as South Africa's president to unify the country and to stop the economic slippage that the nation faced. But that's not how he'll be remembered. He is seen everywhere as a symbol of peace and determination, of sheer willpower and belief. His speeches are invariably a fine amalgam of structure, wit, emotion and spirit, with an argument that focuses on what people can achieve if they really want to. He is Africa's most respected and well-known figure.

George Martin

Music of the future is in your hands. Cherish it; it is a vital part of humanity ..."

Commencement address, Berklee College of Music, Boston, Massachusetts, USA, Thursday 13 April 1989

Sir George Henry Martin was born on 3 January 1926. He is a British record producer, arranger and composer, although some refer to him as "the fifth Beatle". And indeed, he was involved in the production of all of The Beatles' original songs and played piano on some of the band's tracks.

Martin's musical expertise was fortuitous, and eventually essential, in bridging the gap between the ideas of the band and the type of music or sound the "fab four" wanted to achieve. Martin's skill can only be truly appreciated it you consider for just one moment that there is really no Beatles song that is the same as the next.

Lessons from George Martin

When you have been successful, people want to know the details. How did you succeed? What did you do? What's your story? George Martin's distinctive musical arrangements and ideas appear on many Beatles recordings. On "Eleanor Rigby", for example, Martin scored and conducted an emotive string accompaniment. It was also his idea to put a string quartet on "Yesterday". With the song "Penny Lane", featuring a trumpet solo, Paul McCartney apparently hummed the melody, George Martin wrote the music down and a classical trumpeter played it. These and other stories are the details that people want to hear. They're fun and they paint a picture. They create a warmth. As with good talk show hosts, the audience will gain little gems of interest as the interview progresses that go towards making the subject's story powerful. Or, in your case, as you stand on your stage, your audiences will learn what makes you tick.

Flatter your audience a little. Why not? In this address to students at Berklee College of Music, Martin said: "I like your attitudes, too. I do not find snobbishness here between different kinds of music. This college is a superb example of a healthy, impartial approach that knows no barriers, no pigeonholes, no classical looking down the nose, no rock and roll sneering at their opposite numbers. You show the existence of only two kinds of music: good and bad."

A Legacy

George Martin's main legacy is of course his brilliant, unsurpassed body of work with The Beatles. It's an extraordinary accomplishment and over forty years after the Beatles disbanded, the music is still regarded as fresh. Much of the work is held as classic, as a consequence of which Martin is regarded by most as one of the greatest music producers ever and the Beatles the greatest group.

Martin won many accolades including Grammy and Brit Awards and in 1998 he received the British Phonographic Industry's recognition as "Man of the Year". In 1999 he was inducted into the Rock and Roll Hall of Fame and into the UK Music Hall of Fame in 2006. The Royal College of Arms granted him his own heraldic shield featuring, of course, beetles.

John McCain

I wish Godspeed to the man who was my former opponent and will be my president. And I call on all Americans, as I have often in this campaign, to not despair of our present difficulties, but to believe, always, in the promise and greatness of America, because nothing is inevitable here. Americans never quit. We never surrender. We never hide from history. We make history."

Concession speech, Biltmore Hotel, Phoenix, Arizona, USA, Tuesday 4 November 2008

John Sidney McCain III is a United States senator from Arizona and was born on 29 August 1936. Notably, he was the Republican nominee for the United States Presidency in the 2008 election.

John McCain followed his father and grandfather, both four-star admirals, into the United States Navy, graduating from the US Naval Academy in 1958. While on a bombing mission over Hanoi in 1967, he was shot down, injured and captured by North Vietnamese forces. He remained a prisoner of war until 1973 and he experienced severe torture, the effects of which are with him still and stop him from raising his arms easily.

McCain ran for the Republican presidential nomination in 2000 but lost the primary contest to George W. Bush Jr. In 2008 he gained the nomination, but lost the general election to Barack Obama.

Lessons from John McCain

Make each speech count. If you don't, you may realize that you should have done, but far, far too late. This applies to the corporate sector just as much as it does to the world of politics. There are many times when we've witnessed very senior executives at the helm of organizations who know, absolutely know (even if they're not told), that what they have just delivered is poor or less than good. Sometimes they ask how their speech was and the acolytes nod and commit to damnation with faint praise. Offline, some get told that they "could have done better". But what a waste of opportunity!

McCain conceded defeat to Barack Obama in a speech of (unusual and) striking grace and generosity that called for all Americans to unite behind and support the new president-elect. His speech paid tribute to Obama's accomplishment of becoming the country's first African-American leader and for leading an extraordinary campaign.

Interestingly, McCain seemed more relaxed in his concession speech than at any point during his campaign. The timing of his words and the overall delivery were excellent. Many believe that if, during the campaign, he had sounded like he did in his concession speech, he might have won the election or, at the very least, he might have come much closer to victory.

Powerful phrases and powerful words make a speech strong. McCain was moving and emotive in some of his phraseology. This is great material: "Whatever our differences, we are fellow Americans. And please believe me when I say no association has ever meant more to me than that. It is natural – it's natural, tonight, to feel some disappointment. But tomorrow, we must move beyond it and work together to get our country moving again … We fought as hard as we could. And though we fell short, the failure is mine, not yours."

Respect your adversaries. McCain showed a defeated soldier's nobility in his praise of Obama for inspiring millions of Americans. He surprised his audience by recognizing that Obama's election would help the country heal its racial wounds. Obviously, this kind of speech is always hard to write and to deliver. Winners nearly always look strong. It was for McCain to do the hard thing: not only to accept loss and graciously congratulate the winner, but also to encourage the rest of the country to support the new president-elect in what was going to be a different and a very tough time.

This is a strong speech delivered with humility and grace. In it he said: "In a contest as long and difficult as this campaign has been, his [Obama's] success alone commands my respect for his ability and perseverance. But that he managed to do so by inspiring the hopes of so many millions of Americans who had once wrongly believed that they had little at stake or little influence in the election of an American president, is something I deeply admire and commend him for achieving." That takes courage to say, let alone in such a strong and, one must imagine, heartfelt way.

A Legacy

Following his defeat, McCain returned to the Senate amid varying views about what role he might play there. He was seen by the new administration as a man of honour and with a genuine willingness to help effect change. In mid-November 2008, he met president-elect Barack Obama and the two discussed shared issues. Before and since his inauguration, Obama consulted with McCain on a variety of matters, to an extent rarely seen between a president-elect and his defeated rival.

President Obama's inauguration speech included an allusion to McCain's theme of finding a purpose greater than oneself.

Robert Menzies

The home is the foundation of sanity and sobriety; it is the indispensable condition of continuity; its health determines the health of society as a whole."

"The Forgotten People" broadcast, Macquarie Network, Australia, Friday 22 May 1942

Sir Robert Gordon Menzies was born on 20 December 1894 and died on 15 May 1978. He was the founder of the Australian Liberal Party, Australia's sixteenth prime minister and, during his second term, had the honour of becoming the country's longest-serving prime minister.

From the 1940s until he retired in 1966 it could be argued, and often is, that Menzies was the major influence in Australian politics. He was also, without question, regarded as a brilliant speaker. He saw a need to define the middle class which, he rightly assumed, was the country's backbone – morally and economically. He was keen to gain support from this social group, on the basis that it was obviously a good political tactic, but also because there was a malaise – it was felt that the country's financial burdens rested much with this group for which there was no recognition or political support.

His broadcast, "The Forgotten People", was an example of his oratorical skills. This speech defines, praises and attempts to protect Australia's middle class and all that it then stood for: pride, modesty and sense. He said: "The case for the middle class is the case for a dynamic democracy as against the stagnant one. Stagnant waters are level and in them the scum rises. Active waters are never level: they toss and tumble and have crests and troughs; but the scientists tell us that they purify themselves in a few hundred yards … But what really happens to us will depend on how many people we have who are of the great and sober and dynamic middle-class – the strivers, the planners, the ambitious ones. We shall destroy them at our peril."

Lessons from Robert Menzies

Make sure that your audience understands your background and accomplishments. Don't assume that just because you're a senior member of an organization, or even the most senior, the audience will know your background or view you as credible. This speech by Robert Menzies began life as a 15-minute radio talk during World War II. It was a very tough time for his country; Singapore had capitulated and Japan's forces were advancing across the Pacific. The threat of invasion was very real. Menzies was no longer prime minister at this time, but a backbencher in opposition. However, he made weekly broadcasts from 1942 to 1946, setting out his values and ideas and keeping his voice in the national conversation. Australians liked his manner, his approach, his conversational tone, his common sense and his content. People remembered him and what he said. He was quoted in the street and in the media. His views counted and the middle class relied on him to be their barometer.

Ensure that you speak about things in which your listeners will be interested, even if they don't agree with everything you say. Describing the virtues of the middle class, Menzies uses well-known phrases, references and arguments. He states categorically that the middle class is the backbone of the country. He praises middle-class thrift, its ambition, its views on education and its contribution to culture. In many ways the broadcast has the qualities of a sermon, much more so than a political address. That's a clever device and it clearly worked. Listeners responded very well to this "sermon" about the need to focus upon home, on family and on the need to break down the barriers of class and social strata. Some of what Menzies said, both in this address and others, was not immediately well received. Bones of contention became the topics of the dinner table, the office and bars. But that added weight to support for his thinking. He was seen as fair and reasonable, someone who understood current issues in a rounded way.

Political language is public language. It is (or perhaps should be) conventional, colloquial – sometimes clichéd. It uses images and points of view that are instantly recognizable to audiences. Its purpose is to ensure agreement and to get an audience to think or act in a particular way, the conclusion of which has to be support for the speaker who is putting forward the case or argument. Menzies was a superb proponent of this.

Some politicians enjoy the battle of language. Menzies was one such politician and was aware that he was not everyone's favourite. While he was speaking in Williamstown, Victoria, in 1954, a heckler apparently shouted: "I wouldn't vote for you if you were the Archangel Gabriel" to which Menzies is said to have replied: "If I were the Archangel Gabriel, I'm afraid you wouldn't be in my constituency."

Own your speech. Even when he was prime minister, Robert Menzies wrote his own speeches. Language mattered to him and his skill with it was a vital asset. His aim was to offer himself up as the person to remedy middle-class grievances. If people listened, he promised, these grievances and the middle class would no longer be forgotten. He constantly reiterated this and eventually, when he was able and in government, he delivered.

Make your voice and tone interesting. This might need training, but it will pay dividends. Record yourself – how do you sound? What do others think? These days, there are many opportunities to improve speech delivery. That doesn't mean that an accent should be lost or a style. But good delivery is absolutely essential. Menzies' voice was well modulated with each word clearly understood; he sounded confident, respectful, friendly and authoritative. But that hadn't happened by accident; it took work.

A Legacy

In the 1930s radio became more intimate and informal, with broadcasters entering listeners' everyday lives and speaking directly and personally to each one. Franklin D. Roosevelt made broadcasts known as "fireside chats" to Americans during the Depression from which people drew comfort and inspiration. Menzies did the same thing. Both politicians showed that radio broadcasts were often far more useful in explaining an issue or arguing a point than a large public event or a newspaper article. In Australia, and due to broadcasts like these, radio became a key communications opportunity for politicians.

Higher education improved dramatically under Menzies' tenure and the existing system (much admired around the world) is largely down to his initiatives. "The Forgotten People" speech was a precursor for Menzies' philosophy for the Liberal Party that he was to establish. It's a philosophy that many people, particularly on the Labour Left, hated but it's also one that won Menzies, and eventually the Liberal Party, huge support.

Menzies was far-sighted, and one of his notable achievements was the increase of immigration, when Australia was desperate for skilled labour. Australia's strength today, in all aspects of the word, is very much down to his vision.

Jawaharlal Nehru

At the stroke of the midnight hour, when the world sleeps, India will awake to life and freedom. A moment comes, which comes but rarely in history, when we step out from the old to the new, when an age ends and when the soul of a nation, long suppressed, finds utterance."

"Tryst With Destiny" speech delivered to the Constituent Assembly of India on the granting of Indian Independence, New Delhi, India, Thursday 14 August 1947

Jawaharlal (Pandit) Nehru was born on 14 November 1889 and died on 27 May 1964. He was the first prime minister of independent India. The name Jawaharlal is from the Persian Javâher-e La'al, meaning "Red Jewel", but Nehru was often referred to as "Pandit" – the Sanskrit word for scholar.

Lessons from Nehru

A powerful speech captures the moment. Nehru's "Tryst with Destiny" speech was made to the Indian Constituent Assembly literally on the eve of India's day of independence. The beginning is strong and demands attention: "Long years ago we made a tryst with destiny and now the time comes when we shall redeem our pledge, not wholly or in full measure, but very substantially. At the stroke of the midnight hour, when the world sleeps, India will awake to life and freedom. A moment comes, which comes but rarely in history, when we step out from the old to the new, when an age ends, and when the soul of a nation, long suppressed, finds utterance."

The speech obviously marks a historic moment and is considered by many in modern India to capture the essence of India's hundred-year struggle for freedom. The rhetoric is powerful and the images are beautiful. As one might imagine, this is a well-crafted speech full of promise and vision. It is often copied, in construction if not in content, by senior business executives and politicians, in setting out their vision for the future of their company or party.

If the moment in time is significant make much of it. The skilful way in which Nehru struck the right note for this historic moment is extraordinary. He spoke lyrically of celebrating victory after a lengthy freedom struggle, while acknowledging the trauma of partition and claiming a future of promise, peace, excellence and a recognized place in the world. He articulated the remaining struggles and emphasized the fact that these struggles would be tough. This is an eloquent and lyrical speech, one that presents its themes clearly and powerfully. It is rightly regarded as one of the best ever and, even today, many Indian children learn it by heart.

Read and learn from the speeches of others. Nehru was a huge personality and holds much responsibility for shaping the vision and image of modern India. He was a scholar and the head of the famous and politically influential Nehru–Gandhi family. His scholarly knowledge is evident in his speeches and, like other great orators, he spent time in preparation, in reading the speeches of other politicians and also in understanding his audiences and why they were standing before him. He didn't show off his scholarly background, but tried to use it to engage and support the emotion of a speech.

Nehru began his political career as a very hesitant public speaker and he had to force himself to learn the art. Often he would read political speeches and listen to politicians on the radio. By 1947 he was smoothly and gently spoken, using colourful and expressive language to suit an occasion.

Make your speeches appear natural. Despite preparing and rehearsing his speeches, Nehru was skilled at making them sound as if they had been made up on the spot. People liked his apparent ability to extemporize. And they adored the fact that all of his speeches displayed his admiration of, and adherence to, the principle of freedom. His delight in the state of India was contagious. As he says in the "Tryst with Destiny" speech: "The appointed day has come – the day appointed by destiny – and India stands forth again, after long slumber and struggle, awake, vital, free and independent …" This is vibrant, crisp and demands attention. But it still sounds natural and unforced.

Choose your words carefully. Make phraseology count. Nehru mentioned the word "freedom" no less than fourteen times in the "Tryst with Destiny" speech and produced several memorable phrases. For example, "at the stroke of the midnight hour", "when the world sleeps, India will awake to life and freedom", "a moment comes, which comes but rarely in history", "freedom and power bring responsibility", "the noble mansion of free India where all her children may dwell".

A Legacy

Nehru played a major role in shaping independent India's government as well as the country's political culture and foreign policy. However, violence soon overtook the initial jubilation of the nation's beginning. Sectarian riots erupted as Muslims in India fled to Pakistan and Hindus in Pakistan fled in terror the opposite way. It is thought that over 2 million people died in north India and at least 12 million became refugees. Kashmir became a bone of contention and fighting broke out between the two new states over the province.

In order to rebuild the country's damaged economy, Nehru introduced a mix of socialist planning and free enterprise measures. He also helped establish the non-aligned movement.

Despite the (perhaps unfair) view of some that Nehru's legacy was a substantial failure to manage a burgeoning state and prevent religious and political schisms, he is nevertheless remembered as India's father. It was without doubt he who began to put the vision of modern India into practice.

Nehru's daughter, Indira Gandhi, served as India's prime minister from 1966 to 1977 and from 1980 to 1984. Her son, Rajiv Gandhi, was prime minister from 1984 to 1989. Both Indira and Rajiv Gandhi were assassinated in office.

Barack Obama

If there is anyone out there who still doubts that America is a place where all things are possible; who still wonders if the dream of our founders is alive in our time; who still questions the power of our democracy, tonight is your answer ... It's been a long time coming, but tonight, because of what we did on this day, in this election, at this defining moment, change has come to America."

"Change Has Come to America" election victory acceptance speech, Grant Park, Chicago, USA, Tuesday 4 November 2008

On 4 November 2008 US senator **Barack Hussein Obama** was elected the 44th president of the United States. Great orators, like great artists, are often only recognized after their death. For Barack Obama's skill as an orator to be appreciated during his life is a testament to the power of his words.

Obama was born on 4 August 1961 in Honolulu, Hawaii. He moved to Indonesia where he attended local schools in Jakarta until the age of ten, then returned to Honolulu to live with his maternal grandparents.

Obama's story is fresh and immediate. He is a graduate of Columbia University and Harvard Law School, where he was the first African-American president of the *Harvard Law Review*. Later he worked as a community organizer in Chicago before earning his law degree and practised as a civil rights attorney in Chicago. Between 1997 and 2004 he served three terms in the Illinois senate. Clearly his experience as a politician was limited, a point that was thrust against him in his campaign to lead the USA. However, that clearly didn't stop him and it was predominantly his rhetoric, his manner and his oratory that persuaded people he was the right person for the job. There were other ingredients as well, including his background and the country's mood for change.

Lessons from Barack Obama

Personalize your words and compliment your audience. Obama's speeches are positive and are prepared to acknowledge the best in people. This sits well with his personality and background. At times unusual and unconventional, but always hugely successful, his life-story gives him a broad appeal beyond the USA. More significantly, it has also provided Obama with a strong sense of self-reliance and self-belief. This life narrative is something that Obama often uses in his speeches, both formally and informally. By opening up about his personal background, engaging and reassuring people, he helps himself connect with his audience. Crucially, this openness is a key element in establishing trust.

Obama's personal story was memorably invoked at the 2004 Democratic Party Convention, when he first came to national prominence, with the words: "I stand here today, grateful for the diversity of my heritage, aware that my parents' dreams live on in my precious daughters. I stand here knowing that my story is part of the larger American story, that I owe a debt to all of those who came before me, and that, in no other country on earth, is my story even possible."

Emphasize shared values and connectedness. Obama's huge popularity stems from the perception that his values, priorities, approach and personality are widely understood and distributed. It often seems that the way in which he shares his story makes it emblematic of an inclusive America, rather than being just one individual's tale. For example, he emphasized this sense of shared values in the 2004 Democratic Convention speech: "Alongside our famous individualism, there's another ingredient in the American saga. A belief that we are connected as one people. If there's a child on the south side of Chicago who can't read, that matters to me, even if it's not my child. If there's a senior citizen somewhere who can't pay for her prescription and has to choose between medicine and the rent, that makes my life poorer, even if it's not my grandmother. If there's an Arab-American family being rounded up without benefit of an attorney or due process, that threatens my civil liberties. It's that fundamental belief – I am my brother's keeper, I am my sister's keeper – that makes this country work."

Show your intention and provide a sense of possibilities. People do things (such as enter politics) for many reasons. Obama's reasons for becoming a politician are entirely consistent with his life before politics and his actions afterwards: to genuinely help people and improve their situation as well as to contribute to the life of his community. His great ability is to connect with people, partly by saying what they want to hear (and what he wants to deliver) and partly by providing a refreshing sense of possibilities. Audiences respond extremely well if presented with possibilities all of which they know they can achieve.

This open, positive approach from Obama is clear from his words spoken at Grant Park, Chicago, the night he was elected president: "If there is anyone out there who still doubts that America is a place where all things are possible; who still wonders if the dream of our founders is alive in our time; who still questions the power of our democracy, tonight is your answer … It's been a long time coming, but tonight, because of what we did on this day, in this election, at this defining moment, change has come to America."

Have a clear message: things *can* be better. But be realistic. Audiences want to hear the positives, but they're not stupid. Obama's campaign slogan "Yes we can" was simple – according to some reports, too simple for Obama, who had to be persuaded to use the phrase by his advisors. But people do tend to want change and improvement; after all, these things are more appealing than stagnation and complacency. Change is a universally popular message, although of course, as we all know, it can't be promised for ever without delivery.

Take your opportunities. Obama delivered the keynote address at the Democratic National Convention in July 2004 and quickly rose to national prominence. Many things contributed to his success, but he was undoubtedly helped by having an opponent who led an unpopular political party, combined with a nationwide feeling that it was a time for substantial change. His campaign, like his speeches, was impressively disciplined and kept to the same messages, not repeated in the same way but highlighted in different ways with a wide variety of stories, examples and analogies. He made his opportunities work because he understood his audiences.

Use language carefully. Personalize your message and connect with people. Obama has bucked the trend: in an age of soundbites and spin, it is the quality of his traditional speeches combined with modern campaigning techniques that have contributed to his rise. While many of the devices in his speeches, such as the repetition of the same phrase at the beginning of successive sentences, were used by orators from Cicero to Kennedy, it is unusual to see this style in the twenty-first century. There are several reasons why Obama can achieve this classical oratory that his contemporaries tend to avoid. First, his words are entirely of their time, not at all disconcerting, elitist or alienating. The language and phrases are real and of the people. Also, his language involves the audience in narratives that are highly personal – or seem so at first hearing. Finally, he refers to the greats who precede him, particularly Lincoln. Obama declares himself the heir to salvationist politics, a bringer of hope and change – and people love him for it.

Reference other great speeches or speakers. Obama's speeches often include references to other speakers, speeches and writings. If managed lazily or badly, this can merely confuse or block the listener. In Obama's case, the process of quoting others helps those in the audience to feel familiar with his words and understand the scale of his ambition. It is a technique often used in history's greatest speeches. For example, in his inaugural address in January 2009, Obama said: "We remain a young nation, but in the words of Scripture, the time has come to set aside childish things. The time has come to reaffirm our enduring spirit; to choose our better history; to carry forward that precious gift, that noble idea, passed on from generation to generation: the God-given promise that all are equal, all are free, and all deserve a chance to pursue their full measure of happiness."

Of course, the subject of a speech and its context need to match the reference, or it can appear absurd. Perhaps this is one reason why relatively few leaders feel bold enough to do it. As well as fear of pretension, lack of ambition may also explain why this technique has fallen out of favour. Or it may simply be that inspiration is out of fashion in the more egalitarian, fast-moving routine of our soundbite times. However, human nature has not changed and still responds positively to bold, powerful references.

A Legacy

To date, Obama's legacy has been a spirit of change and hope in very difficult times – a sense that anything is possible. Elected during a time of war, deep uncertainty and global economic crisis when people wanted resolution, guidance, optimism, humanity, belief, inspiration and, generally speaking, something better, Obama was able to offer this clearly, strongly and consistently. Interestingly, he gained as much favour outside America as he did inside it. He moved people with a strong sense of possibility and practical, personal action, powerfully conveyed in his words.

Conan O'Brien

So, that's what I wish for all of you: the bad as well as the good. Fall down, make a mess, break something occasionally. And remember that the story is never over ..."

Commencement speech, Harvard Class of 2000, Harvard, Cambridge, Massachusetts, USA, Wednesday 7 June 2000

Conan Christopher O'Brien was born on 18 April 1963. He is an Emmy Award-winning American television host and comedian, best known as the anchor on NBC's *Late Night with Conan O'Brien*. He replaced Jay Leno as host of *The Tonight Show* in 2009.

Speakers who use humour, such as O'Brien, need to understand their audiences very well indeed, chiefly to ensure that the humour will work and that people will actually laugh. What they also need to know is that the humour will not distract, trivialize or offend. Poor humour can ruin a speech opportunity and we've probably all seen and heard that happen. It's hard to recover from weak humour or a funny line that isn't.

Lessons from Conan O'Brien

Humour is good for certain speeches, but it can be risky. In this address to Harvard students, Conan O'Brien drew on his trademark self-effacing humour. He uses a series of comedic gems to make a point and tells these stories to great effect, making an immediate and strong connection with his audience. In this instance, it's easier for him because the audience expects him to be amusing and he was invited because he is known for his humour. But that too can be a poisoned chalice if managed badly.

O'Brien begins: "The last time I was invited to Harvard it cost me $110,000, so you'll forgive me if I'm a bit suspicious ..." And he went on, reinforcing the smile and laughter that idea achieved, with: "I wrote a thesis: 'Literary Progeria in the works of Flannery O'Connor and William Faulkner' ... For three years after graduation I kept my thesis in the glove compartment of my car so I could show it to a policeman in case I was pulled over. License, registration, cultural exploration of the Man Child in the Sound and the Fury ..."

He does cover serious topics too, not least the issue of taking the rough with the smooth in life. Audiences can quickly tell if humour is helping make a serious point and they enjoy the process. And there is a big difference between just being funny for funny's sake and using humour as a lever.

A Legacy

A combination of zany humour, recurring sketches and self-deprecation has made Conan O'Brien a big television star. His show *Late Night with Conan O'Brien* has been a favourite with students and critics alike for more than a decade. He is seen as smart, clever, funny. He's mainstream without standing too close to the establishment; he has edge, but he's not discourteous; he is cynical without criticizing everything. His viewing public in America see O'Brien as a fresh face, someone who replaced much of the dust in which late-night television was beginning to be covered. His legacy is growing as someone with probity and panache – someone who is changing the face of America's television, an extraordinary thing to attempt, never mind achieve. He was an excellent choice as speaker for Harvard and there are many words of wisdom and advice alongside his humour. He is never dry or dull.

O'Brien is beginning to become aware of his growing influence in the media and over young people. For example, he endorses the anti-hunger organization Labels Are For Jars, which he co-founded.

O'Brien ended his Harvard Commencement Address with: "But let me leave you with one last thought: If you can laugh at yourself loud and hard every time you fall, people will think you're drunk."

Robert Oppenheimer

Now I am become Death, the destroyer of worlds."

Interview from television documentary *The Decision to Drop the Bomb*, broadcast by NBC, USA, Tuesday 5 January 1965

Julius Robert Oppenheimer (born 22 April 1904; died 18 February 1967) was professor of physics at the University of California before he was invited to work for the American government. Oppenheimer's fame relates to his direction of the Manhattan Project based at the secret Los Alamos National Laboratory in New Mexico. This controversial initiative, set up during (and because of) World War II, was established to build the world's first nuclear weapon. Some gave Oppenheimer a title of dubious honour: "The Father of the Atomic Bomb".

The first atomic bomb test took place on 16 July 1945. It was called the Trinity test, after one of John Donne's sonnets. After the bomb had been detonated, Oppenheimer is said to have quoted the Hindu holy book, the *Bhagavad-Gita* (*Song of the Lord*): "If the radiance of a thousand suns were to burst at once into the sky, that would be like the splendour of the mighty one" and, reportedly, he also murmured: "Now I am become Death, the destroyer of worlds."

The Manhattan Project employed a huge number of people, some 130,000. There were three atomic bombs detonated as a result of the project. The first was exploded at the test site, Jornada del Muerto (Spanish for "Route of the Dead Man"), the second over Hiroshima, and Nagasaki was the target for the third.

Brigadier-General Thomas F. Farrell supervised the Trinity test on behalf of the military. He was with Oppenheimer in the bunker ten miles away from the detonator site. Farrell later wrote: "The effects could well be called unprecedented, magnificent, beautiful, stupendous and terrifying. No man-made phenomenon of such tremendous power had ever occurred before." When the test bomb was about to be detonated, Farrell said that Oppenheimer: " ... grew tenser as the last seconds ticked off. He scarcely breathed. He held on to a post to steady himself ... When the announcer shouted 'Now!' and there came this tremendous burst of light, followed ... by the deep-growling roar of the explosion, his face relaxed into an expression of tremendous relief." According to his brother, at the time of the explosion Oppenheimer simply exclaimed: "It worked".

Lessons from Robert Oppenheimer

A speech does not need to be long, particularly about an occasion that requires little detail. Oppenheimer later repeated the *Bhagavad-Gita* quotation in a 1965 television broadcast: "We knew the world would not be the same. A few people laughed, a few people cried, most people were silent. I remembered the line from the Hindu scripture, the *Bhagavad-Gita*. Vishnu is trying to persuade the prince that he should do his duty and, to impress him, takes on his multi-armed form and says, 'Now, I am become Death, the destroyer of worlds.' I suppose we all thought that one way or another."

The short, moving and emotive piece from the broadcast shows Oppenheimer, by then ill with cancer, clearly displaying huge emotion at recalling the day in 1945 and, possibly, the way that the world had developed and changed for ever over the following twenty years. The words are spoken slowly and deliberately. They are so very powerful and succinct, not least because they are simply said about something momentous. The words require no extra detail, no convoluted explanation. The power of what this was all about can be seen in Oppenheimer's face and in the simple delivery – wistful, distressed, a mix of hope and despair – of the words.

Make sure you use the best quotations and only those absolutely appropriate to your message. Since Robert Oppenheimer was proficient in Sanskrit, he is likely to have read the original text of the Hindu holy book, the *Bhagavad-Gita*. The translation is apparently his own.

A Legacy

After World War II, Oppenheimer was appointed chief advisor to the newly created United States Atomic Energy Commission. Out of guilt perhaps, or a realization of what he'd created, he used his position within the Commission to lobby for the worldwide control of atomic energy and to curb the burgeoning nuclear arms race with the Soviet Union.

During the deeply harmful McCarthy investigations of the 1950s into alleged communist activity in all walks of life, in particular within the United States government, Oppenheimer was stripped of his security clearance and effectively his research career was over. He continued as an academic and with his writing. It was a decade later that President John F. Kennedy awarded Oppenheimer the Enrico Fermi Award (presented to him by President Lyndon B. Johnson) as a gesture of political rehabilitation and recognition.

Shortly after the Trinity test, Oppenheimer became a national spokesman for science in America. The world was in absolute awe of an extraordinary new power. Nuclear physics was now a huge political force as all governments realized the strategic and awesome might of nuclear weaponry, the demand for which has not diminished. The "extraordinary new power" may not be so new anymore, but it is still extraordinary. As are its horrific implications.

Emmeline Pankhurst

You have left it to women in your land, the men of all civilized countries have left it to women, to work out their own salvation."

"Freedom or Death" speech, Hartford, Connecticut, USA, Thursday 13 November 1913

Emmeline (Emily) Pankhurst was a political activist and leader of the British suffragette movement. Although she was widely criticized for her militant shock tactics, her zealous belief and determination are recognized as instrumental in helping to achieve women's suffrage in Britain. She was born on 15 July 1858 and died on 14 June 1928.

Lessons from Emmeline Pankhurst

Adversity and a strong belief can lead to highly persuasive speeches. Emily Pankhurst showed that, if you have an important argument to share, you should be unequivocal. Many speechmakers don't like to be direct. Consequently, a great proportion of the speech is spent on matters that don't directly relate to the main argument or presented in such a way that the audience fails to see the main argument.

Pankhurst made her most famous speech on a fundraising tour of America in the autumn of 1913. As she told one American audience: "They sent me to prison, to penal servitude for three years … I broke my prison bars. Four times they took me back again; four times I burst the prison door open again … Have we not proved, then, that they cannot govern human beings who withhold their consent?" Between spells in prison, Pankhurst occasionally addressed audiences from a stretcher. Whether that was because she was genuinely unwell or not is a moot point. But few people at the time were photographed more often or to better effect. Her speeches are those of a celebrity; she knew that her audiences were curious to see her, regardless of whether they agreed with her or not. And she went out of her way to surprise and shock.

Understand your audience. For example, if you know your audience will readily agree with your points, say them. Equally, on occasion you will need to say things that may shock or surprise. That's fine too, provided that you can support them. Emily Pankhurst delivered her "Freedom or Death" speech before an audience assembled by the Connecticut Women's Suffrage Association, under the leadership of Katherine Houghton Hepburn (the mother of the famous film actress). Pankhurst's audience would have been aware that, a few months earlier, Emily Davison, the Women's Social and Political Union (WSPU) member, had shockingly stepped out in front of King George V's horse when it was running in the Derby, in England. Davison died four days later. The photograph of the Derby incident appeared in newspapers around the world. Pankhurst's task with this speech was to justify the adoption by the WSPU of such militant tactics. "Deeds not Words" was their slogan. In actual fact, the process was too stark and frightening to many, the result being that it alienated much of the British suffragist movement.

State your case clearly. In this 1913 "Freedom or Death" speech, Pankhurst starts by inviting her audience to consider the absurdity of treating someone such as her as a dangerous criminal. It's a clever ploy and, without casting any aspersions, it's a device used by ex-criminals, by politicians or business people who have been discovered to have committed some misdemeanour, by those who have committed great wrongs – but who look, sound and seem much the same as anyone else.

Pankhurst then reminds her listeners of their own tradition of revolution and civil war (remember, she's in America), subtly persuading them that it was inconsistent not to allow women to use violence when they had fought two wars to free themselves and to end slavery: "You won the civil war by the sacrifice of human life when you decided to emancipate the negro. You have left it to women in your land, the men of all civilized countries have left it to women, to work out their own salvation ..." Then, surprisingly, she metaphorically charges head-down into the people who have welcomed her to Hartford. She tells her audience that she doesn't give a damn if she alienates sympathizers, because suffragists in England had enjoyed public sympathy for many years and it never brought them anything at all. Now's the time, she implies, for action. She tries to embarrass her listeners into action. She berates them: "When you have warfare, things happen; people suffer; the noncombatants suffer as well as the combatants. And so it happens in civil war. When your forefathers threw the tea into Boston Harbour, a good many women had to go without their tea. It has always seemed to me an extraordinary thing that you did not follow it up by throwing the whiskey overboard; you sacrificed the women; and there is a good deal of warfare for which men take a great deal of glorification which has involved more practical sacrifice on women than it has on any man. It always has been so ..."

A Legacy

By 1916, more than a year after making this speech, Pankhurst had been imprisoned twelve times but had served no more than thirty days, all of them on hunger strike. According to reports, prison staff never dared to force-feed her. In any event, and in response to public disgust, force-feeding was abandoned in 1913.

The British government was obviously aware of Pankhurst's high profile and that of the WSPU. On the declaration of war against Germany in 1914, the government sought WSPU assistance in gaining support for the war. It agreed to release all WSPU prisoners and paid the organization a large sum to hold a recruiting rally, attended by 30,000 people. Under the slogan "Men must fight and women must work", Pankhurst urged the trades unions to allow women to work in jobs traditionally done by men.

In 1918 women in Britain aged over 30 (but only those who were householders, wives of householders or landholders) were given the vote. Pankhurst's own civil war ended in compromise. It was not until ten years later in 1928 that women in Britain were granted the same voting rights as men.

Randy Pausch

We cannot change the cards we are dealt, just how we play the hand."

"The Last Lecture", Carnegie Mellon University, Pittsburgh, Pennsylvania, USA, Tuesday 18 September 2007

Randolph (Randy) Frederick Pausch was born on 23 October 1960 and died on 25 July 2008, at just 47 years of age. He was an American computer science professor at Carnegie Mellon University (CMU) in Pittsburgh, Pennsylvania. After learning that he was terminally ill in September 2006, he gave an upbeat and thought-provoking lecture at Carnegie Mellon, which became a popular YouTube video and led to other media appearances on, for example, *The Oprah Winfrey Show*. He later co-authored a bestselling book entitled *The Last Lecture*.

Lessons from Randy Pausch

Offer people a role model. Randy Pausch's "The Last Lecture" intrigued and inspired many people with the words: "We cannot change the cards we are dealt, just how we play the hand." It is, of course, highly unusual and impressive that a person with a terminal illness would have the courage, clarity and control to deliver such a lecture, let alone one so interesting and thought-provoking. It took no prisoners in its honesty and directness. Universal virtues of courage, openness, wit and wisdom will always attract and inspire.

Use humour – even when times are serious, and perhaps especially when times are serious. Pausch said: "When there's an elephant in the room, introduce him." He was of course referring to his illness and the fact that when he walked into a room people would either avoid him or try not to mention it. Wry humour, if it works, is a great technique for a speech-maker or lecturer. It allows people to vent their emotion; it draws people together and can also be relaxing, even thought-provoking. It calms, it excites, it pulls an audience in.

Play to your strengths and enjoy yourself. Pausch was an experienced academic and lecturer. He presented well, enjoyed it and understood how to address a group of people.

Give of yourself. Being open and sharing personal experiences (for example, about family members) is a very effective way of engaging an audience. It helps people understand your personality, priorities and perspectives. It adds value to your topic, not in terms of ensuring sadness at a predicament but empathy. It can be a risky process, however, and clearly inappropriate in certain circumstances and cultures.

Deliver something of value. What is the most important or valuable part of your speech? What's the most valuable thing you have heard in a speech? Randy Pausch included in his lecture words of wisdom based on his experience. These included, for example: "loyalty is a two-way street";

"never give up"; "you get people to help you by telling the truth"; "be earnest – it is long-term"; "listen to feedback"; "show gratitude"; "be good at something, it makes you valuable". On their own these phrases are by no means earth-shattering, but in the context of a strong and direct message, charged with emotion yet colloquial and matter-of-fact in their delivery, they work.

A Legacy

Randy Pausch was passionate about bridging art and science, in particular computer science and the performing arts. His teaching was regarded as theatrical in a highly positive sense; feedback from students was excellent. His legacy is two-fold: the specific insights he conveyed in his lecture and the feelings and impressions resulting from the manner of his last lecture. Inspiration, both in what you believe and say and, quite different, what audiences perceive in you, is a vital ingredient of a great speech. Inspiration and wonder go hand in hand. A great speaker can manage to elicit both. As Pausch said: "Never lose the childlike wonder. It's just too important."

Lester Pearson

Our age is one of trouble and tension and violence. It is also one of great progress and achievement. It holds both the promise of a far better life for all men and the threat of no life at all for mankind. Which is it to be?"

Public address on the occasion of the presentation to Pearson of the Victor Gollancz Humanity Award, St Martin-in-the-Fields, London, UK, Tuesday 13 June 1972

Lester Bowles ("Mike") Pearson was born on 23 April 1897 and died on 27 December 1972. He was the fourteenth prime minister of Canada, from 1963 until 1968, and became a Nobel Peace laureate in 1957. When he led Canada he was regarded as a safe pair of hands. His minority government delivered a number of innovative and social benefits: national health care, a pension policy, student loans and a wide programme of education. He was also instrumental in redesigning the Canadian flag, the cause of some considerable controversy at the time. Pearson also focused on the issue of relations between French Canadians and the rest of the population, a situation that remained a problem for many years way beyond his premiership.

Pearson is probably best known for his work at the United Nations and in international diplomacy, at which he excelled. He was an exceptional listener and was able to communicate via well-argued, superbly written speeches delivered with aplomb and conviction. He was known as "Mike", an affectionate nickname given to him by his flying instructor in World War I since he considered Lester to be a totally unsuitable name for any wartime pilot.

Lessons from Lester Pearson

Even if you're not a natural speaker, passion, belief and a well-crafted speech make a huge difference. Pearson was not a natural speaker, but all of his speeches showed a quiet determination, a passion and a firm belief. The issues that mattered to Pearson would be revisited, and each time he would deal with them in a slightly different way so that audiences would see his thinking as refreshing and dynamic. For example, in his 1972 London speech, he says: "John Kennedy said in his presidential inaugural address, 'If a free society cannot help the many who are poor, it cannot save the few that are rich.' He was right; not only in respect of relations between the poor and the rich within a country, but also of relations between countries ... Our age is one of trouble and tension and violence. It is also one of great progress and achievement. It holds both the promise of a far better life for all men and the threat of no life at all for mankind. Which is it to be?"

He went to great lengths to warn that the world was far too complacent. His language is firm and he expresses regret. However, he extols the virtue of alertness with a fervour that is rarely seen in a speech such as this: "We seem to get closer to such a system after the disenchantment and revulsion that follows a world war; or in the fear that comes from the imminent danger of another one. Then we forget. The situation seems to improve, the crisis ends, and we again become careless and quarrelsome and selfish and smug. We return to the normal state of dissension and division and disturbance. We begin to plan 'against' rather than 'for'; to compete rather than to cooperate; to link the love of our own land with claims to superiority over others. We confuse greatness with power: God who made us mighty, make us mightier yet."

A Legacy

In his speech, Pearson used terrific language to paint a vivid picture and create a sombre mood: "Threats to global survival, though they are sometimes exaggerated in apocalyptic language which makes our flesh creep, are real. The prophets of doom and gloom may be proven wrong but it is a chilling fact that man can now destroy his world by nuclear explosion or ecological erosion."

He may be remembered as someone who had an enduring, influential impact on the formation and direction of the United Nations. He would have liked the UN to have had more teeth, a desire shared by many observers since. He fervently believed that there should be considerably more international cooperation in the world and he fought for that with a quiet and determined commitment – never ostentatious or loud.

Pearson's internationalism and passionate support for UN peacekeeping was prominent and is still in very real evidence by Canada's participation in numerous missions and in its reluctance to support non-UN-sanctioned conflict. He believed that assisting the developing world was an absolute and moral duty. These days, Canada's investment in, and programmes on, poverty, food distribution and world health are regarded as amongst the very best, and this is mostly down to Pearson's efforts.

Pearson's modesty was widely known and viewed with affection. He said: "I accept it [the Victor Gollancz Humanity Award] with humility and pride – conscious of the fact that there are so many who have laboured and are still labouring in this field with greater claim to the distinction than I possess; conscious also that the Award commemorates one whose whole life was one of triumphant and unselfish service to humanity. I pay him my tribute, deep and sincere."

Pericles

To you who are the sons and brothers of the departed, I see that the struggle to emulate them will be an arduous one."

Funeral Oration, as recorded by Thucydides, Athens, Greece, Winter, 431 BC

Pericles was born in approximately 495 BC and is believed to have died in 429 BC. He was a prominent Athenian general, a statesman and an orator between the Persian and Peloponnesian wars, a time known as Athens's

Golden Age. He had such a deep and long-lasting influence on Athenian society that Thucydides (who "recorded" this eulogy in his *History of the Peloponnesian War*) acclaimed him as "the first citizen of Athens". At the end of the first year of the Peloponnesian War in 431 BC, Athens held a funeral for all those killed in battle. The funeral oration over the dead on this occasion was delivered by Pericles, who himself died in the horrifying plague that scourged Athens the following year.

The Funeral Oration is the classic statement of Athenian principles, containing the sentiment felt by Athenians towards their dead and those who remained.

The custom was to leave the war dead out for three days under cover, where offerings could be made. At the end of the three days, a funeral procession was held, with ten cypress coffins carrying the remains – one for each of the Athenian tribes. The procession led to the Kerameikos, a public grave, where the bodies were then buried. The last part of the ceremony, the most important, was a speech delivered by a prominent Athenian citizen, on this occasion Pericles.

Lessons from Pericles

Honour, truth and praise for others provide mesmerizing themes. Pericles's oration begins by praising the custom of the public funeral for the war dead, but argues that the "reputations of many brave men" should "not be imperilled in the mouth of a single individual". It ends with equal praise: "The tribute of deeds has been paid in part; for the dead have them in deeds, and it remains only that their children should be maintained at the public charge until they are grown up: this is the solid prize with which, as with a garland, Athens crowns her sons living and dead, after a struggle like theirs. For where the rewards of virtue are greatest, there the noblest citizens are enlisted in the service of the state. And now, when you have duly lamented, every one his own dead, you may depart."

Change tack in your speeches and avoid dull repetition. Pericles departs most dramatically from the example of other Athenian funeral orations and skips over the great martial achievements of Athens's past. Instead, he focuses on "the road by which we reached our position, the form of government under which our greatness grew, and the national habits out of which it sprang".

Use analogies to make a point. The speech does not follow the normal pattern of Athenian funeral speeches. It is regarded by some as a eulogy of Athens itself. Certainly what Pericles says puts Athens's achievements on a pinnacle and he presents these achievements so as to motivate a state and its people still at war: "Some of you are of an age at which they may hope to have other children, and they ought to bear their sorrow better; not only will the children who may hereafter be born make them forget their own lost ones, but the city will be doubly a gainer. She will not be left desolate and she will be safer."

A Legacy

In part, Pericles's legacy can be found in the cultural, artistic, literary, educational and architectural developments which he initiated, sponsored and supported in Athens. Much of the art and architecture still exists, for example some of the surviving structures on the Acropolis (including the Parthenon). Pericles also created a fair and well-defended society. He made Athens proud of itself and he effected strong government which lasted beyond his death. He believed passionately (and with a very modern outlook) that democracy would allow citizens to advance because of merit instead of wealth or inherited class.

Those interested in oratory and great speech structure regard Pericles as the master. His influence on speech delivery has been and still is powerful and relevant. Since his leadership equalled careful, clever and efficient government of Athens, the years between 461 BC and 429 BC are known as the Age of Pericles.

Pericles was responsible for making Athens the centre of the Greek world, giving it a reputation for democracy, fairness and culture. He was a poet and a philosopher, a soldier and a statesman. All that he did, he did for the future of Athens. In the Funeral Oration, he said: "For heroes have the whole earth for their tomb; and in lands far from their own, where the column with its epitaph declares it, there is enshrined in every breast a record unwritten with no tablet to preserve it, except that of the heart."

William Lyon Phelps

A borrowed book is like a guest in the house; it must be treated with punctiliousness, with a certain considerate formality. You must see that it sustains no damage; it must not suffer while under your roof. You cannot leave it carelessly, you cannot mark it, you cannot turn down the pages, you cannot use it familiarly. And then, some day, although this is seldom done, you really ought to return it."

"The Pleasure of Books" radio broadcast, USA, Thursday 6 April 1933

William Lyon Phelps (born 2 January 1865 and died 21 August 1943) was an American author, critic and academic. His education was from Yale and Harvard, after which he taught English Literature at each establishment, Yale much more so than Harvard. His Yale students regularly voted him the university's most inspiring professor.

Phelps was an engaging orator who clearly loved literature and was well able to share the attraction he felt towards a book, an author's work or a genre. Wherever he spoke, inside or outside Yale, he was sure of a full house. His lectures and speeches were seen as uplifting and fresh. Phelps was considered a great educator, a scholar who could always teach something new to his students.

Lessons from William Lyon Phelps

Learn new ways of expressing ideas. Phelps's language and structure are delightful to explore: "There are of course no friends like living, breathing, corporeal men and women; my devotion to reading has never made me a recluse. How could it? Books are of the people, by the people, for the people. Literature is the immortal part of history; it is the best and most enduring part of personality … (But) in a private library, you can at any moment converse with Socrates or Shakespeare or Carlyle or Dumas or Dickens or Shaw or Barrie or Galsworthy. And there is no doubt that in these books you see these men at their best. They wrote for you … You are necessary to them as an audience is to an actor; only instead of seeing them masked, you look into their innermost heart of heart." You will note the allusions and also the gentle, persuasive style that makes many, on hearing this broadcast, run to a bookshelf and devour.

A Legacy

The speech was read as a radio broadcast in America only a very short time before the Nazis in Germany began their systematic destruction of Jewish, communist or "un-German" books.

In December 1938, *Life* Magazine featured a detailed article on Phelps. The magazine considered him to be "America's foremost promoter of the humanities". For over forty years, his teaching was regarded as faultless and exemplary, encouraging students and academic colleagues alike to seek new thinking about a huge number of classic titles. He was responsible, according to contemporaries, for encouraging wide reading among people outside the university or college system.

Phelps imparted to America a love of literature and a delight in reading. He concluded his 1933 broadcast: "Most of my indoor life is spent in a room containing six thousand books; and I have a stock answer to the invariable question that comes from strangers. 'Have you read all of these books?' 'Some of them twice.' This reply is both true and unexpected."

Colin Powell

The Hispanic immigrant that became a citizen yesterday must be as precious to us as a Mayflower descendant."

"I am a Republican" speech, Republican Party Convention, San Diego, California, USA, Monday 12 August 1996

Colin Luther Powell was born on 5 April 1937. Powell was a general in the US Army and latterly a politician. From 2001 to 2005 he was President George W. Bush's secretary of state and was the first African-American to hold that post. His military career was certainly impressive. He served as National Security Advisor and as Commander-in-Chief, US Army Forces Command. He was also Chairman of the Joint Chiefs of Staff during the Gulf War (August 1990–February 1991).

Overall, Powell has been regarded as a talker of common sense and with a gentle persuasiveness that did not always endear him to his hawk-like colleagues in government. Some thought and hoped that he would run for the presidency. However, Powell made it very clear, much to the disappointment of many, that he preferred to spend more time with his family and to relax from political life.

Lessons from Colin Powell

Emotion is powerful. In the "I am a Republican" address, Powell gets his audience onside by relating his own experience of what America can give: "My parents found here a compassionate land, with a compassionate people. They found a government that protected their labor, educated their children and provided help to those of their fellow citizens who were needy. They found their dream in America and they passed that dream on to their children. Here tonight, over seventy years after they landed on these shores, their son has been given the privilege of addressing the Republican Party ..."

If your presentation is anticipated, use that as a powerful lever. Powell's speech was highly anticipated. His supporters were aware that he felt strongly about the "magic" that was America and that he had a strong belief that American was not just about what you took out but, as encapsulated by Jack Kennedy, also about what you put in. The "I am a Republican" address emphasized an approach that lauded achievement, no matter how small, an approach that praised the whole essence of opportunity, delivered by an American who had served his country well, who was recognized as a decent, just man motivated by values, fairness and a just society: "Values fuel families, families that are bound together by love and commitment, families that have the strength to withstand the assaults of contemporary life, to resist the images of violence and vulgarity that flood into our lives every day. Families that come together to defeat the scourge of drugs and crime and incivility that threatens us ..." The speech was designed not only to gain support from the convention, but to convince a far wider audience that Republicans were principled and decent, at a time when they had often been pilloried in the media. Powell's language is dramatic and his use of repetition emphasizes each of his themes. During his speech he uses memorable lists to add power to his message and to reinforce his argument.

A Legacy

A Republican all his adult life, people were surprised and many were delighted that Colin Powell publicly supported Democrat Barack Obama in the 2008 American election. Much of what Obama stands for is an echo of Powell's own views, evident from the content of this speech.

The legacy of Colin Powell is mixed. He was a military man who certainly distinguished himself in the Vietnam War and later became the driver and main architect of America's liberation of Kuwait from Iraqi forces during the first Gulf War. Powell was, and was seen as, a moderate within George W. Bush's administration and this made him some bitter political enemies among senior politicians in the administration.

He may well be remembered for his speech to the UN highlighting the supposed presence of weapons of mass destruction in Iraq. It was that speech, based perhaps on erroneous information and supported by equally inaccurate information from the UK, that set the stage for America's second Gulf War. During the lead-up to the hostilities, Powell was openly opposed to overthrowing Saddam Hussein by force, preferring to continue a containment policy. Powell was also very concerned that the international community should support war with Iraq. More than that, he tried to demand that other nations would back America with armed support. The Bush administration was much more in favour of the more or less unilateral approach, which is what was eventually adopted.

Most observers praise Powell's oratorical skills and he is still in great demand as a speaker.

Yitzhak Rabin

Standing here today, I wish to salute our loved ones – and past foes. I wish to salute all of them."

Nobel Peace Prize acceptance speech, City Hall, Oslo, Norway, Saturday 10 December 1994

Yitzhak Rabin was born on 1 March 1922. He was Israel's fifth prime minister, serving two terms in office, from 1974 to 1977 and again from 1992 until his assassination on 4 November 1995 by a right-wing Israeli radical allegedly opposed to Rabin's signing of the Oslo Accords (the Declaration of Principles).

There were two internationally critical events during Rabin's second term: the Declaration of Principles with the Palestinians and the peace treaty with Jordan. Rabin led all key negotiations with the Palestinians and the Declaration of Principles was eventually signed with the PLO in September 1993. The Peace Treaty with Jordan was signed in October 1994.

Lessons from Yitzhak Rabin

Persevere. We all know that public speaking doesn't always come easily. If necessary, get training or coaching. Yitzhak Rabin did not find public speaking easy and essentially was a socially shy man. His manner of leadership was blunt and he was seemingly unsentimental, a man normally of few words. His speeches were sometimes beautiful to read but they were often, particularly in his early career, poorly delivered by a man who really had to steel himself to get up and speak in public. He improved with time and practice.

Rabin is proof that a polished speaking style is not necessary to be an effective leader. Whether he spoke in Hebrew or English, the measured and sometimes slow pace of his words, his stumbling pronunciation, the flat, dull intonation, his grammar sometimes all over the place, and the fact that he was not at all well read did in fact enhance his public reputation as a practical, straightforward, direct man. Unlike many contemporary politicians, he was by and large trusted by both sides of the political spectrum. He also detested what we now know as spin. And insincerity was met with a coldness that stopped the perpetrator in his or her tracks.

Any occasion, every occasion, demands that you do your very best. Second best doesn't have a place at a lectern. Rabin's Nobel acceptance speech is regarded by many as his finest. It begins slowly and gathers both pace and confidence. The content is impossible to ignore and you know that the speechmaker means every word of his speech. The emotional strength, the slight exposure of hurt, humility and sorrow, of course, shine through. It is a speech made in all modesty and has huge, huge strength for that. It is a remarkable example of understated oratory.

Touch people's hearts and minds. Touching one can't really be done without touching the other. A speech should touch both hearts and minds. There's no shame in this. Any speech has to be understood, has to be respected, has to be remembered, has to be motivational, has to be powerful.

Rabin's speech doesn't hesitate to exploit the audience's emotions. For example, in his description of battle and bravery, he takes the opportunity to recall moving events; most moving is his acknowledgement of the sacrifice of soldiers (from any nation) for their country: "Ladies and gentlemen ... of all the memories I have stored up in my seventy-two years, what I shall remember most, to my last day, are the silences ... That is the moment you grasp that as a result of the decision just made, people might go to their deaths. People from my nation, people from other nations. And they still don't know it ... Which of them is fated to die? ..."

A Legacy

Rabin began to negotiate with the Palestinians on autonomy in Gaza and the establishment of a Palestinian Authority. The negotiations were going well when he was assassinated.

The 1994 award of the Nobel Peace Prize was one of the most controversial of all Nobel Peace Prizes. Rabin shared it with Shimon Peres, his political rival. And he shared it with Yasser Arafat, not the most popular of Peace Prize recipients.

The agreement with Arafat did not bring peace, and few genuinely felt it would. But Rabin, and indeed the political community at large, believed that it was important progress. The world began to believe, not for the first time and most certainly not for the last, that there was a possibility of a true peace between Arabs and Israelis. At the time there was a genuine feeling that Rabin was capable of making such peace reality, maybe not perfect in all its parameters, but nonetheless something solid. Peace was the ambition, he said. Peace was that elusive factor that waits until we get close and then flies away or is destroyed. But it is peace, or attempts to reach peace, that is his legacy.

As he said towards the end of his Nobel Peace Prize acceptance speech: "Standing here today, I wish to salute our loved ones – and past foes. I wish to salute all of them – the fallen of all the countries in all the wars; the members of their families who bear the enduring burden of bereavement; the disabled whose scars will never heal. Tonight, I wish to pay tribute to each and every one of them, for this important prize is theirs."

Rania of Jordan

We live in a world plagued by a poverty of multicultural knowledge, tolerance, and respect ... Companies must play a key role in bridging the East–West divide, in making us better neighbours ... As economies become global, so do our obligations to each other."

Speech at the Skoll World Forum, Oxford, UK, Tuesday 27 March 2007

Rania Al-Yassin was born in Kuwait to Palestinian parents on 31 August 1970. She went to school in Kuwait before studying for a Business

Administration degree at the American University in Cairo, after which she worked at Citibank and Apple Computer in Amman. She married Abdullah bin Al-Hussein, Prince of Jordan, on 10 June 1993 and became Queen of Jordan when her husband became King in 1999.

Corporate responsibility has always been a favourite topic of Queen Rania's. In this 2007 World Forum speech, she called on companies to focus on corporate multicultural responsibility, not least to help with communications and understanding between East and West. This particular speech, like many she makes, balanced a clear and direct style with warmth, humanity and a positive, humanitarian spirit.

Queen Rania sees it as essential that there is better understanding between businesses operating in the Middle East and in, say, the United States. She believes that each can learn from the others, particularly in the field of ethical and moral guidelines, corporate governance standards and community support.

Lessons from Queen Rania

Tap into universal virtues. Queen Rania is often featured for her beauty and celebrity, frequently making the lists in the popular press of the world's most beautiful, most photographed, most influential or most powerful women. Since becoming Queen of Jordan she has skilfully turned this celebrity to her advantage, using her profile to successfully raise awareness and funds for a wide range of causes.

More significantly, there is a simple, optimistic and positive theme that runs through many of her speeches: that the world can be better with greater cooperation, mutual understanding and a desire to change. Her messages come over as relevant and her audiences listen. More to the point, rather than simply listening politely, her audiences, invariably large businesses, offer support or take action.

Queen Rania has campaigned for greater understanding between Muslims and Christians, commenting: "We still prejudge others through labels and not through personal experience and direct contact with them." In her keynote address to the Jeddah Economic Forum in February 2007, she emphasized two priorities. First, the need for Muslims to build a developed and economically secure environment for future generations in the Middle East; second, the need to correct the flawed perceptions that exist in the West of Muslims in general and the region in particular: "As a Muslim, as an Arab, as a mother, and as a member of the global family, I am alarmed at the way in which the Muslim world and our western counterparts are looking at each other with suspicion, fear, prejudice ...then turning away."

Be professional and use the best. Evidence of Queen Rania's professional approach can be seen in the fact that she retained the services of West Wing Writers, a lobbying and public relations firm headed by one of President Bill Clinton's speechwriters.

A Legacy

Queen Rania is a passionate advocate for a wide range of philanthropic organizations and activities. She sees (and others see) her role as raising awareness and funds. She has a prominent family life and has also travelled the world advocating a variety of causes, including education reform and microfinance.

Her messages of change, humanity, mutual understanding and aspiration have reassured people in the early uncertain, turbulent years of the 21st century. She has given free rein to her aspirations and, as a consequence, encouraged others – particularly Arab women – to do the same. That's a strong legacy indeed: "I plan, in the weeks and months ahead, to expand on these ideas – with the aim of championing a culture of trust and respect between Islam and the West. And I do not think I am reaching for the stars ..."

Ronald Reagan

The crew of the space shuttle *Challenger* honored us in the manner in which they lived their lives. We will never forget them, nor the last time we saw them, this morning, as they prepared for their journey and waved goodbye and 'slipped the surly bonds of earth' to 'touch the face of God'."

State of the Union Address replaced by an announcement about the *Challenger* disaster, Washington DC, USA, 5pm EST, Tuesday 28 January 1986

Ronald Wilson Reagan was born on 6 February 1911 and died on 5 June 2004. He was the 40th president of the United States, from 1981 to 1989. The *Challenger* space shuttle disaster occurred on 28 January 1986 when, only a few seconds into its flight, the shuttle exploded over the Atlantic Ocean. All seven crew members died. This was a shocking, low moment for a technologically proud United States.

While a speech has to be delivered in the right way at the right time, great speechwriters are clearly an invaluable asset. Peggy Noonan was a *Wall Street Journal* columnist as well as Reagan's principal speechwriter. This speech, written by Noonan, received huge acclaim from all quarters and reinforced the image of Reagan as a great communicator, a phrase that was often used to describe him.

Lessons from Ronald Reagan

Crises and failures invariably require adaptability and great qualities of leadership. On the night of the disaster, President Reagan had been scheduled to give his annual State of the Union Address. The Address was postponed and, instead, he gave a broadcast on the *Challenger* disaster from the White House. It is a gentle, careful speech and one which echoes how the country felt. It expresses loss and hope: "For the families of the seven: we cannot bear, as you do, the full impact of this tragedy. But we feel the loss, and we're thinking about you so very much. Your loved ones were daring and brave and they had that special grace, that special spirit that says, 'Give me a challenge, and I'll meet it with joy'." The address closed with a beautiful and apposite quotation from the poem "High Flight" by Pilot Officer John Gillespie Magee Jr (killed in action on 11 December 1941) which captured the nation's mood: "We will never forget them, nor the last time we saw them, this morning, as they prepared for their journey and waved goodbye and 'slipped the surly bonds of earth' to 'touch the face of God'."

In difficult situations, you have to read the mood of your audience very well. When expressing hard information about a difficult situation, a speech needs brilliance in its structure, writing, allusion and delivery. It also needs to embrace a wider voice, not just the speaker's, to offer support and empathy. Reagan read the mood of the people well. In this address, he remembered the astronauts and naturally offered support to their families, but in such a way as to widen the voice – fulfilling the wishes of the American people.

With tough or difficult messages, you need to get the audience on your side fast. It was its immediacy and speed that made this address work so well. It instantly recognized that the viewers required comfort and solace. More than that, Reagan saw that people needed help to better understand the tragedy.

With bad or difficult news, very often the worst tactic is to pretend that the "bad things" don't exist. It's a political manoeuvre, but is scorned these days by audiences, particularly given the speed of news promulgation. This is certainly not limited to the world of politics either. Executives hide, or try to camouflage, bad things beneath the detritus of seemingly good policy or rationale. And it's a very frustrating tactic. People aren't stupid. If you are direct, but come up with genuine ideas about the future, then you can win your audience over. You must be seen to be on exactly the same emotional side as those before you. In this speech, Reagan does not necessarily present an argument, but rather offers consolation, solace and, most important of all, an attempt to find meaning in what happened. He prepared the audience for hope without in any way being disrespectful of the families affected by the disaster. Importantly and critically, he built an atmosphere in which everyone could mourn and receive some comfort: "There will be more shuttle flights and more shuttle crews and, yes, more volunteers, more civilians, more teachers in space. Nothing ends here ..."

A Legacy

Several domestic setbacks damaged Reagan's reputation including, for example, poor management of the unions and the mishandling of striking workers. A number of foreign policy forays were also deemed misguided (notably the Iran-Contra affair and the initial repercussions of calling the Soviet Union an "evil empire").

But Reagan is seen by most Americans as a positive leader who managed to get Americans to believe in themselves. He understood the promise of the American Dream and this was a key platform on which he was elected. He inherited a tired and cynical United States that readily took to his optimism, so when he declared that: "everyone can rise as high and as far as his ability will take him", people were more than encouraged. When they saw that he could deliver, they were delighted. Under Reagan's administration more Americans were working than ever before, many new businesses were started up and Wall Street boomed.

At the end of Reagan's administration, not all social ills had been solved or even tackled. However, by persuading Congress to cut taxes and by eliminating unnecessary regulations, he did introduce a period of unprecedented economic growth in the United States.

In 1988 Reagan managed a feat that was often thought impossible: he agreed with Gorbachev to reduce the nuclear stockpiles of each nation. Perhaps this was part of the wind of change to which Reagan had been party. Certainly, this change swept through Eastern Europe and the Soviet Union. Soon after Reagan had left the White House, the Berlin Wall was no more and Gorbachev had dissolved the Soviet Union. It is readily agreed by many that, despite some follies, Reagan improved the American economy, guided American morale upwards and reduced the American people's reliance upon government. It was a situation that was to last long after he had left the White House.

Franklin Delano Roosevelt

The only thing we have to fear is fear itself ... These dark days will be worth all they cost us if they teach us that our true destiny is not to be ministered unto but to minister to ourselves and to our fellow men."

First inaugural address, Washington DC, USA, Sunday 4 March 1933

Franklin Delano Roosevelt was the 32nd president of the United States. Known as FDR, he steered America during some of its darkest, worst times, helping the country to overcome the shock, shame and paralysis of economic depression. This he did primarily via the New Deal policies. He made his leadership count during World War II and, once America joined the allies in fighting Germany and Japan, many saw him as embodying the security and hope for which they yearned. Uniquely, he was elected to the presidency four times. He was born on 30 January 1882 and died on 12 April 1945.

Lessons from Franklin Delano Roosevelt

Show moral courage and immediately set the right tone. There doesn't have to be a war or an emergency for a speaker to show moral bravery. There are small and large situations in all walks of life that require us to step up to the plate and get people to join or support our cause. Roosevelt's speeches were characterized by the need for urgent action and immediate decisions, most of which would have lasting consequences. By the time he came to office in March 1933, the American economy was in tatters. By the time he died, the allies were winning World War II, but the futures of Europe and Asia were still far from certain or secure. However, during his presidency, he not only ensured that the USA resolved some of its greatest challenges, but that it did so in a way that guaranteed its emergence as an economic, cultural, military and political superpower, dominating the rest of the century. This intention, if not the outcome, was evident from his first speech as president – not only because of what he said but of how he said it.

When your message is tough, get to the point. In FDR's first inaugural address, he dispenses with the normal lengthy preamble and gets straight down to business, as if he has been waiting impatiently to do something about the US economy which, by 1933, had already suffered several years of decline and depression. His first words as president were dynamic, direct and vibrantly urgent: "I am certain that my fellow Americans expect that on my induction into the presidency I will address them with a candor and a decision which the present situation of our Nation impels. This is pre-eminently the time to speak the truth, the whole truth, frankly and boldly. Nor need we shrink from honestly facing conditions in our country today."

Connect with your audience. Roosevelt understood that the US presidency is, in relative terms, a weak executive office, constrained by checks and balances (just as America's founding fathers intended). So his powers were relatively limited and relied on the support of others, but expectations were high and circumstances demanded decisive, far-reaching and unprecedented action. The challenge was to reconcile these apparent opposites and Roosevelt understood how this could be accomplished. Political action was essential, but equally important were empathy with and the support of the American people. In the first paragraph of his first speech as president, Roosevelt struck a chord that reassured and encouraged people for the first time during their crisis, with the statement that "The only thing we have to fear is fear itself."

Roosevelt inspired people individually in one-to-one meetings and he could do the same using the mass media. He knew how to speak for different occasions, when to drop his voice or raise it, when to sound like everyone's grandfather and when to sound like a leader, speaking with brio, vim and vigour. During the dark days of the depression, he pioneered the "fireside chat" – the use of radio broadcasts to appeal to the American people, often going over the head of Congress to gain support from the people for his policies. Frances Perkins, his labour secretary, and the first woman ever to attain cabinet rank, was often at the White House when FDR broadcast. She has said that he was oblivious to the twenty or thirty aides in the room, his mind clearly focused on the people listening at the other end. "As he talked his head would nod and his hands would move in simple, natural, comfortable gestures," she wrote. "His face would light up and smile as though he were actually sitting on the front porch or in the parlour with them. People felt this and it bound them to him in affection."

Express shared feelings, sum up the situation and describe your attitude. This is the key to communicating and exercising strong leadership. FDR was a good-humoured family man, experienced, intelligent, personable and self-confident. He possessed great determination, for example, meeting the challenge of crippling polio and ensuring that this weakness should not concern the American people.·

Throughout his presidency, Roosevelt was particularly effective at capturing the public mood, channelling people's thoughts and feelings and expressing the same on behalf of everyone. This is a great oratory skill. For example, in his first inaugural he acknowledged that "this nation asks for action and action now". He then followed through with bold policies. Similarly, addressing a joint session of Congress in the aftermath of the Japanese attack on Pearl Harbor, he memorably described 7 December 1941 as "a date which will live in infamy". He went on to explain that: "I believe that I interpret the will of the Congress and of the American people when I assert that we will not only defend ourselves to the uttermost, but will make it very certain that this form of treachery shall never again endanger us."

A Legacy

Roosevelt's connection with the American people was a strong bond established through his ability to communicate. His language was soothing but he also said precisely what he meant, his message direct and insistent. He says towards the end of his inaugural: "I shall ask the Congress for the one remaining instrument to meet the crisis – broad executive power to wage a war against the emergency, as great as the power that would be given to me if we were in fact invaded by a foreign foe. For the trust reposed in me I will return the courage and the devotion that befit the time. I can do no less."

FDR's political legacy was immense: nothing less than the reinvention of the highest office and the emergence of America as the dominant western power of the twentieth century. He also inspired millions of people in many ways, not least by simply getting them to believe in themselves. Much of this was accomplished through his bold leadership, pragmatic flexibility and decisiveness; his words were in the service of these valuable qualities.

Theodore Roosevelt

> It is not the critic who counts … The credit belongs to the man who is actually in the arena, whose face is marred by dust and sweat and blood; who strives valiantly; who errs, who comes short again and again, because there is no effort without error and shortcoming."

"The Man in the Arena" speech, Sorbonne University, Paris, France, 23 April 1910

Theodore (Teddy) Roosevelt was born on 27 October 1858 and died on 6 January 1919. He was the 26th president of the United States (1901–1909) and led the Republican and Progressive Parties. He is famous for his energy and wide range of interests (including nature, exploration, geography, history and the military) – and an equally wide range of achievements.

Lessons from Theodore Roosevelt

Use your experience. Many speakers don't, which is odd, since their experience is probably the reason why they're making a speech in the first place. Their audience will want to know what they've achieved or how it has a bearing on what they are talking about.

When he spoke, Roosevelt used his depth of experience to portray a man who understood his audience and who could speak knowledgeably about what he felt was most important to America and the ways of the world. In this 1910 "Man in the Arena" speech, Roosevelt used short bursts of phraseology making mention of his own search for achievement: "It is not the critic who counts; not the man who points out how the strong man stumbles, or where the doer of deeds could have done them better. The credit belongs to the man who is actually in the arena, whose face is marred by dust and sweat and blood; who strives valiantly; who errs, who comes short again and again, because there is no effort without error and shortcoming; but who does actually strive to do the deeds; who knows great enthusiasms, the great devotions; who spends himself in a worthy cause; who at the best knows in the end the triumph of high achievement, and who at the worst, if he fails, at least fails while daring greatly, so that his place shall never be with those cold and timid souls who neither know victory nor defeat."

The best speechmakers have enormous energy, physically and mentally. Roosevelt could connect closely with a wide strata of society. He understood the needs of specific American communities and was adept at tailoring his speeches to suit each audience. His enthusiasm and energy led one exasperated ambassador to comment: "You must always remember that the president is about six."

Channel your energy. While Roosevelt had many interests, he also had the ability to balance a broad view with detail. A big picture invariably requires filling to make the picture come alive and he was adept at doing just that. His speeches showed a depth of understanding and expertise that eluded many of his colleagues and predecessors; it's something that is generally only achieved today with a large team of advisors. Roosevelt wanted to make America modern and that required a man both of action and of intellect.

A Legacy

Theodore Roosevelt was the first president to seriously think about saving some of the beauty of the United States for future generations. More than 200 million acres of land were conserved and the effects of that and other similar initiatives, such as designated national forests, bird reservations, parks, monuments and game reserves, lasted long beyond his tenure.

Roosevelt believed in an open government and each day the press were invited into the White House to take photographs and ask questions of the administration's leadership. This was the forerunner of what occurs now under the banner of presidential press briefings.

In foreign affairs, Roosevelt was keen to push back American isolationism and embrace a leading role in the world community. He was aware that the country needed to bolster its military muscle in possible anticipation of international conflict. He built up the armed forces, in particular the US Navy, as a hugely powerful entity establishing America as a major world power. He initiated work on the Panama Canal and negotiated the end to the Russo-Japanese War, for which he won the Nobel Peace Prize.

Domestically, Roosevelt improved American commerce and made improvements in social justice and law and order. He offered Americans a "Square Deal" and that helped millions throughout the country to earn a fair income. And he markedly reduced the national debt.

It was also on Roosevelt's watch that America began to realize that oratory and mass communication would be of considerably greater importance in the future than they had ever been in the past.

Oskar Schindler

Show yourselves to be worthy of the sacrifice of millions from your ranks, avoid every act of revenge ...”

Farewell address to Jewish factory workers, Brnënec, Nazi-occupied Czechoslovakia, Monday 7 May 1945

Oskar Schindler was born on 28 April 1908 and died on 9 October 1974. A Sudeten German industrialist credited with saving 1,200 Jews during the Holocaust, Schindler was an unlikely hero. He was regarded as vain and selfish, keen to make money and to do well for himself alone. However, he became aware, as did others, that the horrendous treatment of Jews by the Nazis was something about which he couldn't just do nothing. However, he was one of the very few who actually took action. Schindler contrived to enable Jews, who would otherwise go to the extermination camps, to work in his enamelware and ammunitions factories located in Poland and the Czech Republic. Very often these “workers” didn't actually do any work, but they were safe under Schindler's jurisdiction.

Towards the end of the war, as the Russians drew nearer to Auschwitz and the other eastern concentration camps, the SS began evacuating the remaining prisoners. Schindler persuaded the SS officials to allow him to move his Jewish workers to Brnënec (Brünnlitz) in Nazi-occupied Czechoslovakia, sparing them from certain extermination.

Schindler, once wealthy, ended the war with very little; bribes and money to care for his charges had eaten into his previous fortune, leaving him with almost nothing.

Lessons from Oskar Schindler

Emotion can occur easily, spontaneously. For Oskar Schindler, saying less about a situation revealed much more about how he felt and how he wanted his audience to feel. At the war's end, Schindler gathered everyone together in order to say farewell. It was a moving and memorable speech. He spelt out what was happening in the immediate world to presumably confused and exhausted people: “I would like to turn to all of you, those of you who have been with me throughout these many difficult years and have feared that this day would never come, to all of you, who in a few days will return to your destroyed, plundered homesteads, searching for survivors from your families – I appeal to all of you to strictly maintain order and discipline. This will minimize panic, the consequences of which would be unpredictable ...”

If the messages are stark, the language can be stark. At the very time when those in his audience might be seeking revenge and retribution, the opportunity is quashed with humility and a plea: "I will continue to work around the clock to do everything for you that is within my power. Do not go into the houses around here to forage and steal. Show yourselves to be worthy of the sacrifice of millions from your ranks, avoid every act of revenge and terrorism …"

The sentences are often long, which gives an idea of the pace and power with which the speech was delivered. Schindler told his workers where he kept his guns and ammunition and gave them keys to a nearby factory, where they could find material to make clothing. "I must leave now," he said simply at the speech's end. "Auf Wiedersehen."

On his way out, he was hastily presented with a gold ring. The brief acknowledgement was embarrassing for him and those who stood awkwardly by his side and in front of him. His "workers" stared at this man who had saved their lives. Inside the ring were the words "He who saves one life – it is as if he has saved the entire world." Apparently, according to eye witnesses, Schindler turned away and wept, as did many in the audience, which included a number of German soldiers.

A Legacy

Virtually destitute, Schindler did not prosper in post-war Germany. In fact, he was reduced to receiving assistance from Jewish organizations. Eventually, he emigrated to Argentina in 1948, where his businesses did not thrive at all and he went bankrupt. He returned to Germany in 1958 and once more his business ventures were unsuccessful. In 1968 he began receiving a small pension from the West German government.

He was divorced late in life from his long-suffering wife, Emilie, and, surprisingly and shockingly, died alone and destitute in Hildesheim, Germany. He is buried at the Catholic cemetery at Mount Zion in Jerusalem. On his grave, the German inscription reads: "The Unforgettable Lifesaver of 1,200 Persecuted Jews".

What Schindler did was to establish that good could be done in times of terror and horrendous difficulty. He wasn't a particularly religious man and neither was he a particularly "good" man, but his legacy is a superb example of "doing something".

What brought Schindler, and what he did, to the world's attention was the novel *Schindler's Ark* by Thomas Keneally and, subsequently, the Steven Spielberg film of 1993. The film, which was a box office success and which won seven Academy Awards, brought to the world's attention this supreme act of kindness and humanity.

An important legacy of Schindler is the organization established by Spielberg before, as he said, it was too late – the Survivors of the Shoah Visual History Foundation. This is a non-profit body, the aim of which is to provide an archive for the filmed testimony of as many survivors of the Holocaust as possible – testimony from people such as those that Schindler saved.

Gerhard Schröder

The past cannot be 'overcome'. It is the past. But its traces and, above all, the lessons to be learned from it extend to the present."

"I Express My Shame" speech, Berlin, Germany, Tuesday 25 January 2005

Gerhard Fritz Kurt Schröder was born on 7 April 1944. He is a lawyer and was Chancellor of Germany from 1998 to 2005. His government was a coalition between the German Social Democratic Party (SPD) and the Greens, a party that has a large following in Germany.

Following the 2005 federal election, and after many weeks of clinging on to almost non-existent power where he was angling for joint leadership, he stood down as Chancellor in favour of rival Angela Merkel of the Christian Democratic Union.

On 1 August 2004, the 60th anniversary of the 1944 Warsaw Uprising, Schröder apologized publicly to Poland for "the immeasurable suffering" of its people during the specific conflict in question and World War II in general. He was the first senior German politician to be invited to an anniversary of the uprising.

In the "I Express My Shame" speech, Schröder makes the point, obviously and perhaps too easily, that, "Chelmno, Belzec, Sobibor, Treblinka, Maidanek and Auschwitz-Birkenau are names that will for ever be associated with the history of the victims as well as with German and European history". That could be a disposable, easy-to-say line, but it isn't. Schröder goes on to be specific and, in a sense, the address is designed, without cynicism, to be therapeutic – for him, for his local listeners, and for the wider audience.

Lessons from Gerhard Schröder

Saying sorry in any speech is always difficult and for this reason it can be extraordinarily powerful. Many politicians and business executives don't use the "s" word – ever. It is often believed, certainly in political circles, that an admission of guilt or the expression of apology must lead to resignation. Of course, it's easier to apologize when the fault is unequivocally not yours, but that of your predecessors. In this speech, Schröder expressed Germany's shame for the Holocaust, at exactly the time that Europe began the commemoration of the 60th anniversary of the liberation of the Auschwitz extermination camp. The ceremony was held in a Berlin theatre, not at Auschwitz, and was attended by survivors, survivors' families, politicians, ministers of many faiths and Jewish leaders. Standing before a screen showing images of Auschwitz, Schröder's speech contained forthright sentiments, possibly the most forthright concerning the Holocaust ever heard by a leader of post-World War II Germany. The apology came over as strong, determined and genuine. It was, more than anything, unconditional.

Be direct. The speech is primarily directed at those who had and have the most to remember, the survivors of Auschwitz. It's a speech delivered with great care and it contains "shock and awe" moments that make the listener hold his or her breath. Note Schröder's use of lists, the "power of three", to build a case. The speech opens: "Survivors of Auschwitz-Birkenau … It would be fitting for us Germans to remain silent in the face of what was the greatest crime in the history of mankind. Words by government leaders are inadequate when confronted with the absolute immorality and senselessness of the murder of millions. What is left is the testimony of those few who survived and their descendants. What is left are the remains of the sites of these murders and the historical record. What is left also is the certainty that these extermination camps were a manifestation of absolute evil." This focus and deliberation would have been painful to hear, let alone deliver: "Above all, it needs to be said that the Nazi ideology was something that people supported at the time and that they took part in putting into effect."

Sometimes the topic of a speech makes it hard to deliver, as a whole, or in parts. Even very experienced speechmakers struggle with emotion and there's absolutely no shame in that. If a moment becomes too big to manage, then pause, breathe and continue. Most audiences will work with you. Schröder began slowly and a little hesitantly, but he grew into the speech and was clearly moved by what he said (as were many of his listeners), delivering his words with dignity and power. In closing Berlin's commemoration ceremony, the Chancellor urged all Germans to fight anti-semitism, emphasizing that Germany's responsibility for World War II, must not, would not, be forgotten.

A Legacy

In Schröder's speech he says: "The past cannot be 'overcome'. It is the past. But its traces and, above all, the lessons to be learned from it extend to the present …" The chairman of the World Jewish Congress, Israel Singer, used the same occasion to assert that, in Europe, the lessons of the past were being forgotten, if indeed they had ever been learned. Said Schröder: "It is true, the temptation to forget is very great. But we will not succumb to this temptation …" He said that the memory of the Nazi genocide "is part of our national identity" and that "Remembering the era of National Socialism and its crimes is a moral obligation – we owe that not only to the victims, the survivors and the relatives, but to ourselves."

At the time of the speech there had been an upsurge in anti-semitism in Europe, not least in Germany, with synagogues and cemeteries vandalized and the election of far-right neo-Nazi parties into German regional assemblies. Schröder promised that German leaders would protect the country's growing Jewish community "with the power of the state against the anti-semitism of the incorrigible".

Lee Scott

We are working with our suppliers to make our products more sustainable. But we are also helping them become more sustainable businesses in their own right."

"Sustainability 360: Doing Good, Better, Together" lecture to the Prince of Wales Business and Environment Programme, London, UK, Thursday 1 February 2007

H. Lee Scott Jr was the president and chief executive officer of Wal-Mart from January 2000 to January 2009. He was included in *Time* magazine's lists of the 100 most influential people of 2004 and 2005.

Scott, born in 1949 in Missouri, USA, joined Wal-Mart in 1979. He is known to have said that no one can run the world's largest company – it has to be led. To him that meant being a combination of talk-show host and taskmaster, speaking directly (and often) to staff, suppliers and stockholders. Face-to-face communication and "walking the walk" were both imperative in his view of business leadership.

Wal-Mart is a very big business, by anyone's reckoning. The business is still America's largest company – and also the nation's biggest energy consumer. However, latterly it has faced criticism for its labour policies and for its attitude towards sustainability and the environment. Despite these criticisms, and some have been deep, highly publicized and fierce, Wal-Mart has continued to receive the market's ringing endorsement, with the firm now the world's largest retailer based on revenue. Under Scott's care, Wal-Mart has redefined its social and corporate responsibilities – not just in America but worldwide. This speech is part of that drive: "We believe working families should *not* have to choose between a product they can afford and a sustainable product. We want our merchandise to be both affordable *and* sustainable … It's not just about reducing our environmental footprint … It's about stepping out – even without all the answers – and aggressively promoting sustainability among all the stakeholders of our company. We are calling this approach Sustainability 360."

Lessons from Lee Scott

Charm and genuine warmth work. When you address an audience, you should realize of course that people are usually there for you. Sometimes there are obligations and pressures whereby people have no choice but to be in attendance, but usually they are there because they want to hear what *you* have to say. Lee Scott knows this very well and honours his audiences much as does John Chambers of Cisco Systems and a number of other great orators.

Scott presents his points in a disarmingly easy and comfortable way. It's not a lazy style (which can be enormously irritating) but one which helps listeners feel engaged; they know implicitly that he is addressing his views to them as if for the first time. He is refreshing and his good humour and genuine charm are appealing; both are clearly conveyed. You can see this just by reading many of his speeches; it's all the more evident when he is actually performing them.

Use numbers wisely – to illustrate, inform or focus an argument. Keep the content of a speech as simple as possible. Many speeches are just too complicated, too long, too dull, too selfishly delivered, too much off the point, too slow, too fast, with too little verve or vigour and too limited in their sense or ambition. The use of numbers doesn't always sit well in any speech; too many figures are forgettable and tend to counter any added value they may give. PowerPoint doesn't have to be filled with every imaginable colour and with text in a font that cannot be read by anyone sitting beyond the front row. In the "Sustainability 360: Doing Good, Better, Together" speech, Scott uses figures very well to illustrate something that's happening on a huge scale. That makes the argument interesting and it gives the content relevance.

A Legacy

This speech reaffirmed the significance of sustainability issues in business. It was felt that Wal-Mart hadn't done enough to join in the global movement to limit waste and to recycle. Wal-Mart's activity and promise of sustainability in action caused wide ripples because, were the promises translated to reality, it would affect the whole retail world. And the retail world would have to follow suit – not least in the realm of the supply chain.

The company's attitude to, and communications on, sustainability have greatly improved. The desire to change operations and, at the same time, to make money seems to have met with approval on both sides of the cashdesk. In a very short time, the Wal-Mart programme of sustainability has saved huge sums of money and even larger amounts of waste. Waste policies have changed and recyclable materials have improved markedly in the majority of product lines, particularly packaging and storage.

Scott's speech highlighted the need for businesses to listen to social concerns – and then act properly and fast. He concluded: "We want to do good , better, together ... I believe we will make sustainability ... sustainable."

Ricardo Semler

Every one of us can send emails on Sunday night, but how many of us know how to go to the movies on Monday afternoon? If you don't know how to go to the movies from 2 to 4, you're in trouble because you've just taken on something that unbalances life, but you haven't rebalanced it with something else."

"Leading by Omission" speech, MIT Sloan School of Management, Cambridge, Massachusetts, USA, Thursday 22 September 2005

Ricardo Semler was born in 1959 in São Paulo, Brazil. As CEO and majority owner of Semco SA, an innovative Brazilian engineering company known for its radical form of industrial democracy, Semler is famous for driving company value and creating a superb working environment. The company is involved in such diverse ventures as the manufacture of mixing equipment, cooling towers, property management in Latin America and environmental consulting. Semler has managed huge revenue increases under his tenure and his innovative business management policies have attracted worldwide interest.

He has written two books on the transformation of Semco and workplace re-engineering: *Maverick: The Success Story Behind the World's Most Unusual Workplace*, an international bestseller published in 1993, and *The Seven-Day Weekend: Changing the Way Work Works*, published in 2003.

Lessons from Ricardo Semler

Give people an insight into something new – explain how things can be better. Semler asked in the "Leading by Omission" speech: "Why are automobiles made essentially the same way today as they were in Ford's first assembly line 100 years ago?" His answer is straightforward and intriguing: "The problem is that there's something fundamental about organizations and ... leadership that makes it almost impossible for people inside a business to change their own industry."

Semler's style is engaging. He manages to blend an informal style with an air of authority and insight. Many of his speeches are filled with anecdotes and stories, each proving or underlining a point. His thinking is often leftfield and audiences find that they are refreshed by new perspectives on an old problem. His stories are often personal and humorous as well as highly relevant and thought-provoking: "We'll send our sons anywhere in the world to die for democracy, but don't seem to apply the concept to the workplace. This is a tragic error because people on their own developing their own solutions will develop something different ..."

Move around. Semler plans at length what he's going to say, thinks carefully about his audience and asks detailed questions of those organizing the event at which he's speaking. He does this so that he needs no notes and so that he can move around the stage and the room. This not only imbues his speeches with energy, it also enables Semler to focus and heighten the audience's attention when he pauses or stops.

If you do intend to move around during a speech, don't wander aimlessly. An actor wouldn't. Have a place to go and go there for a reason. Make the moves intentional so that people in the room can understand what the move is for.

Be credible. It helps that Semler's business, Semco, is highly successful. And intriguing. It follows unusual business rules. This gives confidence to the audience and credibility to Semler. Simply put, people listen harder and think more when the person giving the advice is already proven to be successful and is, let's be honest, interesting. A speech has to be interesting.

A Legacy

Semler's approach to management is known to be based on empowerment. He fervently believes in trust and trusting people to do the right thing for the business in which they work. Freedom to act and to make mistakes is important to his belief in a democratic approach to management. It's more than that though. It's all about challenging conventional notions of how to manage organizations and approach the world of work. Semler doesn't rely on, or hide behind, jargon and business school theses. He is well educated (Harvard University) but prefers to talk in accessible language, with easily understandable examples. His appeal is that he makes topics relevant and their explanation clear.

Semler shifted workplace democracy to a different level when he took over his father's manufacturing business in the 1980s. It is well documented that he disposed of preconceived management treatises and it is this unorthodox management style that has made the world of management look hard at Semco and how it achieves what it does.

Semco's employees establish their own levels of pay and hours of working. Supervisors are reviewed by their direct reports. There are no formal plans, no organization charts, no written rules, no vision statements, no company "shalts and shalt nots", no ten "reasons to be cheerful" pinned on walls. Staff can take naps when they choose. They elect the company's management team. They also agree or disagree whether to buy a new business or close another.

The model isn't everyone's favoured approach but it has given management techniques a now well-known shot in the arm. In *The Seven-Day Weekend*, Semler says: "Semco is bucking not only the traditional business model, we're resisting a code of behavior at the very core of Western culture. No wonder our ideals are hard for outsiders and other companies to embrace."

Margaret Chase Smith

I don't want to see the Republican Party ride to political victory on the Four Horsemen of Calumny – Fear, Ignorance, Bigotry and Smear ..."

"Declaration of Conscience" address, The Senate, Washington DC, USA, Thursday 1 June 1950

Margaret Chase Smith (born 14 December 1897; died 29 May 1995) was a Republican senator and the first woman to be elected to both the US House and the Senate. She was also the first woman to have her name put forward for the presidency at a major party's convention (in 1964 at the Republican convention, where the nomination was won by Barry Goldwater). When she left office, Margaret Chase Smith had the record as the then longest-serving female senator in United States history.

In the period after World War II and, in particular in the late 1940s, McCarthyism came to the fore. Many thousands of Americans were accused of being Russian spies, Russian supporters, or fascists, after which they would become the subject of aggressive and often devious, certainly unpleasant, investigations. In the process people lost jobs, careers and reputations were ruined and families lost friends and accommodation.

Some, including Smith, became sickened by the ruination of many a suspect's livelihood and sometimes life. Although many in the country supported McCarthy, others became disillusioned with the deeply abhorrent witch-hunt.

In a clear attack upon McCarthyism (and McCarthy himself), Smith made her "Declaration of Conscience" speech in the Senate, calling for an end to "character assassinations". She was appalled that the country

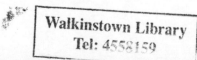

was missing "some of the basic principles of Americanism: The right to criticize; the right to hold unpopular beliefs; the right to protest; the right of independent thought". She said that "freedom of speech is not what it used to be in America", and she poured scorn upon "cancerous tentacles of 'know nothing, suspect everything' attitudes".

Lessons from Margaret Chase Smith

Beautiful language and excellent construction leads any argument. Smith introduced her topic: "I speak as briefly as possible because the issue is too great to be obscured by eloquence. I speak simply and briefly in the hope that my words will be taken to heart. I speak as a Republican. I speak as a woman. I speak as a United States senator. I speak as an American ..." The phraseology is simple and sets a tone of thinly veiled anger and frustration. There is clearly a bombshell coming. Again, the repetition builds the tension, builds a case, builds the drama.

Recognize your audience's priorities. Smith wasn't sure how her speech would be received or who would support it. On 9 February 1950, Senator McCarthy had made his unpleasant "Speech at Wheeling", which attacked President Truman's foreign policy agenda by stating that the State Department and its secretary, Dean Acheson, harboured "traitorous" communists. There is some dispute about the number of communists McCarthy claimed were being "harboured". Some said over two hundred, although McCarthy revised that figure to around fifty. The list was never made public and few believed it existed or could be verified. However, he caused damage and spread poison.

Smith made the "Declaration of Conscience" speech a few months later, in June. In it she insisted that the US Senate should re-examine, as a matter of absolute priority, the methods of McCarthy's House Un-American Activities Committee (HUAC) and, without naming him, the man himself.

Her point was that xenophobia had no place in modern America and it needed to stop before freedoms were totally lost. She declared that there were those with power who were ignoring the American people's basic rights: "The exercise of these rights should not cost one single American citizen his reputation or his right to a livelihood, nor should he be in danger of losing his reputation or livelihood merely because he happens to know someone who holds unpopular beliefs ..."

Understand that your speech is a performance and match your style with your speech's content and context. Margaret Chase Smith's speech was credible and persuasive. She said aloud what many now thought. She made plain that it was a travesty that those who voiced their beliefs risked being labelled traitor, spy, fascist.

McCarthy sat two rows behind her in the Senate. Smith began her short address by clearly decrying the fact that this very chamber was becoming: "a forum of hate and character assassination". She demanded a return to "the right to independent thought" and a revised Republican Party that could truly be "the champion of unity and prudence". This was powerful, carefully prepared rhetoric. Her voice was not particularly loud, but she projected well and her determination commanded enormous respect.

At the end of her short speech, she and others around her in the chamber expected that McCarthy would offer a reply and angrily denounce everything that Smith had said. Instead, and surprisingly, he left the building without saying anything, at least publicly. A few of Smith's colleagues offered brief support for what she had said, but the chamber remained quiet, such was the genuine fear of getting on the wrong side of Senator McCarthy.

Shortly afterwards, the media endorsed Smith's courageous words. It has to be remembered that McCarthy had built a web of committees and spies who could denounce anyone with ease, politicians included, so to come out against him took courage.

A Legacy

Newspaper editors and a growing section of the population admired Smith's bravery in standing up to home-grown tyranny and an atmosphere of hate and fear. President Truman was very impressed. "Mrs Smith," he allegedly told her, "your 'Declaration of Conscience' was one of the finest things that has happened here in Washington in all my years in the Senate and the White House."

McCarthy and his followers tried to discredit Smith, but in 1954 he was censured and his reputation suffered, although he remained a politician until his death in 1957. There ended what she had denounced in her speech as an attempt to ride "the Four Horsemen of Calumny – Fear, Ignorance, Bigotry and Smear".

For many years afterwards, the conclusion to her speech was remembered and frequently repeated in newspapers: "As an American, I want to see our nation recapture the strength and unity it once had when we fought the enemy instead of ourselves ..."

Socrates

The hour of departure has arrived and we go our ways. I go to die
– and you to live. Which is better, God only knows."

Trial defence speech, *Apologia* (*The Apology of Socrates*) by Plato, Athens, Greece,
399 BC

Socrates (born in approximately 469 BC) was a Greek philosopher and
is credited as one of the founders of western philosophy – surprising,
perhaps, given that he left no written records. He is an enigmatic figure
known only through other people's accounts of him, mostly those of Plato
(Socrates's pupil). It is through Plato's writing that we have such a strong
impression of the man.

Socrates was born in Athens and fought in the Peloponnesian War
with Sparta, but in later years became a believer in the power of peace,
non-violence, philosophy and argument. It is said that he spent his latter
years principally in Athens's public places, engaging his fellow citizens in
philosophical discussions and persuading them to consider self-analysis.
It's this self-analysis and dissection of a problem that became the central
theme of much of Socrates's thinking and teaching.

The term Socratic Questioning is used to describe a form of learning and discussion where a teacher doesn't give out information directly
but instead asks a series of questions. The student answers the questions
through deeper questioning and an awareness of the limits to his or her
knowledge.

At the age of 70 Socrates was charged with heresy against Athens and
the corruption of local youth. The case was possibly as a result of jealousies and the fact that he was influential and regarded as an intellectual
troublemaker. After the trial, when the prosecution was held as successful, he was expected to exile himself with the blessing of those who had
convicted him. However, in about 399 BC, to the great surprise of Athens
at large and particularly of his accusers, he chose instead suicide (through
a draught of hemlock) and martyrdom.

The Apology of Socrates is Plato's version of the speech given by Socrates
as he defended himself against the charges of being a man who, according
to his accusers: "corrupted the young, refused to worship the gods and
created new deities". "Apology" here is used in its early meaning (apologia)
– a defence against an accusation about a personal cause or belief.

Lessons from Socrates

Insist on the truth. Socrates asks his jury to judge him not by his oratorical skills, but only by the truth. He insists that he will not cloud the jury's judgement. Truth is, says Socrates, what counts. He commits to speaking directly and in ordinary colloquial language. Perhaps he's being ironic because, despite these protestations, the orator is superbly eloquent. Yet he is not sufficiently persuasive. Even so, the argument for its own sake is wonderful to read, its language ebbing and flowing, its prose a delight.

Physical disadvantages won't keep a great speechmaker down. Socrates was not good-looking. According to statues, he was overweight and had a high forehead, a large bulbous head, a snub nose, staring, bulging eyes, fleshy lips. Yet Plato is insistent that his looks took nothing away from his charm or ability to hold a crowd mesmerized by his oratory.

Push the understanding of a topic to its absolute limits. Socrates was aware that man's knowledge was limited and therefore there was a corresponding limit to conclusive argument. It frustrated him enormously: "If you had waited a little while, your desire would have been fulfilled in the course of nature ... I am speaking now only to those of you who have condemned me to death. And I have another thing to say to them. You think that I was convicted through deficiency of words – I mean, that if I had thought fit to leave nothing undone, nothing unsaid, I might have gained an acquittal. Not so; the deficiency which led to my conviction was not of words – certainly not. But I had not the boldness or impudence or inclination to address you as you would have liked me to address you, weeping and wailing and lamenting and saying and doing many things which you have been accustomed to hear from others and which, as I say, are unworthy of me."

Speech endings should not be long or painfully drawn out. Speeches should close without excessive excuses or a craving for forgiveness, pity, absolution or other devious method of gaining applause. Socrates ends *The Apology* with a famous close: "Now if you suppose that there is no consciousness, but a sleep like the sleep of him who is undisturbed even by the sight of dreams, death will be an unspeakable gain ... Now if death is like this, I say that to die is to gain; for eternity is then only a single night. But if death is the journey to another place, and there, as men say, all the dead are, what good, O my friends and judges, can be greater than this? If indeed when the pilgrim arrives in the world below, he is delivered from the professors of justice in this world and finds the true judges who are said to give judgment there … What would not a man give if he might converse with Orpheus and Musaeus and Hesiod and Homer? … The hour of departure has arrived and we go our ways. I go to die – and you to live. Which is better, God only knows."

A Legacy

In an October 2001 *Newsweek* article Steve Jobs said: "I would trade all of my technology for an afternoon with Socrates."

Socrates's influence throughout history, on education, philosophy and thought, has been embracing and vast. His star pupil, Plato, founded the Academy in 385 BC, a school that initially had no particular doctrine to teach. Plato posed problems to be studied and solved by other philosophers. Plato's own protégé, Aristotle, became tutor to Alexander the Great and in 335 BC Aristotle established his own school – the Lyceum. These developments would not have occurred without Socrates.

The Socratic method of discussion, questioning and answering is used even now to examine complicated topics in order to expose the issues in the subject and the speaker. It is used as a form of therapy and as a way of debating detailed legal, medical and philosophical issues. Most modern aspects of argument and debate, where balance and truth are drivers, are a direct result of Socrates's approach and thinking.

Ted Sorensen

We shall listen, not lecture; learn, not threaten … In the final analysis, our nation cannot be secure around the world unless our citizens are secure at home."

"The New Vision", 2008 Democratic Party Presidential Nominee Acceptance Address, speech prepared for imaginary delivery, Denver, Colorado, USA, 28 August 2008

Theodore Chaikin (Ted) Sorensen (born 8 May 1928) is a retired lawyer and writer. He is best known as President John F. Kennedy's special counsel, advisor and brilliant speechwriter. Kennedy once called Sorensen his "intellectual blood bank".

President Kennedy's inaugural address, written by Sorensen, demanded that all Americans: "Ask not what your country can do for you; ask what you can do for your country." This call to action is the phrase still most closely associated with the Kennedy administration.

Lessons from Ted Sorensen

Great writing takes time, but it matters. It matters very much. When we hear a great speech, great writing just hits us between the eyes. *Washington Monthly* magazine invited Sorensen to write the speech he would most want the next Democratic nominee to give at the party convention in Denver in August 2008. He was requested that he do this with no candidate in mind and that he "give no consideration to expediency or tactics" – in other words that he write what he wanted to write. A free hand. The address reads as beautifully as it would be heard were it to have been spoken by a politician with oratorical skills like, say, Obama.

Simplicity and memorable phrases work. This "can do, will do" speech voices the concern that the current generation of Americans might leave to the country's children a nation in a considerably poorer condition than it was received. The speech is very powerful, emotional and memorable – the usual ingredients. Points are repeated as a way of reinforcing a sense of possibilities. The reader, the audience, is engaged and stays locked in. Sorensen knows so very well when to illicit pride and emotion. He knows how to involve and to engage. He knows how to interest. His logic of argument turns and twists, aims and fires. Brilliant, brilliant.

Make your beginning slightly different. Get people listening from the outset. Engage immediately. This is so very important. Stop the Coca-Cola can being opened. Stop the popcorn being eaten. Stop the conversations between one executive and his/her neighbour. Stop the shout across the room. Demand attention. Demand a hearing.

How you start and finish a speech is just as important as the sandwich filling: "It has been a long campaign – too long, too expensive, with too much media attention on matters irrelevant to our nation's future. I salute each of my worthy opponents for conducting a clean fifty-state campaign." And Sorensen continues by setting out goals, but with a sentence structure that is easy on the ear. We're drawn towards the notion: "In this campaign, I will make no promises I cannot fulfil, pledge no spending we cannot afford, offer no posts to cronies you cannot trust and propose no foreign commitment we should not keep … Nor will I shrink from calling myself a liberal, in the same sense that Franklin and Theodore Roosevelt, the Kennedys and Harry Truman were liberals – liberals who proved that government is not a necessary evil, but rather the best means of creating a healthier, more educated and more prosperous America."

Great rhetoric, brilliant writing, is invaluable in keynote speeches. It's useful to employ the services of someone who writes great speeches. Why not? There's no shame in having a speechwriter. It's a skilled job and not everyone is good at it. You may or may not be. Even if you are, employ someone who can make what you write better.

Sorensen has always stressed the importance of having an idealist as president. He argues that this makes it easy to write the right material for the right speech at the right time. You know when you're hearing great writing and great argument. Delivery is key, but delivery without structure or content is light and sometimes counts for nought. Even at the close of this speech (when many speeches run out of steam), the power holds absolutely firm. The whole is wonderfully expressed; there is no dip whatsoever. It's riveting from start to finish: "I'm told that John F. Kennedy was fond of quoting Archimedes, who explained the principle of the lever by declaring: 'Give me a place to stand, and I can move the world.' My fellow Americans – here I stand. Come join me and together we will move the world ..."

A Legacy

After Kennedy's assassination in 1963 Ted Sorensen helped President Lyndon B. Johnson for several months. He wrote LBJ's first speech to Congress in addition to his first State of the Union address. Sorensen also wrote *Kennedy*, a bestselling biography published in 1965. Speechwriting figured prominently in Kennedy's success. What he said he was going to do, rather than what he had done, became an important product of Kennedy's administration. Some say that he might have delivered more of the promises, but he certainly helped his audiences to understand the issues of the day, made them proud to be American and began to explain the nation's role in the world. More than that, he explained the country's expectations of the individual. Sorensen celebrated the art of rhetoric and oratory.

Charles, Earl Spencer

Someone with a natural nobility who was classless and who proved … that she needed no royal title to continue to generate her brand of magic …"

Funeral eulogy to Diana, Princess of Wales, Westminster Abbey, London, UK, Saturday 6 September 1997

Charles Edward Maurice Spencer, 9th Earl Spencer, was born on 20 May 1964 and is one of Queen Elizabeth II's godchildren. He was also the brother of Diana, Princess of Wales and he became internationally known for the eulogy he delivered at his sister's funeral.

Lessons from Charles Spencer

First, capture the mood of the occasion. A eulogy is a speech or piece of writing usually in praise of someone. Charles Spencer's eulogy for his sister was powerful and moving; it successfully captured the range and depth of public emotions at the time, which ran incredibly high. It was certainly not the kind of speech expected by either the royal family or the media. However, rather than express a few forgettable phrases, Spencer struck out hard at a fair few people who he thought had treated his sister unfairly. In this number he included Prince Charles. The world adored Diana and felt angry at the way it was alleged that she had been treated by Charles and other members of the royal family.

The words of this speech are often simple and in their simplicity gain strength: "All over the world she was a symbol of selfless humanity. All over the world, a standard-bearer for the rights of the truly downtrodden, a very British girl who transcended nationality."

Surprise your audience. Spencer changes from referring to Diana as "she" to referring to her as "you". It was a clever and moving device because it personalized the eulogy and made it and the sentiments absolutely direct. He says, for example: "There is a temptation to rush to canonize your memory. There is no need to do so. You stand tall enough as a human being of unique qualities not to need to be seen as a saint." This makes the speech certainly more personal, but also private and emotional. The speech also contains phrase repetitions, which add immense power.

Strong speeches are remembered. At the beginning of the speech Spencer uses the "repetitive three" device to build a powerful sense of loss: "I stand before you today the representative of a family in grief, in a country in mourning, before a world in shock."

A Legacy

The eulogy drew a spontaneous ovation from the crowd watching the ceremony on screens outside Westminster Abbey. Charles Spencer says he has no problem with those who criticize him for the surprising, emotive and critical speech. Later, he said: "You can't speak your mind and then be offended when people don't agree with what you're saying." The passionate, 8-minute eulogy was heard by a worldwide audience of nearly 3 billion people.

The speech forced the royal family to thaw a little in their attitude to Diana and her death and some say that a review of how its senior members behaved was as a direct result of Spencer's words. Certainly, the royal family supported his sentiment after the funeral much more than it had beforehand. Spencer encapsulated a mood and his words cleverly echoed what many thought.

Sun Yat-sen

We advocate pan-Asianism in order to restore the status of Asia. Only by the unification of all the peoples in Asia on the foundation of benevolence and virtue can they become strong and powerful."

Pan-Asianism speech, Chamber of Commerce, Kobe, Japan, Friday 28 November 1924

Sun Yat-sen was born on 12 November 1866 and died on 12 March 1925. He was the Chinese revolutionary and political leader often referred to as the "Father of Modern China". He was a force behind the overthrow of the Qing Dynasty in 1911 and in 1912 became provisional president at the foundation of the Republic of China. Later, he co-founded (and became the first leader of) the Kuomintang – the Chinese Nationalist Party. As a uniting figure in post-Imperial China, Sun remains unique among twentieth-century Chinese politicians for being genuinely revered in both mainland China and also Taiwan.

Sun Yat-sen believed in strengthening China from within by drawing on the country's natural resources, together with the adoption of new technologies. This wasn't always an easy process since many of China's leaders preferred to stick with the more traditional versions of Chinese society. In his ideology, which he termed the Three Principles of the People, Sun Yat-sen saw the fundamental aspects of nationalism, democracy and socialism as the drivers to make a modern China work. He believed passionately in the power and virtues of Asia when others around him were extolling only the virtues of the West. As he says in this speech: "Asia, in my opinion, is the cradle of the world's oldest civilization ... The origins of the various civilizations of the modern world can be traced back to Asia's ancient civilization. When Asia reached this point, the tide started to turn and the turn meant the regeneration of Asia."

The crux of the speech declares: "... There was a period of a thousand years when China was supreme in the world. Her status in the world then was similar to that of Great Britain and America today. What was the situation of the weaker nations toward China then? They respected China as their superior and sent annual tribute to China by their own will, regarding it as an honour to be allowed to do so ... But in what way did China maintain her prestige among so many small and weaker nations? Did she send her army or navy, i.e., use Might, to compel them to send their contributions? Not at all. It was not her rule of Might that forced the weaker nations to send tribute to China. It was the influence of her rule of Right ..." The rule of Right is what drove Sun Yat-sen's moral drive for China.

Lessons from Sun Yat-sen

Great speeches live long after they are made and provide a record of an initiative, an idea or a guiding vision. Sun Yat-sen made this speech in Kobe in 1924, a few months before his death, and it was to become his final testament. The Kobe Chamber of Commerce and three newspaper companies organized the occasion and he spoke to a Japanese audience of more than two thousand people. His conclusion became an important historical statement: "You, the Japanese nation, have an option: either to become a cat's paw of the western rule of might, or a fortress for an Eastern rule of righteousness. It is up to the Japanese people to carefully choose which way you want to go."

A Legacy

In China and Taiwan, Sun Yat-sen is still hailed as a huge inspiration to politicians and citizens, though he was not always seen as right or even as a leader of strength. In truth he spent much of his time in exile and few of his early initiatives succeeded. He much enjoyed, and was influenced in his thinking by, visits to America; he attached great importance to the ideas of Abraham Lincoln. Lincoln's Gettysburg Address called for "government of the people, by the people, for the people" and this, according to Sun Yat-sen, was the inspiration for his Three Principles of the People.

The Kuomintang reclaimed Sun Yat-sen and reinvigorated his memory. They built a huge mausoleum for him near their new capital of Nanjing and made his funeral largely a political event. Sun Yat-sen's writings became the central ideology of the Kuomintang on the mainland and in Taiwan. The communists, after their victory over nationalist forces in 1949, also claimed him for themselves, citing his insistence that a communist alliance was essential to the political development of China.

A portrait of Sun Yat-sen continues to appear in Tiananmen Square for May Day and the National Day. Many Chinese believe unequivocally that it was Sun Yat-sen who set out the blueprints for modern China.

Margaret Thatcher

It is sometimes said that because of our past we, as a people, expect too much and set our sights too high. That is not the way I see it. Rather it seems to me that throughout my life in politics, our ambitions have steadily shrunk. Our response to disappointment has not been to lengthen our stride, but to shorten the distance to be covered. But with confidence in ourselves and in our future what a nation we could be!"

"The Lady's Not For Turning" speech, The Conservative Party Conference, Brighton, UK, Friday 10 October 1980

Margaret Hilda Thatcher, Baroness Thatcher, was born on 13 October 1925. She was prime minister of the United Kingdom from 1979 to 1990 and is the only woman to have held the post.

When Thatcher became prime minister she had a mandate to reverse the UK's severe economic decline. Her political philosophy and economic policies emphasized reduced state intervention, free markets and entrepreneurialism. She was also a powerful nationalist, which gained her support after the 1982 Falklands War and led to re-election in 1983. It was, however, her tough, uncompromising approach and rhetoric – for example, taking a hard line against trade unions, the European Commission, Irish terrorists, the Soviet Union and her political opponents – that earned her the nickname the "Iron Lady". In 1984, she survived an assassination attempt.

Her outspoken, dynamic approach often meant that she polarized opinion: she was either loved or loathed and that polarity exists still. After her unprecedented re-election for a third term in 1987, the divisions grew, eventually becoming apparent in her cabinet. She resigned as prime minister in November 1990.

Lessons from Margaret Thatcher

Be clear, direct and, more often than not, uncompromising. Leave people in no doubt where you stand. Compromise is often overrated: after all, compromise means that nobody gets what they really want. Better to provide a clear alternative and consistent remedy, and then stick with it. If necessary, you can always answer questions and mollify a stance later, but people like firmness – provided a rationale is offered.

Give your supporters what they want. Thatcher understood brilliantly the people who supported her. This enabled her to give them what they wanted – a clear vision, progress towards their goals, priorities and change. Memorably, she says in the "Lady's Not For Turning" speech: "If I could press a button and genuinely solve the unemployment problem, do you think that I would not press that button this instant? Does anyone imagine that there is the smallest political gain in letting this unemployment continue, or that there is some obscure economic religion which demands this unemployment as part of its ritual?"

Be bold but always look for help. Initially, Margaret Thatcher was not a great orator, a view supported by her much-publicized tuition in public speaking and media handling. There was sometimes an unusual and surprising disconnect between her words, supported by her attitudes expressed in private, and the delivery of those words. Her speeches balanced toughness with understanding, ruthless logical argument with humour, but her delivery occasionally did not. However, once she was flowing with a sharp argument (at which she excelled), she was unbeatable as an orator of courage, strength, guidance and leadership: "If our people feel that they are part of a great nation and they are prepared to will the means to keep it great, a great nation we shall be, and shall remain. So, what can stop us from achieving this? What then stands in our way?"

Provide a compelling, logical analysis along with a commanding and personal prescription. As prime minister, Thatcher had the precise skills of logic and intelligence that you would expect from a scientist (a chemist) and a barrister. She frequently explained the reasons why a particular situation had arisen, before moving on to a clear vision of where she thought things should go. She could sell her views just as powerfully as she could demolish those of her opponents. She said in this speech: "Without a healthy economy we cannot have a healthy society. Without a healthy society the economy will not stay healthy for long ..."

A Legacy

Of all the post-war British prime ministers, it can be argued that two have shaped modern Britain more than anyone else: Clement Attlee, who pioneered the welfare state and characterized the caring, community-oriented side of British life, and Margaret Thatcher, who reinvigorated Britain's economic and entrepreneurial life as well as emphasizing individual responsibility and national identity.

Showing tender humility and patient understanding was never Thatcher's style, which even her admirers acknowledge could make her seem sharp and appear strident or uncaring. Unfortunately for Thatcher, issues of style alienated and antagonized people, often even before they thought about her policies or arguments, and this caused her practical problems. Even so, when people wanted leadership and dynamism, she provided it – winning three consecutive elections.

Leon Trotsky

The historical power which the prosecutor represents in this court is the organized violence of a minority over the majority. The new power, whose precursor was the Soviet, is the organized will of the majority calling the minority to order. In this distinction lies the Soviet's revolutionary right to existence, a right that stands above any legal or moral doubt."

Speech of Leon Trotsky, on trial for his life, to the Tsarist Court, St Petersburg, Russia, Friday 2 November 1906

Leon Trotsky was born on 7 November 1879 as Lev Davidovich Bronstein in Yanovka in the Russian Empire (modern-day Kirovohrad Oblast in the Ukraine). Trotsky was a leader of the Russian Revolution, second only to Lenin and an influential Marxist theorist. During the early days of the Soviet Union, he served first as People's Commissar for Foreign Affairs and later as the founder and commander of the Red Army and as the People's Commissar of War. He was also among the first members of the Politburo.

After leading a failed struggle against the policies and rise of Joseph Stalin in the 1920s and the increasing role of bureaucracy in the Soviet Union, Trotsky (lucky then to escape with his life) was expelled from the Communist Party, deported from the Soviet Union and eventually assassinated on 21 August 1940 while in exile in Mexico by one of Stalin's agents – Ramón Mercader.

Following the revolution of 1905, Trotsky became leader of the St Petersburg Soviet. In December, the Soviet issued a proclamation refusing to repay foreign debts and loans made by the Tsarist government. The Soviet was then surrounded by the army and its leaders were arrested and tried in 1906 on charges of supporting an armed rebellion. During his trial, Trotsky made an impassioned case for socialism, a force that was to influence politics for much of the twentieth century – in particular, the period from 1917 to 1989. This speech by Trotsky was important – to save his life and to give vent to his position on the future of Russia.

At the trial, Trotsky delivered some of the best speeches of his life and cemented his reputation as a powerful public orator. Despite – or possibly because of – this, he was convicted and sentenced to deportation, before escaping to London in 1907. This was a time of violence, utter poverty, strikes, insurrection and betrayal. A huge population was nervous, frightened and unsure.

Lessons from Leon Trotsky

Recognize and directly address your opponents' issues. Then take them apart, but not in an aggressive way. After all, your speech is unlikely to be in a law court. Trotsky was a master at understanding the other side of an argument and then demolishing it. It's a good oratorical device. He often did this with questioning. His line would typically be: "So what would you have us do? If we did things your way these would be the problems ... which is why this is the best way forward."

Explain your actions or views and build a powerful case for change. Trotsky lived in revolutionary times when people feared change almost as much as they disliked the status quo. He understood this and explained, patiently but energetically, what was wrong with the current social mores and how things could be better.

Unlike the bureaucratic dogma and totalitarianism that characterizes most communist regimes in history, Trotsky's speeches showed an idealistic fervour and passion – particularly in the time before the 1917 Russian revolution: "The Soviet, as a new historical power, as the sole power at a time of total moral, political, and technical bankruptcy of the old apparatus, as the sole guarantee of personal immunity and public order in the best sense of that term, considered itself entitled to oppose its force to such elements. The representatives of the old power, which is wholly based on murderous repression, has no right to speak with moral indignation of the Soviet's violent methods ..."

Recognize your strengths and your supporters' priorities. Trotsky knew that some people would never agree with him, so rather than compromising or trying to assuage their concerns he preferred to stick with the priorities he shared with his supporters. This meant that for the years before 1917 he stayed a Menshevik/Bolshevik with very limited power; but after the revolution and his return to Russia in 1917, from the United States, he was perfectly placed to organize his supporters and take control through workers' councils (or soviets).

A Legacy

Trotsky's main legacy is seen as his contribution to Marxist ideology. He was a thinker and, although he could be brutal and ruthless, he was also an idealist. He had a total belief that he was right – there was little room for self-doubt. Yet despite his intelligence, his position, influence and support, his self-belief and the force with which he expressed his ideas, he was eventually killed by his great rival, Stalin.

There was a time when Trotsky was powerful enough to have side-lined or outmanoeuvred Stalin. So, while intelligence and rhetoric are powerful, it is also important to recognize the reality of a situation. The true reality, not that which others paint. Anything else is simply vain, misplaced idealism.

George Washington

... The name of American, which belongs to you, in your national capacity, must always exalt the just pride of Patriotism."

"Farewell Address", *Independent Chronicle*, USA, Sunday 18 September 1796

George Washington was born on 22 February 1732 and died on 14 December 1799. He was the first American president and held office from 1789 to 1797. In 1792, as he was preparing to retire at the end of his first tenure in office, he wrote a farewell address to the American people with the aid of James Madison (America's eventual fourth president – from 1809 to 1817). However, faced with the unanimous objections of and protestations by his cabinet, Washington agreed to stand for another term. It was at that point that he revisited his previous address and rewrote it, this time with the aid of Alexander Hamilton. Historians believe that while some of the style might be Hamilton's, the ideas are undoubtedly Washington's.

The "Farewell Address" was written as a speech and intended as George Washington's valediction to public service for the new republic. It was, however, never spoken by Washington in public, but was published as an open letter in the form of a speech. During the darkest days of the civil war in 1862, the Senate was petitioned to read the speech to commemorate the 130th anniversary of Washington's birth. Secretary of the Senate John W. Forney was invited to read the text.

Once more, this time in early 1888 – the centenary of the Constitution's ratification – the Senate recalled the ceremony of 1862 and had its presiding officer read Washington's Address on 22 February. Within a few years, the Senate had made the practice an annual, and much relished, occasion. Each year since 1896, the Senate observes Washington's birthday by choosing one of its members, from alternating parties, to read the 7,641-word statement in legislative session. The delivery generally takes about 45 minutes. At the end of each reading, the appointed senator writes his or her name and a few remarks in a black, leather-bound book maintained by the secretary of the Senate.

Lessons from George Washington

Provide a clear structure that supports specific themes. Reinforce these themes, *not* ad nauseam, but in a way that you know will be crystal clear to your audience. Above all, more than anything, be clear. Washington's speech had three notable and specific themes. The first was a warning against what he saw as potentially harmful political factionalism. He urged Americans to unite for the good of the whole country, not simply a state or group. The second theme was a warning to avoid permanent foreign alliances, particularly in Europe. Therein, he considered, lay danger and debt. Washington's third theme was religion and morality, which he called "indispensable supports" of political prosperity. It's a theme to which senior politicians in the USA and Europe frequently refer, particularly in America, and Washington is often quoted in the process.

Memorably, Washington called morality "a necessary spring of popular government". Did his audience pay attention then? Quite possibly. Do they now?

Offer genuine gratitude where gratitude is warranted. Great speakers will thank those people (or conditions) who (or which) have made possible a cause, an argument, a case, a business decision, a plan. Not a shopping list of people or things – think the oft dreaded Oscar-style acceptance speech – but a genuine attempt to draw in those factors that (and those people who) have given help or occasioned support. Credit for anything can rarely go to one person alone. Washington begins the "Farewell Address" with a line of thanks and humility: "In looking forward to the moment which is intended to terminate the career of my public life, my feelings do not permit me to suspend the deep acknowledgment of that debt of gratitude which I owe to my beloved country for the many honors it has conferred upon me."

Be true to your own ideals and, where possible, provide words of enduring support, guidance or encouragement. Falsehoods rarely last. The underpinning of any such gamble will always, eventually, collapse and fall away, exposing something far less than your audiences expected or demanded. Among Washington's greatest assets were his strength of character, leadership skills, experience and, by 1796, the authority and prestige he had accumulated in 45 years of public service. The "Farewell Address" uses these assets to give credibility and authority to his points.

A Legacy

Crucially, one of the main tasks of a leader (whether in business or politics, in the eighteenth or twenty-first centuries) is succession planning – the need to support one's successors. It's a key task and a rare skill. George Washington's speech addressed what he saw as pressing issues that have since been recognized as perennial concerns in American life (unity and purpose, foreign policy and morality).

His words have guided lawmakers and politicians ever since his time in office – and particularly since their annual reading in the Senate after 1896. People still reflect on the great words of union and freedom: "The unity of Government, which constitutes you one people, is also now dear to you. It is justly so; for it is a main pillar in the edifice of your real independence, the support of your tranquillity at home, your peace abroad; of your safety; of your prosperity; of that very Liberty, which you so highly prize ..."

Daniel Webster

Mr President – when the mariner has been tossed for many days in thick weather, and on an unknown sea, he naturally avails himself of the first pause in the storm, the earliest glance of the sun, to take his latitude, and ascertain how far the elements have driven him from his true course. Let us imitate this prudence."

"Second Reply to Hayne" address to the United States Senate, Washington DC, USA, Tuesday/Wednesday 26/27 January 1830

As US secretary of state, **Daniel Webster** negotiated the Webster-Ashburton Treaty that defined the border between the United States and Canada. His First and Second Replies to Senator Hayne in 1830 were generally regarded as being among the most eloquent speeches ever delivered in Congress. Many hold that view still. Webster was born on 18 January 1782 and died on 24 October 1852.

Lessons from Daniel Webster

Achieve mastery with rehearsal and practice. Webster is recognized as the first American orator, and his speech at Plymouth Rock on 22 December 1820, on the second centennial of the landing of the Pilgrims, gave him this recognition. Webster prepared well for his speeches, which he delivered speaking mainly from memory, guided only by brief notes. He mastered thoroughly the fundamental principles of government and how various parts of the USA and indeed other nations felt about key national and international issues. His speech in 1825 at the setting of the cornerstone of the monument at Bunker Hill contained possibly the clearest statement to be found anywhere of the principles underlying the American War of Independence. In that speech he famously says: "We wish that this column, rising towards heaven among the pointed spires of so many temples dedicated to God, may contribute also to reproduce in all minds a pious feeling of dependence and gratitude. We wish, finally, that the last object to the sight of him who leaves his native shore, and the first to gladden his who revisits it, may be something which shall remind him of the liberty and the glory of his country."

When relevant, make strong beliefs the bedrock of your speech. Those who witnessed the "Second Reply to Hayne" address considered Webster's closing oration, beginning on 26 January 1830, to be a brilliant speech. Commentators since have made it plain that they think it the most famous speech in Senate history. In a full Senate chamber, it is said that Webster used his powerful voice to great effect as he began a speech spanning two days known as his "Second Reply to Hayne". In response to Senator Hayne's argument that the nation was simply an association of disparate sovereign states from which individual states could withdraw at will whenever they so wished, Webster thundered that it was not. Instead, he declared that this was a "popular government, erected by the people; those who administer it are responsible to the people; and itself capable of being amended and modified, just as the people may choose it should be."

Make sure that your speeches have impact. Five minutes of brilliance are better than an hour of unnecessary material – provided, of course, your point is made and your argument is strong. Say things succinctly because they are important to your audience. While Webster could touch his audience's emotions, his speeches were also superb and carefully reasoned arguments. People couldn't wait to read the 1830 speech duels with Senator Hayne. The impact of Webster's oration extended throughout the country, establishing him as a national statesman who would lead the strong debate over the nature of the Union for many years.

Lyrical language worked then. Carefully used, it works still. But it takes time to consider and to prepare. Webster began his speech beautifully: "Mr President – when the mariner has been tossed for many days in thick weather, and on an unknown sea, he naturally avails himself of the first pause in the storm, the earliest glance of the sun, to take his latitude, and ascertain how far the elements have driven him from his true course. Let us imitate this prudence, and, before we float farther on the waves of this debate, refer to the point from which we departed, that we may at least be able to conjecture where we now are." Webster then quotes from a Senate Resolution and, of course, he knows that everyone will want to hear the extract. He sets it up so well.

Mix your style. Avoid the monotone. Webster's style and approach mixed gentle spirit with pointed anger. This extract from the speech shows how he uses language to make a self-effacing point superbly well. While it is perhaps flowery by today's standards, it does its job with great aplomb and there is much to be learned from the carefully crafted style: "There yet remains to be performed, Mr President, by far the most grave and important duty, which I feel to be devolved on me by this occasion. It is to state, and to defend, what I conceive to be the true principles of the Constitution under which we are here assembled. I might well have desired that so weighty a task should have fallen into other and abler hands. I could have wished that it should have been executed by those whose character and experience give weight and influence to their opinions, such as cannot possibly belong to mine. But, Sir, I have met the occasion, not sought it; and I shall proceed to state my own sentiments, without challenging for them any particular regard, with studied plainness, and as much precision as possible ..."

A Legacy

Isaac Bassett, the son of a Senate messenger, described Webster's behaviour and style when speaking: "He was so conscious of his power and had all of his mental resources so well in hand that he never was agitated or embarrassed; his garments in the Senate chamber were unsurpassed. Before delivering a speech, he often appeared absent-minded. Rising to his feet he seemed to recover perfect self-possession, which was aided by thrusting the right hand within the folds of his vest, while his left hung gracefully by his side. His dark complexion grew warm with inward fire." Wouldn't it be great to have that said about you?

Webster's description of the US government as "made for the people, made by the people and answerable to the people" was later echoed by

Abraham Lincoln in the Gettysburg Address in the words "government of the people, by the people, for the people". Webster edited the "Second Reply to Hayne" speech for the purposes of printing a pamphlet, thereby turning a piece of rhetoric into a persuasive and widely read document. He spent as much time on the editing process as he had preparing for the speech itself. In altering his speech for printing, Webster was consciously turning what had been an example of effective spoken oratory into a document that would be persuasive to readers everywhere. He spent time adapting his speech because he was aware that techniques, idiom, colloquial language, inflection and pauses that might be impressive to listeners would not have the same effect when viewed on the printed page. A good lesson for us all today.

Jack Welch

... It's important for you to know that you don't have to make a choice between owning a company that puts up great numbers and a company that is socially responsible. You own both."

"A Company To Be Proud Of" address to stockholders at the 1999 General Electric Annual Meeting, Cleveland, Ohio, Wednesday 21 April 1999

John Francis (Jack) Welch Jr was born on 19 November 1935. He was Chairman and CEO of General Electric between 1981 and 2001 and he built a huge reputation for his business acumen and leadership at that company. His efforts and direction helped to streamline GE and make it a much more competitive business. In 1981 he gave a speech in New York called "Growing Fast in a Slow-Growth Economy". This is often acknowledged by the media as the beginning of an absolute focus among executives (including Welch) on the issue of shareholder value.

Lessons from Jack Welch

If you sound tough, then you'd better be able to back it up with exceptional management skills. Welch's bluntness shines through most of his speeches and he has given most of the credit for making him fiery, argumentative and wanting to win to his Irish mother. When making speeches, Welch is always excellent at telling business stories to make a point. His speeches also convey the joy of his career's experiences and his audiences, whether his own people, other executives or politicians, find that love of the job contagious. Welch carefully supports his statements with facts, his plans with examples, his decisions with effective action.

Cleverness is good, as long as you know what response you'll get. This speech is clever in that it certainly dwells on performance figures for GE – this was, after all, an annual general meeting and he was chairman – but also moves away from those figures to talk about other, more human, factors relating to what the company had done for its wider communities around the world. This AGM audience hears good company numbers and then is made to feel doubly good because of the strength of belief in putting something back: "We broke another big round number in 1998 in addition to the $100 billion in revenues ... At the President's Summit held in Philadelphia in 1997, a very persuasive leader, General Colin Powell, challenged ... our Industrial Systems business ... to raise the bar of GE volunteerism and commit to a pace of one million hours a year of volunteer service to America's youth by April of 2000. GE people like big round numbers like this and they love to take big swings at what we call 'stretch' targets. They knocked this one out of the park ..."

Convey the force of your personality when you speak. Welch is a great storyteller and that can make an orator great. With his muscular, broad frame and pale face this man doesn't really look like the typical business leader. He has always had a slight stutter, a handicap emanating from childhood, yet he presents his points through sheer force of personality, coupled with a contagious passion for winning and a superb attention to detail that many executives lack. These qualities inspired many people inside and outside GE when he was managing that business, and the inspiration continued as he made a living from corporate and public speaking on international management issues. He is regarded as a superb orator – from the outset his public speaking fees were among the highest in the world.

A Legacy

At GE, Welch's philosophy was that a company should be either number one or number two in its industry, or else leave the market completely. This was a simple, direct and ambitious approach, one focused on achieving results and building shareholder value. It was a philosophy copied by many management boards throughout America and, because of Welch's growing status and reputation, elsewhere in the world.

Welch's reputation was primarily founded on the tough candour he displayed in his meetings with executives. But he was also seen as fair. He's also known for dismantling GE's nine-layer management hierarchy and bringing a sense of informality to the company. And he adopted Motorola's Six Sigma quality programme in late 1995 which, in turn, helped lead the company to massive revenues. In 1999 he was named Manager of the Century by *Fortune* magazine.

Elie Wiesel

So much violence, so much indifference."

"Perils of Indifference: Lessons Learned from a Violent Century" address, The White House, Washington DC, USA, Monday 12 April 1999

Elie Wiesel, born Eliezer Wiesel on 30 September 1928, is a political activist, writer and academic. Arguably his most famous book is *Night*; it's a memoir describing his terrible experiences during the Holocaust and his imprisonment in concentration camps.

In the summer of 1944 Wiesel, along with his father, mother and sisters, were deported by the Nazis to Auschwitz in occupied Poland. On arrival at the extermination camp, Wiesel and his father were selected by SS Dr Josef Mengele for slave labour.

Life in the camp was unbearable. There was little food, the brutality was horrendous and despair was deep and long lasting. Wiesel and his father were eventually evacuated from Auschwitz to Buchenwald in Germany. There, Wiesel's father, mother and younger sister died. In April 1945 Buchenwald was liberated by American troops.

Lessons from Elie Wiesel

Fervour and belief are vital if you want to convince your audience. Elie Wiesel gave his impassioned speech at the White House as part of the Millennium Lecture series. The language is rich and Wiesel provides a carefully structured narrative. The audience is gripped by the emotion, the stark horrors and the humanity, but primarily because the speaker tells a series of fascinating stories, each of which has a mix of the light and dark.

Significantly, and painfully in many ways for the audience, an unanswered question echoes beyond the speech: Will people always remain indifferent to others' pain? The answer echoes back.

The theme of a speech can be a tough one. In his White House speech, Wiesel recalls the American liberators. It's a moving moment on several levels, particularly because it reinforces his point about utter indifference. The "he" in the following extract is Wiesel: "Fifty-four years ago to the day, a young Jewish boy from a small town in the Carpathian Mountains woke up ... He was finally free, but there was no joy in his heart ... Liberated a day earlier by American soldiers, he remembers their rage at what they saw. And even if he lives to be a very old man, he will always be grateful to them for that rage, and also for their compassion. Though he did not understand their language, their eyes told him what he needed to know – that they, too, would remember and bear witness."

Return to your point throughout your speech. Wiesel ends his speech with hope, having explained gently, sometimes angrily and often hopelessly, the general indifference to man's inhumanity to man: "When adults wage war, children perish. We see their faces, their eyes. Do we hear their pleas? Do we feel their pain, their agony? Every minute one of them dies of disease, violence, famine. Some of them – so many of them – could be saved." Throughout the speech he prods and examines the issue of indifference to violence. He has commented since that, generally speaking, people rarely care enough or consistently enough to make a big difference to those in the world who suffer terribly at the hands of others. Sometimes, he says, not far from where we sit now. Certainly, he acknowledges, individuals and some groups of course do care and do make a difference but, he wonders, will people always practise indifference to violence and suffering? Is it part of our selfish condition not to stop it happening?

A Legacy

Since 1976 Elie Wiesel has been the Andrew Mellon Professor in the Humanities at Boston University. He was also the Founding Chair of the United States Holocaust Memorial. In 1986 he was awarded the Nobel Peace Prize. The Norwegian Nobel Committee called him a "messenger to mankind" of "peace, atonement and human dignity".

Wiesel went to Auschwitz with television host Oprah Winfrey in 2006, a visit that was broadcast as an extraordinary and powerful piece of television. In the same year he supported George Clooney at the UN Security Council when the humanitarian crisis in Darfur was addressed. During the early 2007 selection process for the Kadima candidate for president of

Israel, Prime Minister Ehud Olmert is said to have offered Wiesel the nomination. Wiesel turned the offer down and the role went to Shimon Peres.

On the occasion of the "Perils of Indifference" speech at the White House, Hillary Clinton said: "It was more than a year ago that I asked Elie if he would be willing to participate in these Millennium Lectures … I never could have imagined that, when the time finally came for him to stand in this spot and to reflect on the past century and the future to come, we would be seeing children in Kosovo crowded into trains, separated from families, separated from their homes, robbed of their childhoods, their memories, their humanity."

Woodrow Wilson

It is a fearful thing to lead this great peaceful people into war … but the right is more precious than peace and we shall fight for the things which we have always carried nearest our hearts … for democracy, for the right of those who submit to authority to have a voice in their own governments … for a universal dominion of right by such a concert of free peoples as shall bring peace and safety to all nations and make the world itself at last free."

"War Message", Congress, Washington DC, USA, Monday 2 April 1917

Dr **Thomas Woodrow Wilson** was born on 28 December 1856 and died on 3 February 1924. He was the 28th president of the United States, from 1913 to 1921.

On 3 February 1917 Wilson informed Congress that diplomatic relations with Germany had been cut. Then, on 2 April of the same year, he delivered the "War Message" to a hastily gathered Joint Session of Congress, asking for agreement to a declaration of war against Germany. The Joint Session agreed, some say because Wilson's "War Message" was incontrovertible. Wilson had insisted that formally joining the conflict was a necessary effort to make America "safe for democracy". Entry into a world war was not a foregone conclusion but, as he said in his "War Message": "American ships have been sunk, American lives taken in ways which it has stirred us very deeply to learn of; but the ships and people of other neutral and friendly nations have been sunk and overwhelmed in the waters in the same way. There has been no discrimination …"

Lessons from Woodrow Wilson

Reinforce your most important points. The speech reiterated what was required of America and where its duty lay, both in defending itself and also in helping to defend others. He believed that the war was a threat to decent, civilized countries and fair behaviour. It was this speech to Congress that, without question, helped to shorten the war: "The world must be made safe for democracy. Its peace must be planted upon the tested foundations of political liberty. We have no selfish ends to serve. We desire no conquest, no dominion. We seek no indemnities for ourselves, no material compensation for the sacrifices we shall freely make. We are but one of the champions of the rights of mankind ..."

Preparation is different for different people, but preparation *is* vital. The country was aware that war might be looming and that huge change was in front of the United States. Wilson had marked 2 April as the day that he would present his case to Congress. He spent the day reading, rehearsing and rewriting his address. That evening, as he reached the lectern, the applause that he received was, it is said, the greatest that any president had received in front of Congress.

Wilson's "War Message" had three great components: style, substance and dramatic impact. As a speech, it is brilliantly constructed and shows Wilson to be a masterly writer. He chooses phrases that are both great to read and undoubtedly powerful to hear. Not all speeches are made in the context of taking a country to war. But that's not the issue. If you're making a speech, your topic is presumably important to you and to your audience. Your speech deserves careful construction and strong preparation.

Oratory always centres on a worthy theme; it must appeal to and inspire the listeners' ideals. Wilson's "War Message" builds to a crescendo. It explains a situation, reinforces that explanation and then delivers what everyone in Congress knew was coming next. It then rationalizes the hope that, once the decision to fight is made, the country will go forward (to what, few knew) with dignity: "To such a task we can dedicate our lives and our fortunes, everything that we are and everything that we have, with the pride of those who know that the day has come when America is privileged to spend her blood and her might for the principles that gave her birth and happiness and the peace which she has treasured. God helping her, she can do no other." The speech taps into what most Americans and their leaders will have felt in their heart of hearts, whether they liked the prospect or not. It is an inspiring speech and one which, rightly or otherwise, matches the prevalent ideal of freedom.

Speaking difficulties can be overcome or hidden. Many great speakers, or people in prominent positions who have been or are obliged to make speeches or presentations, have had (or have) speech problems – stutters, stammers, lisps and dyslexia. The list is long and could be said to include, for example: King George VI, Winston Churchill, Lewis Carroll, Rudy Giuliani, Truman Capote, Robert Kennedy, Emperor Claudius, Humphrey Bogart, Athenian General Alcibiades, Marilyn Monroe, James Stewart, Tiger Woods, Demosthenes, Aesop, Lenin, Aristotle, Isaac Newton, Aneurin Bevan, Jack Welch, James Earl Jones and Alan Turing.

Wilson suffered from dyslexia and attention deficit hyperactivity disorder. He taught himself shorthand to compensate for his inability to write longhand quickly. When possible, he spoke with very few notes, but rehearsed and practised any speech no matter where or to whom it was to be made.

A Legacy

Wilson averred that World War I should be, must be, a "war to end all wars". He knew that the only way to real peace was to get the aggressive nations to sue for peace as an option to war. His ambition was to encourage peace on terms that would prohibit similar future conflicts. His plans didn't come to fruition and 21 years after the end of one world conflict, the next began.

President Wilson's ideas, in particular those relating to domestic policy, were popular both within Congress and also amongst the American people. His implementation of (particularly foreign) policy didn't always go to plan, though. For example, famously, he could not succeed in persuading Congress to validate the United States' membership of the League of Nations. However, American foreign policy was revised and devised under his administration and he was instrumental in leading the United States to become a key influence in international politics.

Wilson was awarded the Nobel Peace prize before the end of his presidency. He was delighted, but becoming a Nobel laureate didn't match the satisfaction he would have gained from bringing the USA into the League of Nations. However, his efforts can be said to have led to the eventual United Nations. This, many would agree, is a key legacy.

Woodrow Wilson's first administration progressed jurisdiction that challenged the banking cartels, industrial practices that favoured business owners, and brought a balance between the rights of the worker and the demands of the employer. These federal changes, whilst not as exciting perhaps as forays into foreign policy, were vital in stabilizing America's economy, creating fairness in industry, agriculture and commerce.

Oprah Winfrey

... God uses good people to do great things."

Eulogy for Rosa Parks, Metropolitan AME Church, Washington DC, USA, Monday 31 October 2005

Oprah Gail Winfrey was born on 29 January 1954. She is primarily an American television presenter, although she also owns great chunks of the media and her philanthropy is well known. It is her internationally syndicated television programme, *The Oprah Winfrey Show*, that has earned her praise and many awards – it is also the highest-rated talk show ever. In 2006 Winfrey became an early supporter of Barack Obama and one analysis estimates that she delivered over a million votes in the 2008 Democratic primary race. What Winfrey says, recommends or does, many follow.

Time magazine named Oprah Winfrey one of the most influential people in the world every year from 2004 to 2008. In 2005, Winfrey was named in a public opinion poll the greatest woman in American history.

On 1 December 1955 in Montgomery, Alabama, a 42-year-old African-American woman, Rosa Parks, bluntly refused to obey bus driver James Blake's order that she must give up her seat to make room for a white passenger. This action was not the first of its kind. Others had won court rulings before the Supreme Court and the Interstate Commerce Commission for similar cases. But Parks's decision not to move sparked the now famous Montgomery Bus Boycott and a nation's imagination.

Rosa Parks became an icon and her decision a symbol of resistance to racial segregation. She collaborated with civil rights leaders, including Martin Luther King Jr, and her association helped launch him to prominence.

Lessons from Oprah Winfrey

Speeches don't have to be complicated. Simplicity (in content, context and emotion) works well if the speech is properly prepared. Many speakers insist on writing something late in the day on a scrap of paper and others cover their speeches in swathes of extraneous material. Simple and direct, simple and direct. Oprah Winfrey's speech tells a story and is simple, direct and from the heart: "That day that you refused to give up your seat on the bus, you, Sister Rosa, changed the trajectory of my life and the lives of so many other people in the world. I would not be standing here today nor standing where I stand every day had she not chosen to sit down. I know that. I know that. I know that. I know that, and I honor that. Had she not chosen to say we shall not – we shall not be moved."

A Legacy

In her book, *Rosa Parks: My Story*, Parks writes: "People always say that I didn't give up my seat because I was tired but that wasn't true. I was not tired physically ... I was not old ... I was 42. No, the only tired I was, was tired of giving in." Oprah Winfrey took that quote as a basis for speaking about Rosa Parks's life.

Many recall and empathize still with Winfrey's eulogy for Rosa Parks: "And in that moment when you resolved to stay in that seat, you reclaimed your humanity and you gave us all back a piece of our own. I thank you for that." It was strong, emotional and carefully worded – each of these – but it was also truthful and, as was reported later, representative of what many others felt.

The extraordinary figures for *The Oprah Winfrey Show* – broadcast in over 130 countries and attracting around 26 million viewers in the US each day – are a legacy in their own right, of course, but Winfrey regularly uses her show and other platforms to talk about people who have sacrificed a great deal and tried to make American society a safer, fairer place, and genuinely a country of equals.

Virginia Woolf

Let me imagine, since the facts are so hard to come by, what would have happened had Shakespeare had a wonderfully gifted sister, called Judith ..."

"Women and Fiction" lecture delivered at Girton and Newnham colleges, University of Cambridge, UK, Saturday 20 October and Friday 26 October 1928

Adeline Virginia Woolf was born on 25 January 1882 and committed suicide on 28 March 1941. She was an English novelist, and is regarded now as one of the foremost modernist literary figures of the twentieth century.

Between the end of World War I and onset of World War II, Woolf was a significant figure in London literary society and a member of the Bloomsbury Group. Her most famous works include the novels *Mrs Dalloway* (1925), *To the Lighthouse* (1927) and *Orlando* (1928), and the long essay *A Room of One's Own* (1929), famous for its insistence that: "a woman must have money and a room of her own if she is to write fiction". It is this essay that formed the lectures she gave in 1928 at the University of Cambridge.

The lectures describe Virginia Woolf's search to find out what women's lives were like in the past; she wonders why women didn't produce "great" literature to the same degree as did men. In her quest, she considers a number of factors upon which successful writing depends, and imagines what might have happened to a gifted sister of Shakespeare (Judith), had such a sister ever existed.

Lessons from Virginia Woolf

Use descriptive stories and analogies to make your point. Woolf wanted to know the conditions necessary for the creation of works of art. For instance, did gender matter? She wanted to know what Shakespeare's sister might have been like. This is a vehicle for a fascinating storytelling process: "I could not help thinking, as I looked at the works of Shakespeare on the shelf, that ... it would have been impossible, completely and entirely, for any woman to have written the plays of Shakespeare in the age of Shakespeare. Let me imagine, since the facts are so hard to come by, what would have happened had Shakespeare had a wonderfully gifted sister, called Judith, let us say."

She saw the women undergraduates in front of her as the avengers of Shakespeare's imaginary sister, a bright and ambitious girl who, in her scenario, is driven to commit suicide as a consequence of her futile attempts to fulfil her creative ambition. "Women and Fiction" is an intimate speech. It is conversational: a series of thoughts.

Audiences understand more than you may imagine. Don't spell everything out. These people watch television and movies and follow story lines pretty well all of the time. Virginia Woolf expects her audiences to understand her thinking without spelling everything out. You don't have to tell people all the specific details of an idea or proposition – that can come later. Remember that people can understand an issue without too much detail or PowerPoint back-up. They can make the quantum leap from one idea or set of arguments to the next without too many bridges.

When appropriate, be conversational. Woolf begins each passage as if resuming a conversation that had been interrupted. It's a good device and one which can make you appear warm and interested in the audience. It's a version of "Now, where were we?" More than anything, the story she tells is memorable. Memorable is good. Woolf enthralled her audience before concluding: "That, more or less, is how the story would run, I think, if a woman in Shakespeare's day had had Shakespeare's genius ... I would venture to guess that Anon, who wrote so many poems without signing them, was often a woman ..."

A Legacy

This speech was made at a time when few women worked for the purpose of being independent. Women were very much secondary from a political, social, economic and educational positioning. Virginia Woolf gives an overview of the history of women's and men's education in England. Why was it, she asked, that men had so much money to educate their sons and women had insufficient money to leave to their daughters? She says: "lock up your libraries if you like; but there is no gate, no lock, no bolt that you can set upon the freedom of my mind". It was this essay and these lectures (*A Room of One's Own*/"Women and Fiction") that refreshed focus on the examination of the future of women in education and society at large. As Woolf said in her lecture: "Now my belief is that this poet who never wrote a word and was buried at the crossroads still lives. She lives in you and in me, and in many other women who are not here tonight, for they are washing up the dishes and putting the children to bed ..."

Virginia Woolf is remembered as a feminist, a modernist and for focusing attention upon the rights of women to lead lives that mirrored those of men.

Muhammad Yunus

I believe terrorism cannot be won over by military action. Terrorism must be condemned in the strongest language. We must stand solidly against it and find all the means to end it. We must address the root causes of terrorism to end it for all time to come. I believe that putting resources into improving the lives of the poor people is a better strategy than spending it on guns."

"Poverty is a Threat to Peace" lecture, given on receiving the 2006 Nobel Peace Prize, Oslo, Norway, Sunday 10 December 2006

Muhammad Yunus was born on 28 June 1940 in Chittagong, in what is modern-day Bangladesh. He was already a successful Bangladeshi banker and economist when he founded the now internationally famous Grameen Bank and, through it, pioneered the concept of micro-credit, which involves loans given to entrepreneurs too poor to qualify for traditional bank funds.

In 2006 Yunus and the bank were jointly awarded the Nobel Peace Prize "for their efforts to create economic and social development from below".

Lessons from Muhammad Yunus

Use your platform to show your passion and explain your beliefs. Yunus used his 2006 Nobel Peace Prize lecture to highlight the importance of finance and economics in preventing social and political problems. His argument included the point that, in his view, economically comfortable people do not tend to riot or behave in an extreme way, whereas poverty-stricken and desperate people may. This may seem an over-simplistic view, but it was a theme that Yunus explored in his speech with intelligence and authority. He knew the environments in which people who had nothing could become proud and happy individuals. He knew that microfinance worked.

While very few of us will have a platform as illustrious as that provided by the Nobel Foundation, it is still sensible to consider how best to convey our views, priorities and – where appropriate – experience. Again, this is the telling of stories to give weight and example to your argument.

Be thoughtful and considered. Yunus is clearly a calm, thoughtful, modest and highly intelligent individual: qualities that had commanded him attention and respect long before he received the accolade of Nobel Peace Prize laureate. If you are presenting a view, proposing a plan of action or simply suggesting a way to behave, then, in most circumstances, you will achieve it more easily with a carefully considered style. People who treat speaking engagements and public platforms as an opportunity and privilege are much more likely to prepare more, think deeper, perform better and succeed than those who don't.

Understand the power of clarity and boldness. Discussing how to fight terrorism is an emotive and highly complex issue. Yunus said: "Poverty is the absence of all human rights. The frustrations, hostility and anger generated by abject poverty cannot sustain peace in any society. For building stable peace we must find ways to provide opportunities for people to live decent lives."

Yunus tackled this topic in his December 2006 lecture with clear understanding and authority. If he had misjudged his words, he would have been criticized for naivety or simply meddling – but he wasn't. His analysis was simple and thought-provoking, clear and bold: Don't treat the symptoms of terrorism, treat the causes; and don't do this with guns, instead use economic and financial measures.

Play to your strengths. Yunus had the qualities of both a successful scholar and a leading business executive; in his Nobel lecture, he unsurprisingly brought to bear the qualities of a lecturer and CEO. He started by acknowledging people's participation and successes; he appeared cool, insightful, rational, experienced and authoritative. Certainly, he used notes but he knew his material inside out and therefore the notes were a safety net only (never a bad plan). He also ended with the premise with which he'd begun: "Grameen has given me an unshakeable faith in the creativity of human beings. This has led me to believe that human beings are not born to suffer the misery of hunger and poverty."

A Legacy

Yunus serves on the board of directors of the United Nations Foundation, a public charity created in 1998 which builds and implements public-private partnerships to address the world's most pressing problems.

On 18 July 2007 Nelson Mandela, Graça Machel and Desmond Tutu convened a group of world leaders in Johannesburg. Called The Global Elders, this new group was designed to contribute its wisdom, independent leadership and integrity to some of the world's most pressing problems. Alongside founding members of this group, such as Kofi Annan,

Gro Harlem Brundtland, Jimmy Carter, Li Zhaoxing and Mary Robinson, was Muhammad Yunus. This was clear recognition that boldness, innovation and change can be achieved with a calm, insightful and intelligent approach and a quiet spirit.

Yunus has already created a legacy of real social change in Bangladesh. And it's not just in the developing world that he has had an impact. In 2000 Hillary Clinton remarked that Yunus had helped the Clintons introduce micro-credit schemes to some of the poorest communities in Arkansas.

Greatness Omitted

As you can imagine, we had to leave out some great speeches and speakers from this book, much to our chagrin and disappointment. Also, we restricted ourselves to the inclusion of only one speech from any one speaker and that, too, caused some dismay. Of course if we hadn't set some rules, then American presidents, literary giants, Cicero or civil rights orators from around the world could have overwhelmed the book.

We knew from the outset that our choices were likely to be controversial and, we believe, that's a healthy thing. We have already received looks of horror or a sharp "tut" of dismay when people learned of certain inclusions and exclusions. Our intentions were to provide a book that is interesting and thought-provoking and also to cast a light on two vital subjects, oratory and rhetoric. These issues are perennially important, but increasingly neglected and only infrequently discussed nowadays. They matter because of their role in moving and influencing people and making sure that people are reassured, engaged, inspired or simply satisfied.

Our approach was to seek examples of (very) different styles of oratory and rhetoric. We knew that this would court controversy, but sometimes controversy is there to be courted. Our choices were, of course, highly subjective.

Sadly (but, perhaps, encouragingly) there were some great speakers and speeches that did not quite make it on to The 100. We thought that it might be useful to show that we did, at the very least, consider the following omissions carefully. Perhaps one day they might be included in another book.

63 BC: Catiline Orations – Cicero
AD 30: Sermon on the Mount – Jesus
AD 632: The Farewell Sermon – Mohammed
1095: Council of Clermont – Pope Urban II
1630: City Upon a Hill – John Winthrop
1741: Sinners in the Hands of an Angry God – Jonathan Edwards
1789: Speech to the House of Commons on Slavery – William
    Wilberforce
1803: Speech from the Dock – Robert Emmet
1823: The Monroe Doctrine – James Monroe
1851: Ain't I A Woman? – Sojourner Truth
1858: House Divided – Abraham Lincoln
1860: Speech to the Soldiers – Giuseppe Garibaldi

1861: Cornerstone Speech – Alexander Stephens

1861: First Inaugural Address – Abraham Lincoln

1862: Blood and Iron – Otto von Bismarck

1865: Second Inaugural Address – Abraham Lincoln

1877: Surrender – Chief Joseph

1889: On Conserving Ancient Monuments – Lord Curzon

1893: Sisters and Brothers of America – Swami Vivekananda

1900: Acres of Diamonds – Russell Conwell

1901: Votes for Women – Mark Twain

1906: I Warn the Government – F. E. Smith

1913: First Inaugural Address – Woodrow Wilson

1915: Ireland Unfree Shall Never be at Peace – Patrick Pearse

1917: Free is my Birthright – Bal Gangadhar Tilak

1918: Fourteen Points – Woodrow Wilson

1922: Trial Speech – Mohandas Gandhi

1930: Muslims of India – Muhammad Iqbal

1933: Passage of the Enabling Act address– Otto Wels

1936: Address to the League of Nations – Haile Selassie I of Ethiopia

1936: Rendezvous with Destiny – Franklin Delano Roosevelt

1939: The Luckiest Man on the Face of the Earth – Lou Gehrig

1939: Broadcast to the Nation – Neville Chamberlain

1940: Arsenal of Democracy – Franklin Delano Roosevelt

1940: Blood, Toil, Tears and Sweat – Winston Churchill

1940: This Was Their Finest Hour – Winston Churchill

1940: Never Was So Much Owed By So Many To So Few – Winston Churchill

1941: Four Freedoms – Franklin Delano Roosevelt

1941: What is an American? – Harold Ickes

1941: A Date Which Will Live in Infamy – Franklin Delano Roosevelt

1943: Do You Want Total War? – Joseph Goebbels

1944: The D-Day Prayer – Franklin Delano Roosevelt

1944: Paris Liberated– Charles de Gaulle

1945: Imperial Surrender – Hirohito

1946: Sinews of Peace or The Iron Curtain speech – Winston Churchill

1948: The Light Has Gone Out of Our Lives– Jawaharlal Nehru

1949: Four Point Speech – Harry Truman

1949: Why I Killed Gandhi – Nathuram Godse

1949: The Light on the Hill – Ben Chifley

1950: Man Will Not Merely Endure, He Will Prevail – William Faulkner

1952: Checkers Speech – Richard M. Nixon

1953: History Will Absolve Me – Fidel Castro

1956: We Will Bury You – Nikita Khrushchev

1957: Longest Speech in the United Nations – Krishna Menon

1959: There's Plenty of Room at the Bottom – Richard Feynman

1960: Wind of Change – Harold Macmillan

1961: Farewell Address – Dwight D. Eisenhower

1961: Wasteland Speech – Newton Minow

1961: Mouseland Speech – Tommy Douglas

1962: Segregation Now, Segregation Tomorrow, Segregation Forever – George Wallace

1962: Rice University Address – John Fitzgerald Kennedy

1963: We All Breathe the Same Air – John Fitzgerald Kennedy

1963: Ich bin ein Berliner – John Fitzgerald Kennedy

1964: A Time for Choosing – Ronald Reagan

1966: Day of Affirmation – Robert F. Kennedy

1967: Vive le Québec Libre – Charles de Gaulle

1967: Time to Break Silence – Martin Luther King Jr

1968: I've Been to the Mountaintop – Martin Luther King Jr

1968: Rivers of Blood – Enoch Powell

1974: Richard Nixon's Resignation Speech – Richard M. Nixon

1981: Speech Against the Death Penalty – Robert Badinter

1982: Education of a Film Maker – Satyajit Ray

1982: Rekindling of Enthusiasm – J. R. D. Tata

1987: Tear Down this Wall – Ronald Reagan

1987: Today and Forever – Robert Bourassa

1988: Sermon on the Mound – Margaret Thatcher

1989: Gazimestan speech – Slobodan Milosevic

1990: Resignation speech – Geoffrey Howe

1992: Culture War speech – Pat Buchanan

1993: The Fatwa speech – Salman Rushdie

1996: I am an African – Thabo Mbeki

2000: Speech at Israel's Holocaust Memorial – John Paul II

2002: Notre Maison Brûle et Nous Regardons Ailleurs – Jacques Chirac

2003: Let Us Not Forget – Dominique de Villepin

2006: Chocolate City – Ray Nagin

2008: Apology to the Stolen Generations – resolution by the Parliament of Australia, Kevin Rudd

2008: Yes We Can – Remarks at New Hampshire Primary night – Barack Obama

2008: A More Perfect Union – Barack Obama

2009: Speech at Cairo University – Barack Obama

And there were other speeches that sat on our desks for a long time. Should we, shouldn't we? They, too, are worthy of a passing mention:

Rocky Anderson's Anti-war Patriots Rally speech
Maya Angelou's On the Pulse of Morning speech
Kofi Annan's Nobel Prize Acceptance speech
Neil Armstrong's One Small Step commentary
Stanley Baldwin's Disarmament speech
Nancy Birdsall's On Growth and Poverty Reduction speech
Tony Blair's War with Iraq speech
Napoleon Bonaparte's The Egyptian Campaign speech
Sarah Brady's Signing of the Brady Gun Control Bill address
John Brown's Address to the Court at his Trial
Pearl Buck's Nobel Lecture on The Chinese Novel
Edmund Burke's He is a Member of Parliament speech
Edmund Burke's Conciliation with America speech
Stokely Carmichael's Black Power speech
Carrie Chapman Catt's The Crisis speech
Beth Chapman's Stand Up for America Rally address
Cher's Tribute to Sonny Bono
Shirley Chisholm's Equal Rights for Women speech
Hillary Clinton's Women's Rights are Human Rights speech
Russell Conwell's Acres of Diamonds speech
Mario Cuomo's Religious Belief and Public Morality speech
Marie Curie's On the Discovery of Radium speech
Edouard Daladier's The Nazis' Aim is Slavery speech
Crystal Eastman's Now We Can Begin speech
Anthony Eden's The Suez Crisis speech
General Dwight D. Eisenhower's D-Day Order
Queen Elizabeth II's On the Death of Princess Diana speech
Dianne Feinstein's A Time to Act on Global Warming speech
Mary Fisher's A Whisper of AIDS address
Jane Fonda's Broadcast Over Radio Hanoi to American servicemen
J. K. Galbraith's The Affluent Society presentation
William Lloyd Garrison's On the Death of John Brown speech
Emma Goldman's What is Patriotism? speech
Frances E. W. Harper's Enlightened Motherhood speech
Adolf Hitler's Declaration of War Against the US
Jesse Jackson's Common Ground and Common Sense speech
Ladybird Johnson's Tribute to Eleanor Roosevelt
Erica Jong's On Free speech
Helen Keller's Strike Against War speech
Edward M. Kennedy's Chappaquiddick speech
Edward M. Kennedy's Eulogy for Robert F. Kennedy
Edward M. Kennedy's Faith, Truth and Tolerance in America speech

Sources of further information and acknowledgements

The brief excerpts and short quotations included in this book have been used to review and assess each of the speeches. In many cases the speaker (or their estate) retains copyright in the speaker's original work. If you would like to review the speeches in greater detail they can be read in full through many publicly available websites and sources, including those given below.

Salvador Allende   The speech can be viewed online at: http://en.wikisource.org/wiki/Salvador_Allende's_Last_Speech

Susan B. Anthony   The speech can be viewed online at: http://gos.sbc.edu/a/anthony.html

Corazón Aquino   The speech can be viewed online at: www.newsflash.org/2004/02/hl/h1102820.htm

Mustafa Kemal Atatürk   The speech can be viewed online at: www.ambasciataditurchia.it/Sub_Pages/on_the_tenth_anniversary.htm www.ataturksociety.org/10thyear.html www.theturkishtimes.com/archive/02/11_01/f_speech.html

Aung San Suu Kyi   Aung San Suu Kyi's translation of the speech can be viewed online through the Burma Library website at: http://burmalibrary.org/docs3/Shwedagon-ocr.htm or http://burmalibrary.org/docs3/Shwedagon-ocr.htm

Henry Ward Beecher   Interesting background information can be viewed at: www.mrlincolnandnewyork.org/inside.asp?ID=44&subjectID=3 http://en.wikipedia.org/wiki/Henry_Ward_Beecher

Aneurin Bevan   The speech is reported in Hansard, columns 1268 to 1283. Extracts can also be viewed online at *The Guardian* newspaper's website: www.guardian.co.uk/theguardian/2007/may/03/greatspeeches2

Benazir Bhutto   The speech can be read online through the International Institute for Strategic Studies: www.iiss.org/EasysiteWeb/getresource.axd?AssetID=2602&type=Full&servicetype=Attachment

Lee Bollinger   The speech at Columbia University can be viewed online at: www.columbia.edu/cu/news/07/09/lcbopeningremarks.html

Napoleon Bonaparte   The speech can be viewed online at: www.fortunecity.com/victorian/riley/787/Napoleon/France/Napoleon/oldguard.html
www.famous-speeches-and-speech-topics.info/famous-short-speeches/napoleon-bonaparte-speech-farewell-to-the-old-guard.htm
www.historyplace.com/speeches/napoleon.htm
www.en.wikisource.org/wiki/Farewell_to_the_Old_Guard

Sir Neville Bonner   The speech is available through the Australian Government's Hansard record of the Constitution Convention. Details of the Hansard record can be found at: www.aph.gov.au/hansard. Also, the speech can be viewed online at: www.abc.net.au/news/features/obits/bonner/ccaddress.htm
www.norepublic.com.au/index.php?option=com_content&task=view&id=888&Itemid=24
Background information can be found at: http://en.wikipedia.org/wiki/Republicanism_in_Australia#1998_Constitutional_Convention

Adrien Brody   The Oscar acceptance speech can be viewed online at American Rhetoric's website: www.americanrhetoric.com/speeches/adrienbrodyoscarspeech.htm

George H. W. Bush   The Inaugural Address is available from The American Presidency Project, and can be viewed online at their website: www.presidency.ucsb.edu/ws/index.php?pid=16610

John Chambers   The speech is available through the Commonwealth Club of California. It can be viewed online at: www.commonwealthclub.org/archive/01/01–04chambers-speech.html

César Estrada Chávez   The speech is available through the César E. Chavez Foundation. It can be viewed online at: www.chavezfoundation.org/_board.php?mode=view&b_code=001008000000000&b_no=14

Winston Churchill   The speech can be viewed online at: http://en.wikisource.org/wiki/We_shall_fight_on_the_beaches
Also, an edited version of the broadcast can be heard at: www.youtube.com/watch?v=611T2ZYg-4E

Marcus Tullius Cicero   The speech can be viewed online at: http://
www.perseus.tufts.edu/cgi-bin/ptext?doc=Perseus%3Atext%3A1999.02.002
1%3Ahead%3D%238
It can also be found in *The Orations of Marcus Tullius Cicero*, translated by
C. D. Yonge, published by George Bell & Sons, 1903

Bill Clinton   The First Inaugural Address is available from The
American Presidency Project, and can be viewed online at their website:
www.presidency.ucsb.edu/ws/index.php?pid=46366

George Clooney   The speech can be viewed at: www.youtube.com/
watch?v=JRpNS9cM60s
Extracts and interesting background information can also be
viewed through the BBC at: http://news.bbc.co.uk/1/hi/world/
americas/5347660.stm

Sebastian Coe   Excerpts from the speech and information can be found
online at: www.london2012.com/news/archive/post-bid-2005/coe-a-
games-for-the-youth-of-the-world.php
The speech can be viewed online at: http://news.bbc.co.uk/
player/nol/newsid_4650000/newsid_4657400/4657475.
stm?bw=bb&mp=wm&news=1&nol_storyid=4657475&bbcws=1

Colonel Tim Collins   Excerpts from, and information about, the
speech can be viewed online at: http://en.wikipedia.org/wiki/Tim_Collins_
(soldier)#Eve-of-battle_speech
http://news.bbc.co.uk/1/hi/uk/2866581.stm

Emperor Constantine   As well as being heard at Christian church
services the Nicene Creed can be heard online through many sources,
including: www.newworldencyclopedia.org/entry/Council_of_Nicea and
www.spurgeon.org/~phil/creeds/nicene.htm

Bill Cosby   The address can be viewed online through Blackpast.org:
www.blackpast.org/?q=2004-bill-cosby-pound-cake-speech

Walter Cronkite   The speech can be viewed online at: www.youtube.
com/watch?v=kDQAgPjv94M www.thirdworldtraveler.com/United_
Nations/Chronkite_UN.html
www.dwfed.org/pp_cronkite.html

Severn Cullis-Suzuki The speech can be viewed online at: www. youtube.com/watch?v=5g8cmWZOX8Q
Also, see www.sustainablestyle.org/sass/heirbrains/03suzuki.html
Background information can be found at: http://en.wikipedia.org/wiki/ Severn_Cullis-Suzuki

Clarence Darrow The closing arguments can be viewed online at: www.law.umkc.edu/faculty/projects/ftrials/sweet/darrowsummation.html

Demosthenes The speech can be viewed online at: http://en.wikisource. org/wiki/The_Public_Orations_of_Demosthenes/On_the_Crown and www. mlahanas.de/Greeks/Texts/Demosthenes/OnTheCrown.html

Deng Xiaoping The speech at can be viewed online at: http://english. peopledaily.com.cn/dengxp/v013/text/c1010.html

Charles Dickens The speech can be viewed online at: www.scribd. com/doc/9436936/Charlesdickensspeechesliterarysocial and www.dickens-literature.com/Speeches:_Literary_and_Social/50.html

Benjamin Disraeli The speech is in Hansard CCXXVII (3d Ser.) 652–61. It can also be viewed online at the following websites: www. historyhome.co.uk/polspeech/suez.htm; www.famous-speeches-and-speech-topics.info/famous-speeches/benjamin-disraeli-speech-suez-canal. htm

Frederick Douglass The speech can be viewed online at: www. redandgreen.org/July_5th_Speech.htm
http://docsouth.unc.edu/neh/douglass55/douglass55.html#p446

Queen Elizabeth I The speech can be viewed at: http://en.wikipedia. org/wiki/Spanish_Armada
www.youtube.com/watch?v=cSV7zSjbrts
www.luminarium.org/renlit/tilbury.htm

Ralph Waldo Emerson The speech can be read online at: http:// en.wikisource.org/wiki/The_American_Scholar

Benjamin Franklin The speech to the constitutional convention can be viewed at: www.liberty1.0rg/benjamin.htm and www.usconstitution. net/franklin.html
Another useful source of information is *Notes of Debates in the Federal*

Convention of 1787 Reported by James Madison by W.W. Norton & Co., Ohio University Press, 1987, pp. 652–4

Galileo Galilei   The speech and interesting background information can be read at: http://courses.science.fau.edu/~rjordan/phy1931/GALILEO/galileo.htm

Indira Gandhi   The speech can be viewed online at: http://gos.sbc.edu/g/gandhi2.html
It can also be found in *Selected Speeches and Writings of Indira Gandhi, September 1972–March 1977* by Indira Gandhi, Publications Division, Ministry of Information and Broadcasting, Govt. of India, 1984. pp. 312–3.

Mohandas K. Gandhi   The speech can be viewed online at: http://en.wikipedia.org/wiki/Quit_India_speech
www.mahatma.com/php/showNews.php?newsid=7&linkid=12
www.wordpower.ws/speeches/gandhi-quit-india.html

Bill Gates   The address is available online from Harvard University's website: http://harvardmagazine.com/commencement/harvard-commencement-address
It can also be viewed at: www.youtube.com/watch?v=GQf-uGxWt_A

Charles de Gaulle   The speech was broadcast on the radio by the BBC. It can be viewed online at: www.charles-de-gaulle.org/article.php3?id_article=283 and www.guardian.co.uk/theguardian/2007/apr/29/greatspeeches1

Rudy Giuliani   The speech can be viewed online at: www.nyc.gov/html/records/rwg/html/2001b/un_remarks.html
http://avalon.law.yale.edu/sept11/un_004.asp

Patrick Henry   The speech and background information can be viewed at: www.jmhochstetler.com/guides/PatrickHenrySpeech.pdf
www.history.org/almanack/life/politics/giveme.cfm
www.theamericanrevolution.org/ipeople/phenry/phenryspeech.asp

Adolf Hitler   The speech to the Reichstag can be viewed online through Humanitas International: www.humanitas-international.org/showcase/chronography/speeches/1939–10–06.html

Ho Chi Minh The speech can be viewed online at: http://coombs.anu.
edu.au/~vern/van_kien/declar.html
It has also been published in *Ho Chi Minh: Selected Writings, 1920–1969*
published by Foreign Languages Publishing House, Hanoi, 1973,
pp. 53–6.

General Sir Mike Jackson The speech was broadcast by the BBC. It
can be viewed online at: www.timesonline.co.uk/tol/news/world/iraq/
article663229.ece
www.telegraph.co.uk/news/uknews/1536245/The-Richard-Dimbleby-
lecture.html?pageNum=3

Thomas Jefferson The Inaugural address is available from The
American Presidency Project, and can be viewed online at their website:
www.presidency.ucsb.edu/ws/index.php?pid=25803

Muhammad Ali Jinnah The speech can be viewed online at: www.
pakistani.org/pakistan/legislation/constituent_address_11aug1947.html

Steve Jobs The speech can be viewed online at: http://news.stanford.
edu/news/2005/june15/jobs-061505.html
http://en.wikisource.org/wiki/Steve_Jobs's_Commencement_address_at_
Stanford_University
It can also be seen on Youtube at: www.youtube.com/
watch?v=UF8uR6Z6KLc

Barbara Jordan The Keynote Address can be read online at:
edchange.org/multicultural/speeches/barbara_jordan_1976dnc.html,
and www.womenspeecharchive.org/files/1976_Democratic_National_
Convention_1192213012206.pdf

John F. Kennedy The Inaugural Address is available from The
American Presidency Project and can be viewed online at their website:
www.presidency.ucsb.edu/ws/index.php?pid=8032

Robert F. Kennedy The speech can be viewed online at: http://
en.wikisource.org/wiki/Speech_on_the_Assassination_of_Martin_Luther_
King,_Jr.

Muhtar Kent The speech can viewed online at: www.thecoca-
colacompany.com/presscenter/viewpoints_kent_wharton.html

Nikita Khrushchev   The speech can be viewed online at: www.marxists. org/archive/khrushchev/1956/02/24.htm
www.guardian.co.uk/theguardian/2007/apr/26/greatspeeches1
Also, background information can be found at: http://en.wikipedia.org/ wiki/On_the_Personality_Cult_and_its_Consequences

Martin Luther King Jr   The speech can be viewed online at: www. youtube.com/watch?v=iEMXaTktUfA
It can also be found at: www.usconstitution.net/dream.html
http://avalon.law.yale.edu/20th_century/mlk01.asp

Junichiro Koizumi   The speech can be viewed at: http://www.mofa. go.jp/policy/un/assembly2005/state_pm.html
http://www.un.int/japan/statements/koizumi050915.html

James Lavenson   Excerpts from the speech can be viewed online at: www.amazingpeople.co.uk/Blog/strawberries.htm and www.indianeye. org/2008/02/07/selling-strawberries-inspirational-business-series/

Lee Kuan Yew   The speech can be viewed online at: www. bridgesingapore.com/externalreports/37th-jawaharlal-nehru-memorial-lecture-lee-kuan.pdf
http://app.mfa.gov.sg/2006/press/view_press.asp?post_id=1523

Abraham Lincoln   The Gettysburg address is available from the United States of America's Library of Congress. It can be viewed online at their website: www.loc.gov/exhibits/gadd

David Lloyd George   The address was published in *The Times* newspaper on 22 July 1911. It can also be viewed online at: http://wwi. lib.byu.edu/index.php/Agadir_Crisis:_Lloyd_George%27s_Mansion_House_ Speech and http://teachers.sduhsd.k12.ca.us/tpsocialsciences/world_ history/world_war1/mansion.htm

Huey P. Long   The speech can be viewed online at: www.senate.gov/ artandhistory/history/resources/pdf/EveryManKing.pdf
Also, interesting background information can be found at: www. senate.gov/artandhistory/history/common/generic/Speeches_Long_ EveryManKing.htm

General Douglas MacArthur   The *Duty, Honor, Country* speech is available from the General Douglas MacArthur Foundation and can be viewed online at: www.west-point.org/real/macarthur_address.html

Malcolm X   The speech can be heard at: www.youtube.com/watch?v=CRNcirylmqg
The text versions differ from the audio version and can be viewed at:
http://teachingamericanhistory.org/library/index.asp?document=1147
http://edchange.org/multicultural/speeches/malcolm_x_ballot.html

Nelson Mandela   The speech can be viewed online at: www.anc.org.za/ancdocs/history/rivonia.html
www.guardian.co.uk/world/2007/apr/23/nelsonmandela
Excerpts and background information can also be found at:
http://en.wikiquote.org/wiki/Nelson_Mandela#I_am_Prepared_to_Die_.281964.29
www.menziesvirtualmuseum.org.au/transcripts/ForgottenPeople/Forgotten1.html

George Martin   The Commencement Address can be viewed at: http://www.berklee.edu/commencement/past/gmartin.html

John McCain   A video of the speech can be viewed online at: www.youtube.com/watch?v=vBgFCqPSzgA
It can also be found at: www.america.gov/st/elections08-english/2008/November/20081105104120abretnuh0.2753979.html
www.cfr.org/publication/17704/

Sir Robert Menzies   The speech can be viewed online at: www.liberals.net/theforgottenpeople.htm

Jawaharlal Nehru   The speech from the Constituent Assembly Debates can be viewed online at: www.guardian.co.uk/theguardian/2007/may/01/greatspeeches
www.hindustantimes.com/news/specials/parliament/Tryst%20with%20Destiny.pdf

Barack Obama   The election victory speech at Grant Park can be viewed on line at: www.barackobama.com/2008/11/04/remarks_of_presidentelect_bara.php

Conan O'Brien   The commencement speech can be viewed online at: http://carriedaway.typepad.com/carried_away/2003/08/_conan_obriens_.html and www.geocities.com/conanando/conan.html

Robert Oppenheimer   The speech can be viewed online at: www.youtube.com/watch?v=n8H7Jibx-c0
www.atomicarchive.com/Movies/Movie8.shtml
Also, background information can be found at: http://en.wikiquote.org/wiki/Robert_Oppenheimer

Emmeline Pankhurst   The speech can be viewed online at: www.guardian.co.uk/theguardian/2007/apr/27/greatspeeches1 and www.thelizlibrary.org/undelete/library/library00641.html

Randy Pausch   The speech can be viewed online at: www.youtube.com/watch?v=ji5_MqicxSo

Lester Pearson   The speech can be viewed online at: www.unac.org/en/link_learn/canada/pearson/speechgollancz.asp

Pericles   The speech can be viewed online at: http://en.wikisource.org/wiki/Pericles%27s_Funeral_Oration_(Hobbes)
http://en.wikisource.org/wiki/Pericles%27s_Funeral_Oration_(Jowett)

William Lyon Phelps   The speech can be viewed online through The William Lyon Phelps Foundation at: www.wlpf.org/Books/Books.htm

Colin Powell   The speech can be viewed online through the Public Broadcasting Service (USA) at: www.pbs.org/newshour/convention96/floor_speeches/powell.html

Yitzhak Rabin   The speech can be viewed online at: http://nobelprize.org/nobel_prizes/peace/laureates/1994/rabin-lecture.html
http://www.mfa.gov.il/MFA/Peace%20Process/Guide%20to%20the%20Peace%20Process/PM%20Rabin%20-%20Nobel%20Prize%20for%20Peace
http://info.jpost.com/C005/Supplements/Rabin/sp.05.html
Also, background information can be found at: http://nobelprize.org/nobel_prizes/peace/laureates/1994/rabin-bio.html

Queen Rania of Jordan   The speech can be viewed online at: www.youtube.com/watch?v=E07Mtg60V58

http://queenrania.jo/content/modulePopup.aspx?secID=&itemID=1425&ModuleID=press&ModuleOrigID=news

Ronald Reagan The speech can be viewed online at: www.youtube.com/watch?v=gEjXjfxoNXM
http://en.wikisource.org/wiki/Ronald_Reagan_Announces_the_Challenger_Disaster
www.reaganfoundation.org/reagan/speeches/challenger.asp

Franklin Delano Roosevelt The First Inaugural Address is available from The American Presidency Project, and can be viewed online at their website: www.presidency.ucsb.edu/ws/index.php?pid=14473

Theodore Roosevelt The speech given at the Sorbonne University in 1910 is available from The Theodore Roosevelt Association. It can be viewed online at their website: www.theodoreroosevelt.org/research/speech%20arena.htm

Oskar Schindler The original text is available through the Yad Vashem Library. The speech can be viewed online at: www.americanrhetoric.com/speeches/oskarschindlerfarewelltojewishfactoryworkers.htm
Also, background information can be found at: http://en.wikipedia.org/wiki/Oskar_Schindler
www.jewishvirtuallibrary.org/jsource/biography/schindler.html

Gerhard Schröder The speech can be viewed online at: www.historyplace.com/speeches/schroeder.htm
Also, information and excerpts can also be viewed at: http://news.bbc.co.uk/1/hi/world/europe/4204465.stm
http://www.guardian.co.uk/world/2005/jan/26/germany.secondworldwar

Lee Scott The speech can be viewed online at: http://walmartstores.com/FactsNews/NewsRoom/6238.aspx and www.cpi.cam.ac.uk/pdf/BEP%20London%20Lecture%202007.pdf

Ricardo Semler The speech can be viewed online at: http://mitworld.mit.edu/video/308

Margaret Chase Smith The speech can be viewed online at: www.senate.gov/artandhistory/history/resources/pdf/SmithDeclaration.pdf
www.mcslibrary.org/program/library/declaration.htm

Socrates   The speech can be viewed online at: http://en.wikisource.org/wiki/Apology_(Plato)
Also, information can be found at: http://en.wikipedia.org/wiki/Apology_(Plato)

Ted Sorensen   The speech was published in *The Washington Monthly*, and can be viewed online at: www.washingtonmonthly.com/features/2007/0707.Sorensen.html
www.americanrhetoric.com/speeches/tedsorensen2008dnchopeful.htm

Charles, Earl Spencer   The eulogy can be viewed online at: www.internet-esq.com/diana/index.htm and also www.eulogyspeech.net/famous-eulogies/Charles-Spencer-Funeral-Speech-for-his-Sister-Diana.shtml

Sun Yat-sen   The speech can be viewed online at: http://en.wikisource.org/wiki/Sun_Yat_Sen%27s_speech_on_Pan-Asianism

Margaret Thatcher   Highlights of the speech can be viewed at: www.youtube.com/watch?v=rQ-M0KEFm9I
The full text can be read at: www.guardian.co.uk/politics/2007/apr/30/conservatives.uk
www.margaretthatcher.org/speeches/displaydocument.asp?docid=104431

Leon Trotsky   The speech can be viewed online at: www.workersliberty.org/node/3735

George Washington   The Farewell Address is in The George Washington Papers held at the University of Virginia, and can be viewed online at: http://gwpapers.virginia.edu/documents/farewell/transcript.html
The Address can also be viewed online at the US National Archives website: www.ourdocuments.gov/doc.php?flash=true&doc=15&page=transcript

Daniel Webster   Webster's reply to Senator Hayne can be viewed online through the US senate website at: http://senate.gov/artandhistory/history/resources/pdf/WebsterReply.pdf

Jack Welch   The speech can be viewed online at: http://callcentres.com.au/GE2_Jack_Welch.htm#Proud%200f
The speech and background information can also be found in *The GE Way Fieldbook* by Robert Slater p.205ff.

Elie **Wiesel**   The speech can be viewed at: www.youtube.com/
watch ?v=LqFlEeK0Jyg and www.famous-speeches-and-speech-topics.info/
famous-speeches/elie-wiesel-speech-the-perils-of-indifference.htm

Woodrow Wilson   The War Message is in the USA National Archive
Records, and can be viewed online at their website: www.ourdocuments.
gov/doc.php?flash=true&doc=61&page=transcript

Oprah Winfrey   The speech can be viewed online at: http://
speechpedia.org/OprahWinfrey/2005/10/31/Eulogy-for-Rosa-Parks/
www.americanrhetoric.com/speeches/oprahwinfreyonrosaparks.htm
Also, interesting background information can be found at: http://
en.wikipedia.org/wiki/Rosa_Parks

Virginia Woolf   Virginia Woolf's book *A Room of One's Own* was based
on the lectures. It was published by Harcourt Brace Jovanovich in 1929.
It can also be read as an ebook online through eBooks@Adelaide at:
http://ebooks.adelaide.edu.au/w/woolf/virginia/w91r/

Muhammad Yunus   The speech can be viewed online at: http://
nobelprize.org/nobel_prizes/peace/laureates/2006/yunus-lecture-en.html
http://muhammadyunus.org/content/view/79/128/lang,en/

The authors

Simon Maier has been involved in delivering events for 23 years throughout the world and for every imaginable purpose. In the mid-1980s he led much of the event activity in the UK for the privatization of several blue chip companies, and has ever since been responsible for a wide variety of corporate and public events.

As its managing director, Simon led Saatchi-owned ICM to record turnover and profit levels and then did much the same for a number of other leading event and experiential businesses, including his own.

He is frequently invited to comment on what makes a great speech and a speaker great, in the course of which he explains how people can have the first and become the second. Simon is also in demand as a conference facilitator, in which role many CEOs regard him as an event playmaker or quarterback. Despite that, he can't play American football. But he can be contacted on simonmaier@btinternet.com.

Jeremy Kourdi is a writer and executive coach. He was senior vice president at The Economist Group, chairing and participating in a range of international conferences and forums. During his career he has worked with several leading organizations including HSBC, London Business School, IMD, Pearson and the Chartered Management Institute.

Jeremy divides his time between executive coaching and business writing. He has authored twenty books including the best-selling *100 Great Business Ideas* and *Surviving a Downturn*, and several of his books have been translated into other languages including Chinese, German, Hebrew, Indonesian, Korean, Norwegian, Polish, Portuguese, Romanian, Serbo-Croat, Spanish and Thai. Jeremy can be contacted at www.LeadershipExpertise.com.